Sustainable Development & Project Management

Mohamed Eid

Sustainable Development & Project Management

Rethinking Relationships in the Construction Industry; Integrating Sustainable Development (SD) into Project Management (PM) Processes

Lambert Academic Publishing

Impressum/Imprint (nur für Deutschland/ only for Germany)

Bibliografische Information der Deutschen Nationalbibliothek: Die Deutsche Nationalbibliothek verzeichnet diese Publikation in der Deutschen Nationalbibliografie; detaillierte bibliografische Daten sind im Internet über http://dnb.d-nb.de abrufbar.

Alle in diesem Buch genannten Marken und Produktnamen unterliegen warenzeichen-, marken- oder patentrechtlichem Schutz bzw. sind Warenzeichen oder eingetragene Warenzeichen der jeweiligen Inhaber. Die Wiedergabe von Marken, Produktnamen, Gebrauchsnamen, Handelsnamen, Warenbezeichnungen u.s.w. in diesem Werk berechtigt auch ohne besondere Kennzeichnung nicht zu der Annahme, dass solche Namen im Sinne der Warenzeichen- und Markenschutzgesetzgebung als frei zu betrachten wären und daher von jedermann benutzt werden dürften.

Verlag: Lambert Academic Publishing AG & Co. KG
Theodor-Heuss-Ring 26, 50668 Köln, Deutschland
Telefon +49 681 3720-310, Telefax +49 681 3720-3109, Email: info@lap-publishing.com

Herstellung in Deutschland:
Schaltungsdienst Lange o.H.G., Berlin
Books on Demand GmbH, Norderstedt
Reha GmbH, Saarbrücken
Amazon Distribution GmbH, Leipzig
ISBN: 978-3-8383-1578-2

Imprint (only for USA, GB)

Bibliographic information published by the Deutsche Nationalbibliothek: The Deutsche Nationalbibliothek lists this publication in the Deutsche Nationalbibliografie; detailed bibliographic data are available in the Internet at http://dnb.d-nb.de.

Any brand names and product names mentioned in this book are subject to trademark, brand or patent protection and are trademarks or registered trademarks of their respective holders. The use of brand names, product names, common names, trade names, product descriptions etc. even without a particular marking in this works is in no way to be construed to mean that such names may be regarded as unrestricted in respect of trademark and brand protection legislation and could thus be used by anyone.

Publisher:
Lambert Academic Publishing AG & Co. KG
Theodor-Heuss-Ring 26, 50668 Köln, Germany
Phone +49 681 3720-310, Fax +49 681 3720-3109, Email: info@lap-publishing.com

Printed in the U.S.A.
Printed in the U.K. by (see last page)
ISBN: 978-3-8383-1578-2

ACKNOWLEDGEMENTS

I would like to acknowledge the invaluable help of the following people during the production of this book.

I would like to express my enormous gratitude to my dear parents for their generous encouragement and support.

I wish to thank my supervisor, John Brennan, whose intellectual insights have made this research fulfilling and inspiring, for challenging my abilities and for generating long and fruitful discussions. I have received his continuous support and wish to express my appreciation. I sincerely want to thank Dr. Roger D. Talbot for his significant help and guidance in the early stages of my study. From Dr. Talbot, I have received endorsement, which I truly value.

I gratefully acknowledge Dr. Terry Russell for his substantial help and encouragement and I extend my appreciation to Colin Elliot for his help in the early stages of my research.

I am thankful to Dr. John R. Lee for his generosity with time in supporting and maintaining the online questionnaire. His technical guidance has contributed significantly to its success and efficiency. I should particularly mention my friend Sherif Dahan, to whom I am very grateful, for his help in creating the online presentation of the questionnaire. I also wish to thank Fawzeya El Sawy, Morag Arbuthnott and Steven Wren for their momentous efforts in proof reading. I am in debt to my oldest and best friend Abdel Maguid Barakat for always being there for me one way or another and knowing how to make me smile and laugh in the darkest moments.

Thanks to my colleagues and friends at the Department of Architecture for providing a stimulating and supportive environment, for their friendships, exchange of viewpoints and motivation. My appreciation for their generous co-operation and support goes to the members of staff, especially Professor Iain Boyd Whyte.

Finally, I would like to thank my family members and close friends for their constant encouragement and never questioning my pursuit.

TABLE OF CONTENTS

Part II: Rethinking the Relationships; the Tri-Dimensional Integration

Chapter 5: The Integration   185

Chapter 6: The Questionnaire   244

Part III: The Way Forward

LIST OF ABBREVIATIONS

AFITEP	Association Francophone de Management de Project
AIPM	Australian Institute of Project Management
APM	Association for Project Management
BRE	Building Research Establishment
BSRIA	Centre for Building Services Technology and Information
CABE	Commission for Architecture and the Built Environment
CBP	Centre for Business Practices
CBPP	Construction Best Practice Programme
CDM	Clean Development Mechanism
CH_4	Methane
CIB	Conseil International du Bâtiment / International Council for Research and Innovation in Building and Construction
CIBOARD	Construction Industry BOARD
CIRIA	Construction Industry Research and Information Association
CO_2	Carbon Dioxide
CONNET	CONstruction NETwork (for the European Union)
CRM	Certified Project Manager
CRISP	Construction Research and Innovation Strategy Panel
CRMP	Centre for Research in the Management of Projects
CSEM	Centre for Sustainable and Environmental Management
CSR	Corporate Social Responsibility
DEFRA	Department for Environment, Food and Rural Affairs
DETR	Department of the Environment, Transport and the Regions
DJSI	Dow Jones Sustainability Indexes
DTI	Department of Trade and Industry

EESC	European Economic and Social Committee
EMS	Environmental Management System
EPAT	Environment and Natural Resources Policy and Training Project
EPMF	Engineering Project Management Forum
EU	European Union
EUROPA	European Union Online Website
FIEC	Fédération de L'industrie Européenne de la Construction
GCIS	Government Centre for Information Systems
GDP	Gross Domestic Product
GFCF	Gross Fixed Capital Formation
GNP	Gross National Product
GRACE	Global Resource Action Centre for the Environment
GRI	Global Reporting Initiative
ICE	Institute for Civil Engineers
ICEC	International Cost Engineering Council
ICLEI	International Council for Local Environmental Initiatives
ICOSTE	International COST Engineering Council
IISD	International Institute for Sustainable Development
IPCC	Intergovernmental Panel on Climate Change
IPMA	International Project Management Association
ISO	International Organisation for Standardisation
IUCN	International Union for Conservation of Nature and Natural Resources / World Conservation Union
IULA	International Union of Local Authorities
M4I	Movement for Innovation
N_2O	Nitrous Oxide
NAO	UK National Audit Office
NCDC	National Climatic Data Centre
NESDIS	National Environmental Satellite, Data and Information Services
NOAA	National Oceanic and Atmospheric Administration
OGC	Office of Government Commerce
PM	Project Management
PMBOK	Project Management Body of Knowledge

PMI	Project Management Institute
PQA	Process Quality Associates
RCEP	Royal Commission on Environmental Pollution
SD	Sustainable Development
SIGMA	Sustainability Integrated Guidelines for Management
SMS	Sustainable Management System
SO_2	Sulfur Dioxide
TBL	Triple Bottom Line
UK	United Kingdom
UMIST	University of Manchester Institute of Science and Technology
UN	United Nations
UNCED	United Nations Conference on Environment and Development
UNDP	United Nations Development Programme
UNED-UK	United Nations Environment and Development Committee of the United Kingdom
UNEP	United Nations Environment Programme
UNEPFI	United Nations Environment Programme Finance Initiatives
US/USA	United States of America
VM	Value Management
WBCSD	World Business Council for Sustainable Development
WCED	World Commission on Environment and Development
WRI	World Resources Institute
WSSD	World Summit on Sustainable Development

INTRODUCTION

"Rethinking Relationships in the Construction Industry:
Integrating Sustainable Development into Project Management Processes"

During the time the author has spent both studying and gaining practical experience in the fields of architectural design and construction, it became clear that these extremely resource-intensive industries face serious challenges. What at first seemed like a problem specific to the author's native Egypt now emerges as a global challenge.

The major issues facing the world are mostly from the effect of human development activities. Economic instability, widespread social exclusion and inequalities and global environmental degradation mean the world is fighting for a better quality of life for all present and future generations.

In order to start facing up to these challenges, the global community has to realise that these problems are no longer specific to certain countries at a national level, but in fact, they have now risen to a global scale.

When tackling such huge issues, everyone has a significant role to play. Enhancing our quality of life will not be achieved unless the world's communities rise to the challenge and contribute individually as well as collectively to a better quality of life, each within their field of expertise.

Acknowledging that there are always better ways of practice, and that the

1

wheel of development never stops, this book embarks on researching and studying the construction industry's practices and indeed challenging the impacts of global development on our quality of life.

The research tackles the need for changing the strategies, policies and standards which normally control the practices and guide the projects from inception to completion.

Identifying the Central Problems

Generally, the quality of life which individuals benefit from is demonstrated by the standards of the built environment that surrounds them. Many industries and sectors play a vital role in creating the elements which define the built environment. Architecture, urban planning, transport and construction are collectively responsible for the design, building, location and interconnections of these elements. The construction industry stands ahead of these industries in bearing the responsibility for the building processes of the built environment. If the quality of life is not up to the required standards of a better living, construction practices are therefore identified as the central problem of under performance.

On an international level, the construction industry is a major economic contributor within developed countries and is a rising market for developing nations. It does not only affect the economic side of people's lives, but has also a significant social and environmental impact that is now recognised by world communities.

The need for change goes beyond merely functional considerations. The culture within the construction industry itself has to change. In order to change the culture, it is necessary to start with the strategies and policies which guide the industry's practices. This work studies the fundamental relationships within the construction industry to bear a better understanding of the origins out of which the problems facing the industry arise.

Within the culture of the construction industry, sustainable development is emerging as a new and important agenda for better practice. Sustainable development, is a dynamic process, which simultaneously protects and enhances the global ecosystem while working through three parallel strands; social, environmental and economic. Moreover, it has the virtue of expressing the new global commitment to enhance people's quality of life, in the present, without compromising the opportunities for future generations to enhance their own. The relationship between `Construction` and `Sustainable Development` has created new performance agendas driven by `Sustainable Construction` guidelines.

As technology has blossomed, projects have increased in complexity and project management has proved to be an essential and vital tool for managing and delivering more successful projects on target, time and budget. Construction projects are typified by their complexity, diversity and the non-standardised nature of their production. They are complex undertakings where even an output of modest proportions involves many skills, materials, and literally hundreds of different operations and overlapping activities. The work examines the current status of the relationship between project management and construction projects which is perceived as crucial not only in the planning of the different stages of the project but also from the earliest stages of initiation of any project.

This work presents the case for rethinking the relationships between construction projects, sustainable development and project management. The interconnections are studied on the decision making level and more specifically, through the strategies, policies and standards which define the very nature of the interconnecting relationships.

Research Context

Currently, the state of research in the field of construction practices and regulations covers a wide selection of issues. From a local level to an international and global scale, construction has been described as a fundamental part of human development activities. Some researches focus on the impact it has on our environment, some discuss the social side of construction practices and others examine the economic justification of the emerging markets. This research probes the initiatives regulating the construction practices in terms of its contribution to our quality of life and the standards of its performance.

For sustainable development, it is emerging as the new global commitment to improve the world's quality of living on the three parallel levels; socially, environmentally and economically. This book examines the notions of sustainable development guidelines and their possible contributions on the strategic level of construction practices.

The major contribution of project management to our quality of life justifies its increasing recognition as a profession and practice. Indeed, all fields are

4

affected but specifically so in the case of the construction industry. Identifying the interconnections between project management's involvement in construction projects, whilst maintaining a sustainable construction agenda, is one of the key issues discussed in this research in an innovative way since the relationship between project management and sustainable development guidelines has, so far, not been seriously addressed.

A systems thinking approach to these relationships is based on fundamental criteria that embrace the opportunities for introducing 'change' to an existing functioning system. This is implemented by identifying the places within this system where the earlier the change is introduced to its early fundamental stages, the better and more efficient is the impact expected to derive in terms of the overall performance of the system.

The research examines the potential of a tri-dimensional integration to explore the way forward for construction, project management and sustainable development to contribute effectively to the consensus towards a better quality of life. This is investigated by the research to unveil whether or not it would have fundamental impact on the three professions in general and in turn, enhance their contributions to people's quality of life.

This work is responding to the need for change by examining the relationships between these three professions within the guidelines of Systems Thinking theories to allow a detailed exploration of the outcomes of these interlinking relationships. These are the four main pillars of the research.

Research Methodology and Structure

The methodology of the research is based on a synthesis of a literature review, an examination of three case studies and an online questionnaire all adopting a critical appraisal approach. The literature review consists of a broad data collection with an elaborative analysis of the examined arguments. The examination of the validity of the proposed approaches is demonstrated through the proposed case studies. While the online questionnaire complements the methodology to probe the success of the hypothesis criteria. The methodology's approaches are reviewed through a critical appraisal method which highlights the different sides of the proposed arguments.

The main body of the book is structured around the notions of sustainable construction, as a process that promotes affordable solutions to the problems of the built environment and the significant impact it has environmentally, economically and socially. The research examines the possibility of expanding such notions so as to embrace the proposed 'change' approach from within the fundamental components of sustainable development and the construction industry.

The main principle governing the research methodology is to follow a systems thinking approach to the arguments. By this method, the impact of the proposed hypothesis is examined on the level of the component elements as well as the research framework as a whole.

As the main means to illustrate the concept of the methodology, the research uses a Venn diagram on three-sets to exhibit the existing and proposed relationships between the three main elements of the research. Since the research is based on the interconnections between the four pillars, the Venn diagram demonstrates the integration between three dimensions (three out of four pillars), while the fourth pillar embraces the integration. It is a tri-dimensional integration between three of the four pillars as the three sets of the Venn diagram with the fourth pillar embracing the integration as shown in figure (1*).

By adopting this approach, the research structure is formulated into three main parts: -

Part I: Establishing the Relationships; defining the four pillars of the research.

- Chapter 1: The Construction Industry
- Chapter 2: Sustainable Development
- Chapter 3: Project Management
- Chapter 4: Systems Thinking & Leverage Points

Part II: Rethinking the Relationships; the Tri-Dimensional Integration.

- Chapter 5: The Integration
- Chapter 6: The Questionnaire

Part III: The Way Forward.

- Conclusion

Part I of the research is dominated by the literature review and its analysis. It establishes the background of each of the four pillars on which the research's hypothesis is based. Each pillar defined in a separate chapter. The research analyses the past and current initiatives and studies the progress in theories related to these elements in practice.

Part II is an illustrative analysis of the hypothesis by bringing together the four pillars defined in Part I. The integration proposed in the research allows the creation of a homogenous framework between the main elements of the research for future practice and implementation. The interconnections between the three main elements are described as well as the impact of Systems Thinking, the fourth pillar, has on these relationships.

Having established the existing relationships in part I, the research examines the need for rethinking these relationships in order to enhance the overall performance with a closer look at the Venn diagram and the new areas of interconnections created by the new approach. This part of the research defines the proposed approach in terms of allowing a better understanding of the relationships between the elements and ways of enhancing their interconnections. This is followed by three case studies; demonstrations of practical implementations of the hypothesis on real life initiatives and project management standards. Finally, an online questionnaire was created to channel the views of professionals, practitioners and researchers interested in the approach. This questionnaire is analysed and the respondents' answers are examined against the original hypothesis.

Part III summarises the findings of the research and displays the logic behind the proposed arguments with a list of recommendations and a vision which defines the scope for future research. The wheel of knowledge never stops and, therefore, the work proposes a way forward to proceed with future research and development. Similar to the research structure, each chapter (as a part within the whole) is also defined into three main parts; introduction, main arguments and the way forward as the conclusion.

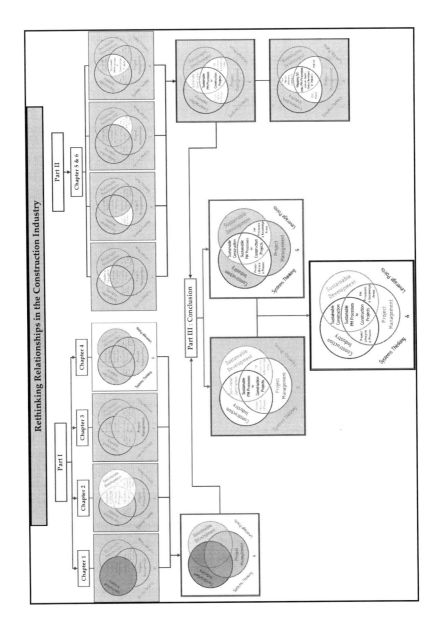

Figure 1*: The Research's Methodology and Structure

9

Figure (1*) above, summarises the research, its structure, its framework and the interconnections between the chapters within the three main parts of the book.

Chapter 1 examines the construction industry; the first pillar of the research and the first element in the proposed tri-dimensional integration. It takes a closer look at the industry's performance on the European scale as well as on the scale of the UK. Both levels share statistics which underpin the importance of the industry not only on the economic level but social and environmental as well. The challenges analysed seem to be the same on both scales; clients' dissatisfaction of the overall performance, low investment in the labour force and, most significantly, high levels of environmental violations.

For the EU, the European Commission published several official reports calling for improving the industry's performance with special emphasis on a new sustainable agenda which has been recently introduced to the industry. On the scale of the UK, the Egan report arises as a fundamental milestone in the road towards a sustainable industry. Despite the criticism which the Egan agenda received, a crucial initiative for `Rethinking Construction` re-addresses the Egan's drivers in order to highlight the potential of a sustainable development approach to its framework.

The research explores the contribution of the construction sector to our quality of life and exhibits the need for a change within the culture as well as within the fundamental aspects of the performance.

Chapter 2 explores Sustainable Development; the second pillar of the research and the second element in the proposed integration. The world communities have committed themselves to provide a better quality of life for their people on the triple bottom line theory of sustainability; social, environmental and economic. Sustainable development is examined in terms of its origins, evolution, agendas as well as the criticism it is encountering. For a sustainable construction industry, the problems facing this agenda are probed with special emphasis on the practical side of projects. For businesses, committing to such agenda requires further analysis of the business case for sustainable development.

This chapter presents a detailed assessment of the business case for sustainability which triggers the hypothesis of this research. Environmentally friendly activities are no longer sufficient for improving the quality of life, such as Eco-efficiency, but a full commitment to the triple bottom line of sustainable development.

Chapter 3 introduces Project Management; the third pillar of the research and the third element of the tri-dimensional integration proposed in this book. The chapter investigates the origins of project management standards, its definitions and fields of applications. A clear relationship exists between project management practice and the successful completion of construction projects. The construction industry has grown to produce complex and more demanding projects in an age of modern technology and fast development. Thus, the involvement of project management standards, within all projects, has proven fundamental criteria for success. The evolution of project management is examined in terms of the different international initiatives to produce a body of knowledge for standardisation of its practices. As an international project management standards authority, the Project Management Institute (PMI) provided the Project Management Body of Knowledge (PMBOK® 2000 Edition) on which the approach of this book is based. The chapter discusses the standards of project management processes listed in the PMBOK in order to identify the opportunities within its standards to integrate sustainable development guidelines. The recently published `Construction Extension to PMBOK` is also examined while arguing that even though it is more specific to the construction industry it still does not live up to any of the sustainable construction agendas.

Chapter 4 defines the theory of Systems Thinking and Leverage Points; the fourth pillar of this research and the proposed facilitator to the tri-dimensional integration put forward in this book. The notions of the theory are defined and its origins from the work of Peter Senge and the interrelatedness of his proposed five disciplines. It discusses the impact of the implementation of the theory on learning organisations and existing functioning systems. The chapter discusses the ways, underpinned by the theories, in which `change` should be introduced to systems in order to ensure attaining the positive desired impact which was originally planned.

The concept of leverage points is defined while the research highlights the list of places to intervene in a system based on their level of efficiency, as illustrated in the research work of Donella Meadows. The theories of systems thinking and leverage points are used to demonstrate that `change` can be introduced even for complex systems such as project management and sustainable construction. Therefore, the chapter also discusses environmental management systems and sustainable management systems and whether or not they level up to the current sustainability world approach.

Chapter 5 marks the second phase of the research, in which the arguments propose to rethink existing relationships between sustainable development, construction practice and project management in an environment of systems thinking theories. The framework for the proposed tri-dimensional integration is explained and highlights the interconnections between the three elements in question. This is followed by a detailed justification for using systems thinking as a catalyst for this integration. The Venn diagram, as a representation of the integration in question, is then analysed in detail and broken down to its component areas representing the interconnections between the three elements of the integration.

The sustainable construction agenda for rethinking construction is challenged from a systems thinking point of view to produce a new understanding of processes. The systems thinking approach influences fundamental changes to procurement processes which are a crucial part of project management processes and the lifecycle of construction projects. A new approach is then proposed to a governmental procurement model currently used by the UK government by identifying the leverage points within the system that would allow an efficient implementation of sustainable development guidelines.

For project management, the emphasis is on changing the PMBOK's approach to project management processes and knowledge areas. The research identifies the significant potential which exists within these processes to embrace a sustainability approach. It maps the opportunities for integrating sustainable development into all the project management processes and knowledge areas listed in the PMBOK through an innovative matrix of integration.

Chapter 6 examines the created questionnaire as an invitation to PM practitioners, professionals, academics and researchers to contribute to the hypothesis of the research, with their expert views and analysis of the approach. The questionnaire was made available for all interested participants through the World Wide Web. This chapter explains the framework and approach of the questionnaire. By analysing the responses, the chapter concludes with a display of the statistical analysis of the responses.

In summary, sustainable development offers an effective route towards the achievement of a better quality of life and equal opportunities for world's communities, cultures and environments. The project management profession has a significant role to play in promoting such an approach whether it be ethically motivated or be based upon practical benefit. This research outlines the arguments that uphold and demonstrate the evidence which endorse such approach.

Societies are composed of three fundamental components; civil, governmental and finally businesses. Project management's involvement in these three components is the major role which requires enhancement and further commitment from PM professionals. This research highlights the way forward for future project management standards and demonstrates that committing to such imperatives and critical agendas, such as sustainable development, can only affect the profession positively and, indeed, enhance its chances to be more responsible towards providing a better quality of life for now and for future generations.

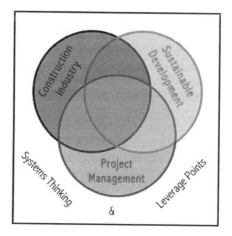

CHAPTER 1

THE CONSTRUCTION INDUSTRY

"Construction provides for many the most basic requirements for a civilised society such as shelter, communication networks (e.g. roads and railways), water supply and waste treatment."

Blockley and Godfrey "Doing It Differently"[1]

The construction industry is of such vital importance that most other industrial areas of world society simply fade in comparison. Construction projects provide the platform for our daily activities with housing and the necessary infrastructure for transport, communication, water supply and sanitation, energy, commercial and industrial activities. The construction industry confronts its major challenge in providing the needs of the growing world population.[2]

The construction industry is the first element in the tri-dimensional

---

[1] David Blockley and Patrick Godfrey, *Doing It Differently; systems for rethinking construction*, London: Thomas Telford Publishing, 2000, pp. 165.

[2] International Council for research and Innovation in Building and Construction, *Agenda 21 on sustainable construction*, Rotterdam, CIB Report Publication 237, July 1999, pp.25. www.cibworld.nl

CIB is the acronym of the abbreviated French (former) name: "Conseil International du Bâtiment" (in English this is: International Council for Building). In the course of 1998, the abbreviation has been kept but the full name changed into: International Council for research and Innovation in Building and Construction. CIB was established in 1953 with the support of the United Nations, as an association whose objectives were to stimulate and facilitate international collaboration and information exchange between governmental research institutes in the building and construction sector.

The Agenda 21 on sustainable construction is intended to be a global intermediary between those Agendas in existence, i.e. the Brundtland Report and the Habitat Agenda, and the required national/regional Agendas for the built environment and the construction sector, current or in course of development. It brings attention to the concepts of sustainable development and sustainable construction, the industry's concerns and its impact, against the background of international agreements such as the Kyoto and Rio Summits.

integration proposed by the author in this research.

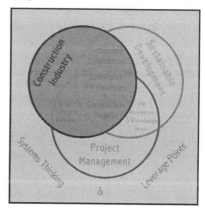

Figure 1.0: The Construction Industry; the first of four pillars, in the research's hypothesis

Figure (1.0) illustrates the hypothesis of the research with special emphasis on the construction industry; the topic of this chapter.

1.1 Introduction

Planet earth and the built environment are suffering from human development which is depleting natural capital at a faster rate than it can be replenished and is producing waste products at rates greater than global ecosystems can absorb.[3] The built environment normally constitutes more than one half of the real capital and in conjunction with construction; they are the main consumers of resources in energy and materials.[4]

The construction industry is the main executer for the elements of the built

---

[3] United Nations Environmental Programme, *Global Environmental Outlook 2000*, Nairobi: UNEP GEO.

[4] International Council for research and Innovation in Building and Construction, *Agenda 21 on sustainable construction*, Rotterdam, CIB Report Publication 237.

environment. When architects design spaces to be added to or even to create the built environment, construction then execute these designs. In general, the stage for our daily life activities relies mainly on the construction industry to produce the elements which define the built environment.[5] Understandably, other industries (e.g. Architecture, Transport, Project Management and Manufacturing) also play vital roles in defining the built environment, but this research concentrates on the construction industry; its practices, policies, strategies and initiatives. This does not undermine the importance of the other industries but it highlights the crucial role that construction is playing in determining people's quality of life and defining the building standards of the built environment.

The construction industry plays a very similar role in all world communities as the generator of the surrounding built environment, ultimately this would lead the research to study and analyse the industry in all world communities. This would be impossible to achieve on the scale of the construction industry worldwide, therefore, this research limits the scope of the study to two interchangeable scales; one derived from the other. This chapter focuses the research on the European Union level of construction strategies as a demonstrative example of successful legislation of change and then develops the focus to the UK construction industry to display the British initiatives in maintaining an industry which thrives to maintain its leadership worldwide.

On the scale of the European Union's construction industry, this chapter describes its current status in terms of performance indicators and statistics, which highlights the contribution of the industry to the general economy, as

---

[5] www.cbe.org.uk the Centre for the Built Environment

well as demonstrates the deficiencies of the industry in contributing to a better quality of life. The EU perspective is good example of a large world community which seeks better performance and a more serious commitment to global issues.

For the construction industry in the UK, a special focus is given to its performances, problems and challenges. The status quo of the UK industry has been challenged by several governmental reports[6] and initiatives to demonstrate the way forward for the industry's contribution to a better quality of life. This research Narrows down the study to the UK's experience because it represents a leading example of successful policy making as well as a positive demonstration on the interaction between government's legislations and stakeholders' needs to implement vital strategies.

This chapter also aims to analyse the problems and milestones facing the industry and its culture, hence describing the need for change. The study analysis the need for a sustainable approach to the current practices as proposed in recent governmental initiatives. This is perceived as the way forward for the industry, showing the way for integrating sustainable development indicators into its own set of key performance indicators. The lessons which could be learned from the EU strategies as well as the UK initiatives are very significant and might well benefit struggling markets such as the construction industry in developing countries or even

---

[6] For the UK, the first of these initiatives challenging the industry's performance is the report of the Construction Task Force -under the chairmanship of Sir John Egan- to the Deputy Prime Minister, John Prescott, on the scope for improving the quality and efficiency of UK construction. The report is entitled *Rethinking Construction*. Published by the formally known as the DETR Department of the Environment, Transport and the Regions) now renamed to DTI (Department of Trade and Industry).
The report can be accessed at http://www.dti.gov.uk/construction/rethink/report/index.htm

communities in the developed world that seek a better quality of life.

1.2 The Construction Industry in the EU

In its broad sense, the construction industry includes housing, non-residential buildings, civil engineering and industrial construction. In addition, the whole supply chain needs to be taken into account; from primary raw materials to complex products and systems. Similarly, the construction process includes all phases; from initial conception, through feasibility studies, design, execution of the works, and maintenance, to demolition (including recovery and recycling of materials, and waste disposal and incineration).

1.2.1 Background Statistics

The construction industry is a major constituent of the European Union's economy.[7] The construction sector is an active and dynamic industry throughout Europe, but one that contains a large number of hazards and risks. It plays a very important role in the economic well-being of the European Union, representing approximately 11% of Community GDP (Gross Domestic Product) in 1996.[8] In spite of a slow-down in the rate of increase of productivity, the construction industry remains the largest industrial sector in the community, ahead of the foodstuffs and chemicals

---

[7] Communication from the Commission of the European Parliament, The Council, The Economic and Social Committee and the Committee of the Regions on: *"The Competitiveness of the Construction Industry"*, Version 3.3, The Documents can be viewed from The European Union Online: http://europa.eu.int/comm/enterprise/construction/compcom/compcom.htm last visited June 2002.

[8] The European Commission Website (The European Union Online; Europa), http://europa.eu.int/comm/enterprise/construction/it/connet/connet.htm accessed June 2002.

[8] CONNET: (CONstruction information service NETwork, http://www.connet.org), A project funded by the European Community through the ETTN (European Technology Transfer Network) initiative.

industries and it is crucial in producing investment goods. It accounted for 10% of GDP and 48.5% of Gross Fixed Capital Formation[9] in 2000.[10] It is also the largest sector in terms of employment, providing jobs for 8.8 million people (7% of the working population), and gives rise to 2.5 million construction related jobs, and 14.3 million other service jobs, acquiring 28.5% of industrial employment. In the EU, 26 million workers depend, directly or indirectly, on the construction sector making it the biggest industrial employer in Europe.[11]

The construction industry is also perhaps the most geographically diverse industry, and one which involves a very large number of small to medium sized enterprises (SMEs) with professionals covering areas from architecture, engineering and construction through to facility management and demolition. [12]

1.2.2 The Challenges for the Construction Industry in the EU

It is a fact that the construction industry and the built environment are the main consumers of resources (i.e. energy and materials) within the European Union where buildings are estimated to consume approximately 40% of total energy. Buildings are also responsible for some 30% of CO_2 emissions – and

---

[9] Gross Fixed Capital Formation (GFCF) consists of resident producers' acquisitions, less disposals, of fixed assets during a given period of time plus certain additions to the value of non produced assets realised by the productive activity of producer or institutional units.

[10] European Construction Industry Federation (FIEC); http://www.fiec.org/main.html last accessed in June 2002.

[11] CONNET: (CONstruction information service NETwork, http://www.connet.org), A project funded by the European Community through the ETTN (European Technology Transfer Network) initiative.

[12] The European Commission Website (The European Union Online; Europa), http://europa.eu.int/comm/enterprise/construction/suscon/finrepsus/sucop1.htm Last visited June 2002.

22

generate approximately 40% of all man-made waste.[13] The destruction of the resource base and the whole scale pollution of the life support systems upon which continued human development depends are among the consequences of operating economic limits beyond ecological limits.[14]

The Intergovernmental Panel on Climate Change (IPCC) is calling for urgent measures to prepare for sea level rises, serious drought, floods and storms which threaten disaster for large areas of the world.[15]

"Construction stands identified as a major part of the problem, as a primary contributor to climate change, resource depletion and pollution."[16]

The construction industry has a major contribution to make to our quality of life as well as national economies. At a European level, and as a major constituent of the European Union's economy, the construction industry has attained a level of competitiveness on a par with its main competitors.[17] In a world of accelerated change, the industry faces a wide range of challenges which must be addressed if it is to maintain, as well as improve, its input to our quality of life. Integrating sustainable development and improving the industry's competitiveness are the major challenges confronting the

---

[13] International Council for research and Innovation in Building and Construction, *Agenda 21 on sustainable construction*, Rotterdam, CIB Report Publication 237, July 1999, pp.25.

[14] Royal Commission on Environmental Pollution: *Energy – the Changing Climate*, RCEP, London, 2000.

[15] Intergovernmental Panel on climate Change, Third Assessment Report, Climate Change Report 2001, *Impacts, adaptation and Vulnerability*, IPCC, Geneva 2001.

[16] Department of the Environment, Transport and the Regions, *Building a better quality of life – a strategy for more sustainable construction*, London, DETR (Now renamed to DTI; Department of Trade and Industry) , 2000.

[17] Communication from the Commission of the European Parliament, The Council, The Economic and Social Committee and the Committee of the Regions on: *"The Competitiveness of the Construction Industry"*, Version 3.3, The Documents can be viewed from The European Union Online: http://europa.eu.int/comm/enterprise/construction/compcom/compcom.htm last visited June 2002.

European Union, underpinned by the importance and significance of the construction industry's role to our quality of life.

The challenge is to make construction environmentally and socially sustainable without compromising its economic viability.[18] Under the generic title of sustainable development three key policy agendas; climate change, social inclusion and competitiveness, are currently converging to present a radical challenge to the construction industry. That challenge is for construction companies to work collectively to integrate vital environmental and social considerations into their financial planning and business management.

Delivering social progress, protection of the environment, better resource use, economic growth and employment require a stable and competitive economy.

Seeking to fulfil that requirement, the European Commission identified key elements to improve the industry's competitiveness to achieve four major objectives, including the development of a coherent quality policy for the sector, the improvement of the regulatory environment and the overall market framework, fostering a substantial and sustained growth in both the level and quality of education and training provision right across the sector and finally, the reorientation and reinforcement of research and development

---

[18] Project Management Institute (PMI) Conference, contributing paper *Rethinking Project Management; The Business Case for Sustainable Construction*, Conference Proceedings, London, June 2001.

in the face of changing needs.[19]

The culture, in which the construction industry exists, revolves around a very competitive market with high emphasis on the risks involved within the industry's practices. It is crucial at this point of the research to analyse the reasons why `Risk Management` represents such a vital element of the industry's culture internationally and therefore was the emphasis of several researches. Appendix 1 represents a thorough study of risk management; its definitions, applications and component processes. The appendix demonstrates that despite of the industry's spotlight on risk management, it can not be responsible for the under performance of the industry. In construction practices, risk management's involvement in projects has been perceived as a vital milestone for successfully completed projects and also the main responsible process for failure in projects. Appendix 1 demonstrates that risk management can not be solely responsible for either case because it does not stand on its own in achieving projects but it functions within a bigger perspective of processes that define the overall project management processes.

Therefore, the culture of the construction industry has to change its attitude towards risk management responsibility; this change translates into a wide range of serious initiatives that lead the industry towards better performance. These initiatives can no longer be based on the development of a better risk management strategy alone, but a wider perspective of the status quo which relies on embracing the bigger influence of general management processes.

---

[19] The European Commission, *The Competitiveness of the Construction Industry*, http://europa.eu.int/comm/enterprise/construction/compcom/objectiv.htm last accessed in June 2002.

25

1.3 The Construction Industry in the United Kingdom

For the European Union economy, the construction industry contributes vital input into how good or bad the economy performs and for the UK the situation is no different. According to the latest statistics of the Department of Trade and Industry (DTI)[20], the main government partner with the construction industry, the construction industry represents a very powerful tool controlling the UK's economic performance, because of its economic influence, employment ratios and its association with several interlinking activities affecting daily lives as well as the quality of life.

"The construction industry has a huge contribution to make to our quality of life. Construction, building materials and associated professional services together account for some 10% of Gross Domestic Product and provide employment for around 1.5 million people."[21]

1.3.1 Background Statistics

The construction industry has, over the years, remained a vital contributor to the quality of life for the public where buildings and structures change the nature, function and appearance of towns, cities and countryside. Construction provides the modernisation of the nation's built environment whether in transport, housing, schools, hospitals or other amenities.

---

[20] The department of Trade and Industry (DTI) is now the official government partner for the construction industry, it was formally known as DETR (Department of the Environment, Transport and the Regions. The Website address has also changed and can currently be found at www.dti.gov.uk , the website acts as a complete platform for the industry's latest information, reports, governmental regulations and statistics. All the documents and reports previously published by DETR can still be found on the DTI platform with publishing reference to their original source of publication (DETR).

[21] Department of the Environment, Transport and the Regions (DETR), *Building a Better Quality of Life (A Strategy for more Sustainable Construction)*, DETR, London, April 2000, pp.7

According to the National Audit Office report `Modernising Construction` [22] published in January 2001, the construction industry represents a sector of economic importance which is worth £65 billion per annum and employs in excess of 1.4 million people. The DTI's Construction Statistics Annual report[23] published in 2002 confirms the importance of the industry in the overall performance of the UK's economy. The industry's performance might not be the best in Europe, compared to its peers in Germany, France or Austria but it still remains one of the strongest in the world, with output ranked in the global top ten. DTI's mission is to monitor and improve the productivity and competitiveness of the UK construction industry.

Similar to the challenges facing the industry on the European level, the UK industry is also affected by global trends and the troubled performance of local and world economies. It is also influenced by the manner in which the construction activities are taking place and their impact on the surrounding environment and people. The potential for this sector to perform better exists within the risks surrounding it. This great potential is often described in government reports and research analysis with a list of challenges which the industry is asked to face up to; in this time of rapid world changes, growing and deflating economies, limited resources, higher standards of customers'/stakeholders' demands, modern technologies, mounting management skills and global commitment to a more sustainable future for social inclusion, competitive economies and greener environment.

---

[22] The National Audit Office www.nao.gov.uk , totally independent of Government, it audits the accounts of all government departments and agencies and reports to Parliament on the economy, efficiency and effectiveness with which government bodies have used public money, report "Modernising Construction", published January 2001, can be found at http://www.nao.gov.uk/publications/nao_reports/00-01/000187.pdf
[23] DTI, Construction Statistics Annual 2002 Edition, can be accessed at http://www.dti.gov.uk/construction/stats/csa.htm

1.3.2 The Challenges for the Construction Industry in the UK

People spend 90% of their lives in buildings; the built environment dominates the surrounding of the population's daily lives. Construction is one of the major, if not the biggest, wide spread example of human development activities. In the UK, half of the CO_2 emissions result from construction and energy use in buildings. Every year, UK construction generates over a tonne of waste per citizen and it is also responsible for 20% of all commercial and industrial noise complaints.[24]

In general, buildings consume energy in their operation and in the extraction and preparation of materials and generate waste and pollution. They have a significant impact on the way society manages its use of non-renewable material resources, such as aggregates, and renewable resources such as timber and water.[25]

The Department of Trade and Industry (DTI), in its latest report 'Building a better quality of life; A strategy for more sustainable construction', describes the construction industry in terms of environmental impact, use of materials and resources and waste production, as a major contributor to climate change, resource depletion, environmental degradation and inefficient use of resources.[26]

In terms of use of materials and resources, the construction industry uses

---

[24] BRE MaSC, *Managing Sustainable Construction – Profiting from Sustainability*, Report produced by MaSC Team, first published in 2002 by CRC Ltd, BRE 2002. Report can be accesses on line at http://projects.bre.co.uk/masc/index.html

[25] DETR, *Construction Research and Innovation Business Plan; Promoting innovation in the construction industry*, London, 1999

[26] DETR, Building a better quality of life; A strategy for more sustainable construction, DETR, London, April 2000

about 6 tonnes of material per person per year in the UK, where 20% of this is for infrastructure and over 50% for repair and maintenance of the existing stock and buildings (i.e. DIY).[27] The extraction of materials involves balancing need against impact which mostly imposes significant environmental costs. Each stage of material extraction and manufacturing involves pollution and transport, which justifies the 10% of national energy consumption used in the production and transport of the construction products and materials (i.e. embodied energy).[28]

In terms of construction waste, 90% of non-energy minerals extracted in the UK are used to supply the construction industry with materials, yet every year some 70 million tonnes of construction and demolition materials and soil end up as waste. Some 13 million tonnes of that comprise material delivered to sites and thrown away unused.[29]

The United Nations' Environmental Program (UNEP) has described human development activities as overwhelming evidence for depleting natural capital at a faster rate than it can be replenished and producing waste products at rates greater than global eco-systems can absorb.[30] Construction activities in the UK, as well as all over the world, push human development activities to the extreme of use of natural resources, environmental damage and waste production. Furthermore, the consequences of operating economic systems beyond ecological limits are the destruction of the resource base and

---

[27] DETR, *Sustainable Development: Opportunities for Change. Sustainable Construction*, DETR, London, February 1998

[28] ibid.

[29] DETR, Building a better quality of life; A strategy for more sustainable construction, DETR, London, April 2000

[30] United Nations Environmental Programme (UNEP), *Global Environmental Outlook 2000*, UNEP GEO, Nairobi, 2000

the whole-scale pollution of the life supporting systems upon which continued human development depends.[31]

It is therefore, evident that construction stands identified as a major part of the problem, as a primary contributor to climate change, resource depletion and pollution.[32]

Construction clearly identified as part of the problem, now needs to be made part of the solution"[33]

A pioneering report by the Construction Task Force under the chairmanship of Sir John Egan published in 1998; "Rethinking Construction"[34] (commonly referred to as the "Egan Report") addressed the problem and described the construction process as presently managed in the UK as highly inefficient and emphasised on the need for a radical change of culture within the industry.

With all its great potential, the construction industry has been performing well enough to maintain its vital role in the national economy, but the potential is much bigger than the industry has currently achieved. The present limited success has been reached at the expense of creating key environmental and social problems and in many cases major economic

---

[31] Royal Commission on Environmental Pollution (RCEP), *Energy – the Changing Climate,* RCEP, London, 2000
[32] DETR, Building a better quality of life; A strategy for more sustainable construction, DETR, London, April 2000
[33] Mohamed Eid, *Sustainable Management Systems; Embedding Sustainable Development into Project Management Processes*, Conference Paper for Sustainable Development Forum, Forum Proceedings, Alexandria , Egypt, January 2003
[34] The Construction Task Force, *Rethinking Construction*, DETR, London, 1998, The Report commonly referred to as the "Egan Report" can be accessed at http://www.dti.gov.uk/construction/rethink/report/index.htm

failures.

"The Challenge is to make construction environmentally and socially sustainable without compromising its economic viability."[35]

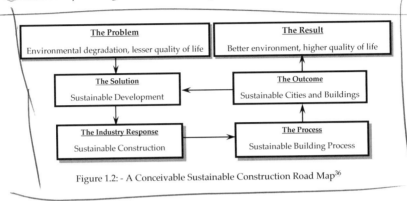

Figure 1.2: - A Conceivable Sustainable Construction Road Map[36]

The answer to the challenges facing the construction industry lies in implementing sustainable development guidelines into construction processes. Several governmental as well as private reports have been discussing the means of implementation to benefit the industry and guide performance towards a sustainable future and therefore leading the public to a better quality of life. Sustainable development might not be the answer to all the problems facing the industry but it definitely answers the challenges on three parallel levels; social inclusion, better and higher environmental standards and viable as well as a competitive economy. (Figure 1.2)

In general, sustainable development means achieving social, economic and environmental objectives at the same time, allowing a more inclusive society

---

[35] Mohamed Eid, *A Sustainable Approach to the Project Management Odyssey*, PMI Research Conference, Seattle, Washington USA, Contributing paper part of conference proceedings, July 2002

[36] International Council for Research and Innovation in Building and Construction (CIB), Sustainable Development and the Future of Construction, Report Working Group 82, CIB Publication 225, Netherlands, May 1998

in which the benefits of increased economic prosperity are widely shared, with less pollution and more efficient use of natural resources.[37]

The economic, social and environmental benefits which can flow from a more efficient and sustainable construction industry are potentially immense."[38]

This approach justifies the need for `Rethinking Construction`, a challenge for construction companies and authorities to work collectively to integrate vital environmental and social considerations into their financial planning and business management, where delivering social progress, protecting the environment, better resource use, economic growth and employment require a stable and competitive economy.[39]

Based on the belief that construction can do better, several initiatives have been introduced including Quality Assurance, Quality Management, Total Quality Management, CDM, Lean and Agile Construction, Partnering, Supply Chain Management, Value Management, and Benchmarking. These are only some the recent initiatives, they mostly address specific issues in the industry or the construction process, but construction people involved both inside and outside the industry believed that we needed an initiative that would address the industry as well as the process of construction as a whole. This initiative originally emerged from clients' concern and dissatisfaction with construction performance, recognising that they are part of the construction process, there was a need to rethink construction as a whole with all stakeholders involved in the rethinking process.

[37] DETR, Building a better quality of life; A strategy for more sustainable construction, DETR, London, April 2000

[38] ibid. pp.7

[39] International Council for Research and Innovation in Building and Construction (CIB), Sustainable Development and the Future of Construction, Report Working Group 82, CIB Publication 225, Netherlands, May 1998

In an effort to improve the construction performance, the Department of the Environment, Transport and the Regions (DETR) – currently called Department of Trade and Industry (DTI) - created a Construction Task Force under the chairmanship of Sir John Egan. On the scope for improving the quality and efficiency of UK construction, the Task Force developed a report called `Rethinking Construction` commonly known as `the Egan Report` published in July 1998.[40]

The following section focuses on the Egan Report because it is the first governmental report which has identified critical internal problems within the industry, categorising the sector as a whole as seriously under-achieving, delivering a low and unreliable rate of profitability and a lack of investment in capital, research and development and training.[41]

1.4 "Rethinking Construction" – The Egan Report

"The construction industry has low profitability and invests too little in capital, research and development, and training....Too many clients are dissatisfied with its overall performance"[42]

This special focus on the Egan Report originates from its importance and significance to the practitioners and researchers of the construction industry. Not only it is considered as a significant milestone in identifying the

[40] DETR, *Rethinking Construction*, The Construction Task Force, DETR, London, 1998. The report commonly referred to as the "Egan Report" can be accessed at http://www.dti.gov.uk/construction/rethink/report/index.htm
[41] Bill Addis & Roger Talbot, *A Guide to Delivering Environmentally-Responsible Projects*, CIRIA Publications, CIRIA Research project 617, London, 2001
[42] DETR, *Rethinking Construction*, The Construction Task Force, DETR, London, 1998

problems behind the under performance of the industry[43], but it has also been the subject of a lot of criticism, analysis, modifications and development in subsequent reports which in some cases were solely based on Egan's agenda and drivers.

These reports include initiatives which reinforce and complement the essential message of the Egan Report such as `Building a Better Quality of Life; a Strategy for Sustainable Construction`[44]. They also include reports that build on the Egan Agenda to commit to sustainability such as the Construction Research and Innovation Strategy Panel (CRISP)'s report entitled `Integrating Sustainability and "Rethinking Construction"`[45] and the recent publication by the Strategic Forum for Construction[46],chaired by Sir John Egan himself, entitled `Accelerating Change` which build on the principles of the Egan Report `Rethinking Construction` but tackles barriers to progress and identifies ways to accelerate the rate of change which is already underway.[47]

With a firm belief that change in the construction industry would lead to radical improvement in the construction process, the Task Force describes the deficiencies of the industry's performance as the reasons behind the need to improve low and unreliable rate of profitability, weak investment in research and development (R&D) and a crisis in training where number of

[43] David Blockley and Patrick Godfrey, *Doing It Differently; systems for rethinking construction*, London: Thomas Telford Publishing, 2000
[44] DETR, Building a better quality of life; A strategy for more sustainable construction, DETR, London, April 2000
[45] CRISP, *Integrating Sustainability and "Rethinking Construction"*, Environmental Resources Management (ERM), CRISP, London, 1999
[46] The Strategic Forum for Construction Official website http://www.strategicforum.org.uk/
[47] The Strategic Forum for Construction, *Accelerating Change*, Construction Industry Council, Published by Rethinking Construction, London, 2002

trainees decreased by half therefore introduced skill shortages with lack of proper career structure for developing supervisory and management grades. It also emphasises on clients' dissatisfaction with projects which are seen as unpredictable in terms of delivery on time, within budget and to the standards of quality expected but the report also highlights that clients are undiscriminating and equate price with cost, selecting designers and constructors almost exclusively on the basis of tendered price alone.

The Task Force had a set of goals for `Rethinking Construction`. The work plan of the Task Force is defined by four goals: first, quantify the scope for improving construction efficiency and derive relevant quality and efficiency targets and performance measures that might be adopted by UK construction industry. Second goal is to examine current practice and the scope for improving it by innovation in products and processes. The third is to identify specific actions and good practice which would help achieve more efficient construction in terms of quality, customer satisfaction, timeliness in delivery and value for money to achieve annual reductions of 10% in construction cost and time. Finally, the fourth goal is to identify projects to help demonstrate the improvements which can be achieved through the application of best practice with defects in projects reduced by 20% per year.

The report identifies five key drivers of change, which are necessary to set the agenda for the construction industry at large[48]: -

1- Committed leadership

Believing in management and being totally committed to driving forward an agenda for improvement and communicating the required cultural and

---

[48] ibid.

operational changes throughout the whole organisation.

2- Focus on the customer

The customer drives everything where he/she defines the exact objective or project's target, the way to finance it and time expectations. Meeting or exceeding customer's expectations and objectives is high on the agenda.

3- Integrated process and teams

The construction industry is not a series of sequential and largely separate operations. There should not be fragmentation of the process. It needs to deliver value to the customer efficiently while eliminating waste.

4- Quality driven agenda

Quality does not only mean zero defects but it also means getting it right the first time, delivery on time according to budget, innovating for the benefit of the client and scraping out waste, whether it is in design, materials or construction on site.

5- Commitment to the people

This means decent site conditions, fair wages, and care for the health and safety of the work force with a commitment to the training and development of committed and highly capable managers and supervisors.

The report never mentions a `sustainable development` approach to the current construction practices although the ways suggested by the report in achieving those targets and key drivers revolve around the three parallel levels of sustainability; socially, environmentally and economically.

With the focus on the five key drivers described above, the suggested ways of achieving the targets start with the industry's need to make radical changes to the processes through which it delivers the project. These processes should be explicit and transparent to the industry and its clients while the industry should create an integrated project process around the four key elements of: project development, project implementation, partnering the supply chain and production of components. This is underpinned by the necessity of the industry to provide decent and safe working conditions, better management and improved supervising skills. To achieve the targets, the industry must also replace competitive tendering with long term relationships based on clear measurement of performance and sustained improvements in quality and efficiency and most importantly, the involved organisations, partners and competing companies should sustain improvements and share learning. [49]

The construction industry should set for itself clear measurable objectives for improvement and then give them focus by adopting quantifiable targets, milestones and key performance indicators (KPIs). [50]

---

[49] ibid.

[50] As an example for providing clear sets of measurable targets and objectives while redeeming the balance on quality through KPIs is the Commission for Architecture and the Built Environment (CABE) as an Executive Non-Departmental Public Body. In its publications CABE provide a list of keys to success in construction projects such as project leadership, understanding projects' heritage and context, building relationships between consultants and contractors, learning from past projects, preparing a clear and realistic brief in terms of costs, time and human resources, committing to sustainability and finally understanding the responsibilities as a client. *Building projects; your role in achieving quality and value*, CABE publications, London, March 2004 www.cabe.org.uk

The Egan report describes the measures of improvement in terms of predictability, cost, time and quality, where clients will then be able to recognise added value and reward companies that deliver it, which means that a method of measuring progress towards its objectives and targets must be created. In addition to that, the construction industry must produce its own structure of objective performance measures agreed with clients.[51]

The report then goes through the different ways of improving the performance of the construction industry on different scales except on the scale of sustainable development or sustainability. The report seemed out of touch with the current significant challenges facing the industry in sustainable development terms.

Although 'sustainable development' was never mentioned in any of the report's chapters, the linkage between a sustainable development agenda and the five key drivers suggested by the report, is eminently clear. This lack of sustainability in the report does not undermine the significant targets suggested in it to improve the industry's performance nor the importance of the report and its key drivers, but by not addressing the issues of sustainability explicitly in the report; it fell short of the industry's expectations for a sustainable future performance. The industry's need for a clearer agenda on sustainable development, which was lacking in the Egan report, was great in terms of commitment and the need to do more. This is why it seems essential to highlight another report that puts the criteria of 'Rethinking Construction' into a sustainable development context.

---

[51] ibid.

Published by the Construction Research and Innovation Strategy Panel (CRISP)[52]; `Integrating Sustainability and Rethinking Construction`[53] is the report which would highlight the linkage between the Egan key drivers and sustainable development's parallel levels of social, economic and environmental performances.

1.5 "Integrating Sustainability and Rethinking Construction"

Written for CRISP by Environmental Resources Management (ERM), this report highlights what sustainability really means in the context of the construction industry. The report outlines how it can contribute towards performance improvement, and confirms that sustainability can and should be directly incorporated with the objectives of Egan. Each of the drivers identified in the Egan report as being vital for the improvement of the quality and efficiency of the UK construction industry is assessed with regard to its potential contribution to the economic, environmental and social objectives of sustainable development. The analysis suggests that, although 'Rethinking Construction' offers a number of opportunities for sustainable construction, sustainability must be incorporated as a key objective for the drivers to have an impact.[54]

---

[52] Construction Research and Innovation Strategy Panel (CRISP) **CRISP** was formed as a joint industry and Government panel in July 1995, to implement the Whole Industry Research Strategy (WIRS). In September 1995 the (then) Department of the Environment established professional support to the Panel, and its first Business Plan was adopted in December 1995. CRISP website is www.crisp-uk.org.uk

[53] CRISP, *Integrating Sustainability and "Rethinking Construction"*, Environmental Resources Management (ERM), CRISP, London, 1999. The report can be accessed on CRISP website at www.crisp-uk.org.uk last visited in January 2003

[54] ibid.

In commissioning this study, the Theme Group recognised the need to ensure that those involved in taking forward the Egan report were aware of the principles of sustainability most relevant to the construction sector. The aim of the work, therefore, is to identify those aspects of sustainable construction which are readily incorporated into the performance improvement agenda set out by the Construction Task Force, and to highlight those areas of sustainable construction which are outside the Task Force's current agenda.[55]

The specific objectives include the review the contributions that a consideration of sustainability can make to performance improvement in the construction industry, identify the opportunities offered by the agenda for change set out in 'Rethinking Construction' for achieving a sustainable construction industry; and finally, identify the barriers that need to be tackled in order to achieve sustainability and the research and innovation initiatives which are required in helping overcome these barriers.

The first stage of the analysis examines how, and to what extent, the current performance improvement agenda addresses sustainability issues.

In table (1.1), each of the drivers identified in `Rethinking Construction`, for improving the quality and efficiency of the UK construction industry, is assessed for its potential contribution to the economic, environmental and social objectives of sustainable development.

The analysis suggests that each of these drivers could help improve the

---

[55] ibid.

industry's contribution to sustainable development, although for this to happen in practice, performance improvement needs to be redefined to incorporate sustainability as a key objective.

1.5.1 Mapping Egan "drivers" onto Sustainable Development

Committed Leadership: Very important to sustainable development on the economic and environmental levels and moderately important on the social level. Strong commitment from senior management is widely recognised as a key factor in improving the environmental performance of major companies. Also necessary for driving through the changes required to make a company more responsive to stakeholders on ethical, social and community issues.[56]

Focus on the customer: Very important to sustainable development on the economic and social levels and moderately important on the environmental level. Customer focus in the construction industry is likely to result in lower running costs (and environmental impacts) associated with energy consumption and maintenance. Providing the best deal for customers where it is also a key issue in corporate social responsibility. Customer demand will be a key influence on other aspects of environmental and social performance.[57]

Integrating the process and team around the product: Very important to sustainable development on the environmental and economic levels and of minor importance on the social level. Improved links between

[56] ibid.
[57] ibid.

41

planning, design and construction will reduce waste, and facilitate use of more sustainable materials and building methods, through better understanding of benefits and sharing of knowledge and skills. Co-operative working environment is likely to increase social interaction and job satisfaction among employees. Partnerships also form the basis for improving environmental and social performance of the supply chain and provide for fair, long- term business relationships.[58]

Quality driven agenda: Very important to sustainable development on the economic and the environmental level and moderately important on the social level. Environmental performance of building components and materials linked with improvements in quality and process efficiency, e.g. standardized components reducing waste; durable materials maximizing product life; energy efficient materials reducing running costs. Approaches to quality management also applicable to environmental and social performances; parallel framework with policy, targets, monitoring and reporting.[59]

Commitment to people: Very important to sustainable development on the social level, moderately important on the economic level and of minor importance on the environmental level. Working conditions, training and development opportunities for employees and contractors is a key issue for companies wishing to demonstrate Corporate Social Responsibility (CSR). Training at all levels of the industry is also important for

---

[58] ibid.
[59] ibid.

sustainability considerations to be integrated in design and construction.[60]

This stage of the analysis also indicates clearly that the scope of 'Rethinking Construction' is insufficient to embrace the full extent of the industry's potential contribution to sustainable development. The Egan agenda is limited to the construction process and falls short of addressing the industry's broader influence on the built environment through linkages with other groups such as planners, building managers, clients/users, and government (the regulators).[61]

The second stage of the analysis aims to identify the sustainability issues' considerations, which might also contribute to performance improvement as defined by 'Rethinking Construction'. This is done firstly by listing the actions or processes the industry would need to implement in order to meet key sustainability objectives. These are then matched against the five 'drivers' in order to identify how, and to what extent, consideration of each sustainability issue might also contribute to performance improvement.

---

[60] ibid.
[61] Mohamed Eid, A review of "Project Management" & "Sustainable Development" for Construction Projects, Edinburgh Architecture Research (EAR) Journal, Volume 27, Department of Architecture, University of Edinburgh, September 2000

Sustainability Issues	Possible Actions	Relevance to Egan Drivers				
		Leadership	Customer	Integration	Quality	People
• Efficiency / productivity of the construction process	• Process Integration. • Product Development • Improved Customer focus • Training • Supply Chain partnering • Quality management systems	***	***	***	***	***
• Minimisation and/or recycling on construction and demolition waste	• Use of reclaimed materials • Waste segregation & recycling • Use of standardised components/durable materials • Extending product life through durability or adaptability	***	**	***	***	*
• Decent working conditions for employees & contractors	• On site facilities • Health and safety measures • Use of local employment	***	*	**	***	***
• Business relations with sub-contractors, customers, suppliers and partners	• Long term partnerships • Non-confrontational contracting • Codes of conduct • Quality assurance/ environmental standards	***	***	***	***	***
• Responsiveness to customers, end users and other stakeholders	• Involvement of communities / end users in project planning & design • Dialogue with other affected by development projects • Environmental reporting	***	***	***	***	***
• Energy efficiency of buildings / completed developments	• Use of energy efficient construction technologies • Planning to reduce car dependency	***	***	**	***	*

Table (1.1):- Key Linkages between Sustainability elements and the Egan report's drivers[77]

The analysis indicates a clear synergy between several of the key sustainability issues (e.g. waste minimisation, decent working conditions and good business relations) and performance improvement as illustrated in table (1.1) and table (1.2).

		Relevance to Egan Drivers				
		Leadership	Customer	Integration	Quality	People
		**	***	*	**	***
• Use of sustainable materials (reduced embodied energy; recycled, renewable, locally sourced)	• Green specifications • Supply chain management	**	*	*	**	*
• Use of renewable energy in buildings	• Passive solar; photovoltaic etc	**	*	*	**	*
• Promoting water efficiency	• Use of water efficient fittings • Water recycling infrastructure	**	**	**	**	**
• Prevention of surface and groundwater pollution from construction & completed developments	• Environmental management systems (EMS)	***	**	*	**	***
• Use of Brownfield instead of Greenfield sites	• Choice of development location	***	*		*	*
• Protection of local landscape and ecological value	• Mitigation measures including landscaping, habitat restoration	**	*	*	**	**

Table (1.2):- Secondary Linkages between Sustainability and the Egan report's drivers[62]

This conclusion is supported by the fact that the same issues are mentioned explicitly in `Rethinking Construction`. However, in each case at least three of the drivers for performance improvement, most notably committed leadership and a quality-driven agenda, need to be in place for this `win-win` result to be achieved.[63]

---

[62] Table (1.1) and (1.2),CRISP, *Integrating Sustainability and "Rethinking Construction"*, Environmental Resources Management (ERM), CRISP, London, 1999
[63] ibid.

A larger number of sustainability issues have less contribution to make to performance improvement and so are less likely to be tackled effectively by the `Rethinking Construction` process. These are sustainability issues for which there are fewer matches between the actions required and the processes for performance improvement. The analysis indicates the sustainability issues least likely to be addressed are use of sustainable materials, renewable energy and brown-field vs. green-field development.

In conclusion, the report concludes that the objectives of sustainability and `Rethinking Construction` overlap in several areas. It also notes that, while the Egan report will not optimise sustainable development, it could help increase it, but for this to happen, sustainability must be acknowledged as a central objective.

1.6 Milestones and the Need for Change in Construction

As addressed in the Egan report, leading companies in other sectors (and a very small number of leading UK construction companies) are already measuring, and taking systematic steps to manage, their sustainability impacts. These companies recognise that a reorientation towards sustainable development is essential for ensuring their long-term viability. However, most companies within the UK construction industry appear to be missing opportunities for taking a more pro-active role, within their broader sphere of influence, in helping to provide a sustainable built environment.[64]

An urgent need – and a considerable opportunity - exists to include sustainable development as an explicit objective into existing and new

[64] DETR, *Rethinking Construction*, The Construction Task Force, DETR, London, 1998

initiatives. This could be facilitated by including indicators of sustainability (such as those being developed by CIRIA[65], BSRIA[66] and others) into the Key Performance Indicators (KPIs) framework put forward in 'Rethinking Construction'.

CURRENT RICS KPIS ?
INCLUSION OF SUSTAINABILITY.

Currently, the industry has identified the need for change; several key researches have established the link between sustainable development and the future of the industry. These researches generally revolve around very similar suggestions and indicators; they argue that the need for change is vital because the challenges exist within a general consensus on the industry's main environmental impacts and agreement that these extend beyond the construction phase to include supply chain issues and the effects of post construction activities such as operation, maintenance and re-use of buildings. They also include less emphasis on the social component of sustainable development and the industry's influence on it; with some agreement among those that did consider that the industry had an important role to play in shaping viable communities. Finally, they include differing views on the scope of the industry's influence on sustainable development; where some considered only the direct impacts of construction activities while others included the industry's wider role in shaping patterns of development.

Historically, a mixture of external pressure, market sensitivity and corporate philosophy has driven this move. Increasingly, business is realising that addressing sustainability issues can also enhance its bottom line. Many companies are taking systematic measures to improve their environmental and social performance in order to ensure their long-term competitiveness

[65] Construction Industry Research and Information Association (CIRIA) www.ciria.org.uk
[66] Leading centre for building services technology and information (BSRIA) www.bsria.co.uk

and license to operate.[67]

The construction industry has successfully passed the milestone of recognising the importance of integrating sustainable development into the core of the industry's practices. Creating sustainable agendas for the industry is a vital step forward towards the implementation of change in the culture of the industry and attitudes towards a sustainable future. The scale of the UK construction industry, its immediate environmental and resource use impacts, coupled with the influence of its products on the nation's quality of life, make it a key player in delivering sustainable development.[68]

The implementation of sustainable development agendas and the business case behind the integration demonstrate that the business case for sustainable construction has many opportunities to create environmental and social improvements whilst increasing profits and market shares which can create new sources of employment and ensure better business benefits and sustainable economic base and beneficial impacts.

The industry is facing up to its weaknesses and building upon its strengths, and, it has not yet used its full potential for change and doing things differently. There are always lessons to be learned from what the UK's construction industry is trying to achieve and there is always potential to do more.

---

[67] BRE MaSC, *Managing Sustainable Construction – Profiting from Sustainability*, Report produced by MaSC Team, first published in 2002 by CRC Ltd, BRE 2002
[68] Mohamed Eid, A review of "Project Management" & "Sustainable Development" for Construction Projects, (EAR) Journal, Volume 27, September 2000

On the European scale, the need for change is now evident, and the European policies introducing `change` have discussed several aspects of the challenges mostly targeting a change for a sustainable agenda for the industry. For the UK's construction industry, where the new initiatives for changing and improving the industry's performance revolve around implementing sustainable development into the industry's practices, it is certainly the same set of challenges as the EU.

The need for change in the industry should start from within the culture of the industry and the people, directly or indirectly, involved in the industry's practices.

There are great opportunities for better performance and the lessons learned from the challenges are undeniably significant.

1.7 The Way Forward

The construction industry is the first element of the tri-dimensional integration proposed in this research. More specifically, the construction practices and processes hold the biggest potential for the integration.

The similarities between the European and the British construction industry are now evident, where they both represent a big share of their own GDPs and play a major role in European as well as British citizens' daily lives. On the European level, the industry was underperforming and there was an urgent need to act upon upgrading the industry to the new global economy and world commitment for sustainable development.

Urgent measures have been introduced by the EU community to introduce a new facelift for the construction industry and introduce a more competitive industry relying on a more stable economy and sustainable guidelines for better performance on social, environmental and economic levels.

The British industry was also facing continuous pressure from disappointed clients and stakeholders' concern for the underperformance of the industry and failure to deliver a better quality of life for all individuals directly or indirectly involved with the industry. Similar to the European challenges, the UK's construction industry had to face up to its weaknesses and failures. The industry was failing clients and underperforming in delivering social inclusion, better environmental commitment and successful economic performance combined with successful business cases.

The construction industry was part of the problem of delivering a better quality of life for people and there was a persisting need to make the industry part of the solution.

Integrating sustainable development into the construction industry practices and indeed into the culture of the industry was, and still is, the biggest challenge facing the industry. Following a global commitment to sustainable agendas for all industries, and most of all the construction industry, the UK construction industry has moved onto the sustainable road map to sustainable construction.

The chapter has discussed the leading research papers studying the means of integration of sustainable development into the industry, by analysing the initiatives and pointing out the points of weakness as well as strengths in these researches. Although the British government is taking the lead in implementing the integration and studying the possible impacts and outcome, there is still more that needs to be done.

The industry has successfully passed several milestones, but the way forward for the industry still needs a lot of work and commitment; where the need for change has developed into proposed actions and means of making the change happen.

The lessons which could be learned from the industry's initiatives are immense, and delivering a more sustainable construction industry has proven to be a great challenge. Many countries could benefit from the UK's ongoing experience with implementing sustainable development especially for developing countries where the potential is even more immense. In terms of changing its culture and understanding of construction practices, the construction industry in developing countries could also meet its challenges by learning from a leading example such as the British construction industry and trying to adopt its experiences and learn from its challenges.

CHAPTER 2

SUSTAINABLE DEVELOPMENT

"American philosopher William James claimed that it (Sustainable Development), like all significant ideas, had passed through three stages: being rejected; being admitted as true but insignificant; and finally, being seen as so important that its opponents claim to have thought of it first."

Alan Holland "Sustainable Development; The Contested Vision"[69]

Following a global concern for the impact of human development activities on the planet as well as on the people, `Sustainable Development` emerged as the new solution to `make things right` and proposed a better quality of life for now and for the future. Sustainable Development (SD) is the second pillar of the integration proposed in this research.

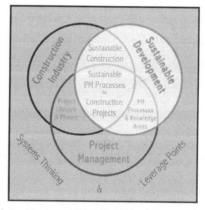

Figure 2.0: Sustainable Development; the second of four pillars, in the research's hypothesis

Figure (2.0) illustrates the hypothesis of the research with special emphasis on sustainable development; the topic of this chapter.

---

[69] Keekok Lee, Alan Holland and Desmond McNeil (Editors), *Global Sustainable Development In The Twenty-First Century*, Edinburgh University Press Ltd., Edinburgh, 2000, pp.05

2.1 Introduction

This chapter discusses the reasons why `Sustainable Development` is considered as the way to a better quality of life for all of us. According to the assessments of the Intergovernmental Panel on Climate Change (IPCC), the Earth's natural climate controls have been altered by humane activities causing a warming process, where global temperatures have risen by at least 0.55°C in the last century.[70] Human induced climate change is now a fact of our lives that needs to be dealt with as quickly as possible. It has an impact on biodiversity, forestry, water, desertification, quality of air and the depletion of the Ozone layer. Our ways of life has been mainly influenced by a long list of disasters, where the 1960s, 70s and 80s brought immense volumes of new knowledge about pollution and the overuse of natural resources.[71]

The following provides an introduction to the evolution of sustainable development's theories and applications, from its emergence, to its current status of practical applications of SD within the EU and the UK with special emphasis on its role within the construction industry. The chapter also discusses the reasons behind the global interest in sustainable development, on the European level and more specifically in the UK. Several significant

---

[70] Information provided by Intergovernmental Panel on Climate Change (IPCC), last visited August 2003 www.ipcc.ch ; The IPCC was established in 1988 by the World Meteorological Organization (WMO) and the United Nations Environment Programme (UNEP). Recognizing the problem of potential climate change, the role of the IPCC is to assess on a comprehensive, objective, open and transparent basis the scientific, technical and socio-economic information relevant to understanding the scientific basis of risk of human-induced climate change, its potential impacts and options for adaptation and mitigation.
[71] Gro Harlem Brundtland, *Our common Future and Then Years after Rio: How Far Have we Come and Where Should We Be Going?* , Article part of the book: Earth Summit 2002, A New Deal, (Edited by Felix Dodds), United Nations Environment and Development-UK Committee (UNED-UK), Earthscan Publications Ltd., 2000, pp.254

European and British documents will be analysed; from governments' regulations to strategies to stakeholders' views, all promoting the introduction of sustainability to touch all citizens in their everyday lives. The contribution of sustainable development to the construction sector will be discussed further, based on the earlier analysis of sustainable construction.

European and British policies for sustainable development are quite similar in their commitment to the implications which sustainable development might introduce within social, environmental and economic trends, but whatever the policies are, sustainable development faces significant challenges in defining its `Business Case`. This chapter will discuss how the business case of sustainable development influences the progress of the implementation of sustainable development in all fields and how `Businesses` react to sustainability trends with special focus on the prospective of Eco-Efficiency into these applications and the potentials it might hold.

Sustainable development goes beyond environmental awareness; it tackles social and economic aspects as well as the environment, hence, the chapter discusses the ways in which sustainable development touches upon our daily activities and the importance it represents in this research. Sustainable development represents a vital element of the integration proposed in order to attain sustainable construction practice and more specifically in the management of projects.

2.2 Introducing "Sustainable Development" (SD)

"Sustainable Development is a development that meets the needs of the present without compromising the ability of future generations to meet their own needs"[72]

This is the first definition of sustainable development, which was part of the World Commission on Environment and Development (WCED) report[73] for the United Nations Environment Programme (UNEP) published in 1987. The Commission was chaired by the then Norwegian Prime Minister, Gro Harlem Brundtland, from whom the report took its name of `Brundtland Report`.

Since the Brundtland Report, several initiatives have been undertaken, worthy of mention as significant attempts to define what Sustainable Development is or should be. At the international level: -

- **Agenda 21:** Formulated at the Rio Summit in 1992[74]

Agenda 21 is one of the resulting documents of the conference along with the Rio Declaration on Environment and Development, the Statement of Forest Principles, the United Nations Framework Convention on Climate Change and the United Nations Convention on Biological Diversity. The Earth Summit influenced all subsequent UN conferences that have examined the relationship between human rights, population, social development, women

---

[72] World Commission on environment and Development (WCED), Our Common future, also known as (The Brundtland Report), United Nations Environment Programme (UNEP) Press, U.S.A, 1987

[73] ibid.

[74] "Rio Summit" is the term generally used to refer to the Earth Summit held in Rio De Janeiro, Brazil in 1992. UN Conference on Environment and Development was the first Earth Summit to be held and organised by the United Nations, twenty years after the first global environment conference. http://www.un.org/geninfo/bp/enviro.html

and human settlements — and the need for sustainable development.

- **Habitat II Agenda:** Habitat II in 1996[75]

Formulated at the UN conference on Human Settlements (Habitat II) held in Istanbul, Turkey in 1996. The conference had two major themes of equal global importance: `Adequate shelter for all` and `Sustainable human settlements development in an urbanizing world`.

And at the Local Level:-

- **Local Agenda 21, Planning Guide:** compiled by the International Council for Local Environmental Initiatives (ICLEI), to provide guidance to local authorities on the formulation of a Local Agenda 21 as prescribed in Chapter 28 of Agenda 21.[76]

Other initiatives at the regional level should also be cited such as the Amsterdam Treaty[77] or the 5th Environmental Action Programme of the European Commission.[78]

From these initiatives, several definitions of sustainable development emerged. These definitions are not different in terms of the issues'

---

[75] Second United Nations conference on Human Settlements (Habitat II), Istanbul 1996, http://www.un.org/Conferences/habitat/
[76] Web Address for Local Agenda 21 and ICLEI, last visited June 2003, http://www.iclei.org/ICLEI/la21.htm
[77] Web Address for Amsterdam Treaty on Environment and Sustainable Development , last accessed in June 2003, http://europa.eu.int/scadplus/leg/en/lvb/a15000.htm
[78] The European Community Programme of policy and action in relation to the environment and sustainable development "Towards Sustainability", last accessed in June 2003, http://europa.eu.int/comm/environment/actionpr.htm

fundamentals they address; in fact, they are united in their goals and objectives.

The first was referred to above as part of the Brundtland Report `Our Common Future`. In the Rio Declaration on Environment and Development 1992, sustainable development is described within the Declaration statement as follows:-

"...with the goal of establishing a new and equitable partnership through the creation of new levels of co-operation among States, key sectors of societies and people, working towards international agreements which respect the interests of all and protect the integrity of the global environmental and development system, recognising the integral and interdependence of the Earth, our home, proclaims that:..."

In 1991, the World Conservation Union (IUCN) along with the United Nations Environment Programme (UNEP) formulated a publication titled `Caring for the Earth`[79] and in its proceedings, sustainable development is described as the path to:-

"Improving the quality of human life while living within the carrying capacity of supporting ecosystems"

From the Local Agenda 21 Planning Guide (ICLEI, 1996), SD is described as:-

"Development that delivers basic environmental, social, and economic services to all residences of a community without threatening the viability of natural, built and social systems upon which the delivery of those systems depends"

Finally, from the EU Amsterdam Treaty (1997):-

"determined to promote economic and social progress for their peoples, taking into

---

[79] Web Address for IUCN "Caring for the Earth", last visited June 2003, http://www.ciesin.org/IC/iucn/CaringDS.html

account the principle of sustainable development and within the context of the accomplishment of the internal market and of reinforced cohesion and environmental protection, and to implement policies that advances in economic integration are accompanied by parallel progress in other fields"

In general, all those attempts to define sustainable development have the same outlook on the concept of SD. Despite the different ways of applying these definitions to the different fields, sustainable development embraces the three broad themes of environmental, social and economic accountability known and referred to as the `Triple Bottom Line`[80] as shown in figure (2.1).

The Triple Bottom Line (TBL) focuses not just on the economic value, but also on the environmental and social. In its narrowest sense, the term 'Triple Bottom Line' is used as a framework for measuring and reporting performance against economic, social and environmental parameters. In its broadest sense, the term is used to capture the whole set of values, issues and processes which must be addressed in order to minimize any harm resulting from human activities and to create economic, social and environmental value. This involves clarity of purpose and goals and taking into consideration the needs of all stakeholders; shareholders, customers, employees, business partners, governments, local communities and the public.[81]

---

[80] John Elkington, *Cannibals with Forks; The Triple Bottom Line of 21st Century Business,* Capstone Publishing, Oxford, 1999
[81] SustainAbility Consultancy, *The Triple Bottom Line (TBL),* www.sustainability.com , last accessed June 2003. Founded in 1987, SustainAbility is the longest established international consultancy specializing in business strategy and sustainable development – environmental improvement, social equity and economic development.

58

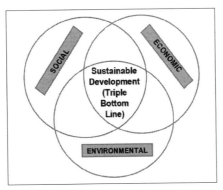

Figure 2.1:- The relationship between the three elements of SD (The Triple Bottom Line)

The ` Triple Bottom Line` and `Sustainable Development` are about ensuring a better quality of life for everyone now, and for generations to come through: social progress and inclusion which recognises the needs of everyone, the maintenance of high and stable levels of economic growth and employment, protecting and if possible, enhancing the environment and using natural resources prudently.[82]

The three parallel levels of the triple bottom line work together to complete the sustainable development parameters. None of them is more important than the other. In fact, it is crucial to understand that the success of applying SD to any field relies mainly on maintaining the equilibrium and balance between the three levels equally and at the same time.

"Sustainable development isn't outstanding environmental performance at the cost of a company, which goes out of business, nor is it outstanding financial performance at the cost of adverse effects on the local environment and communities. It does not

[82] Mohamed E.M. Eid, A review of "Project Management" & "Sustainable Development" for Construction Projects, Edinburgh Architecture Research Journal (EAR) Volume 27, University of Edinburgh, Architecture Department, September 2000, pp.55

demand the perfect solution. Sustainable development is essentially a goal or vision that forward looking organisations are working towards."[83]

In simple terms, sustainable development can be a goal, where it implies great potential for human material well-being (socially and economically) and the environment. This is clearly captured by the two terms `development` and `sustainable`, where the former is concerned with human evolution and activities on both social and economic levels, while the latter is targeting the stress that such development places on the environment.

2.2.1 Criticisms of Sustainable Development

Criticizing the concept of sustainable development has been portrayed mainly in views highlighting; firstly, the conflict in the term `sustainable development` itself and secondly, the conflict of interest between developed and developing countries in the concept of implementation.

Firstly, the critics think that combining `development` with `sustainable` in one term can only create more ambiguity around the concept. It is regarded as a conflict in meaning; asking how the development process can be combined with social, environmental and economic limitations.

"Combining these two words `sustainable` and `development` implies having aspirations to achieve a balanced relationship between human society and the natural environment, one that can be sustained, and at the same time implies striving for a certain kind of development."[84]

---

[83] Movement for Innovation (M⁴I), *Sustainability Indicators*, Department of the Environment, Transport and the Regions (DETR), now known as Department of Trade and Industry (DTI), UK, 1999

[84] Jan J. Boersema and Joeri Bertels, *Sustainable Development in the Developed Countries: Will Theory and Practice Meet?*, published in *"Global Sustainable Development in the 21ˢᵗ Century"*,

But this research demonstrates that sustainable guidelines are more of 'opportunities' rather than 'limitations', where the triple bottom line gives more scope for change in performance on the three levels while allowing growth and development.

"Sustainable Development must not be seen as limitation to economic growth and employment, but rather as an attractive investment strategy for prosperity, welfare and social justice"[85]

Secondly, some critics argue that 'Sustainable Development' and 'Climate Change' are terms created by developed countries to control and limit the growth of developing countries in terms of their use of natural resources, harming the environment, seeking wealth and growth and to better the quality of their life.

"...deep suspicions roused by the sustainability agenda. On the one side are the suspicions that it is a device, whether intentional or not, for blocking 'Southern' development......projects financed by wealthy economies (conservation projects, dam building schemes and the like) are seen as expressions of a distinctly 'Northern' agenda, designed to limit the global environmental impact of economic activity of which they are the primary beneficiaries. This is seen as a value that the developed economies preach but do not practice."[86]

This argument originates from concerns that developed countries have now realised the impacts of their past development activities on the environment and that they fear more negative impacts from the activities of the developing countries when trying to catch up with the globalization

---

edited by Keekok Lee, Alan Holland and Desmond McNeill, Edinburgh University Press, Edinburgh, 2000,pp. 77

[85] The European Economic and Social Committee (EESC), *Opinion of the EESC on the Lisbon Strategy and Sustainable Development*, The European Commission, Official Journal of the European Union, Brussels, April 2003, section 1.16

[86] Alan Holland, *Sustainable Development: The Contested Vision*, Introduction to *"Global Sustainable Development in the 21st Century"*, Edinburgh University Press Ltd., Edinburgh, 2000,pp. 3

initiatives. This is portrayed in the conflict between the `North` and their agenda of ecological modernisation and the `South` and their own agenda of development and poverty reduction.[87]

"Developed economies see the problem as one to be tackled by using cleaner technologies so as to minimise the impact of economic growth upon the environment known as `ecological modernisation` whose central proposition is that economic growth can be adapted to meet environmental goals......In developing economies, on the other hand, a cleaner global environment is a much lower priority than the immediate environmental problems associated with poverty..."[88]

However, the arguments in this chapter demonstrate that the implementation of sustainable development does not mean `static` nor does it mean giving up on the idea of development but in fact, that the implementation cannot harm any economies whether rich or poor. The implementation can only benefit societies, business and governments. It does not limit their growth on any of the three levels of sustainability but, contrary to what the critics argue, it fortifies the approach to development on the same triple bottom lines.

Sustainability helps developing countries to catch up with the developed ones but in a manner that would assure enhanced environmental impact, social inclusion and equality and improved economic performance and business cases.

The chairman of Procter & Gamble (John Pepper) has described this conflict as follows:

---

[87] Michael Redclift, *Global Equity: The Environment and Development*, published in *"Global Sustainable Development in the 21st Century"*, edited by Keekok Lee, Alan Holland and Desmond McNeill, Edinburgh University Press, Edinburgh, 2000
[88] ibid. pp. 101

"We cannot condemn developing countries to a life of poverty so those in the developed countries can maintain their lifestyles. But neither do we have to presume that the only alternative is for the developed world to reduce its quality of life.....but the idea is to mobilise markets in favour of sustainability, leveraging the power of innovation and global markets for the benefit of everyone, not just those in the developed world."[89]

Therefore, the criticism of sustainable development does not represent a genuine cause for concern, because implementing sustainable development strategies can only benefit the whole world. There are no impairments to developing countries in following a much more efficient approach to development socially, environmentally and economically; and neither is there any harm for the developed countries to sustain better environment, social justice and business growing economies.

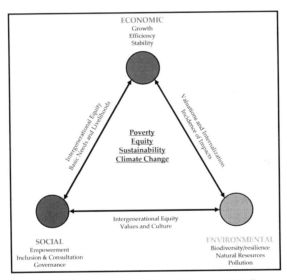

Figure 2.2: Key Elements of SD and Interconnections[90]

Sustainable development goes beyond `greener` environment, `growing`

[89] John Pepper and A.G. Lafley, *CEO and Chairman's Statement in P&G Sustainability Report*, Procter & Gamble, Cincinatti, 2001
[90] Intergovernmental Panel on Climate Change (IPCC), Synthesis Report Climate Change 2001 http://www.ipcc.ch/present/graphics.htm last visited August 2003

economies or `equitable` societies individually, but the three of them balanced collectively. As we have illustrated, the criticism around the concept of sustainable development does not justify not implementing it. In Figure (2.2) the interconnections between the triple bottom line review the significant numerous opportunities where change can be implemented.

The change taking place, whether in developing or developed countries, can only represent the positive impacts on these fields such as climate change, equity, growth, economic stability, empowerment, social inclusion, environmental pollution and biodiversity. These impacts are the opportunities for change that justify the implementation of SD.

The term `Sustainable Development` encapsulates the three parallel levels and pushes towards a higher standard of performance; a new approach.[91]

2.3   The New Approach in a Global Context

In the past, human development activities and engineering were more concerned with quality standards (Cost, Quality and Time) which provided the competitive factors in traditional business processes. Decades later, and as demonstrated in figure (2.3), global interest has focused on the greener approach to businesses and activities; where preserving, or if possible, enhancing the environment, has been on top of the international agenda.

The new paradigm was intended to introduce the golden triangle to a wider

---

[91] Desmond McNeill, "The Concept of Sustainable Development", Keekok Lee, Alan Holland and Desmond McNeil (Editors), *Global Sustainable Development In The Twenty-First Century*, Edinburgh, Edinburgh University Press Ltd., 2000, pp.19-23

perspective of environmental demands, with controlled use of natural resources, monitoring of emissions and biodiversity, which defines its concept. Together with the environmental issues, economic and socio-cultural issues are now encircling the new paradigm to display the new approach in a global context. The new approach reveals economic constraints, social equity and cultural issues and environmental quality in a global context.

The international interest in embedding sustainability into current practices has been triggered by the global commitment to this new approach which demonstrates how human development activities and engineering are widened to encapsulate the triple bottom line guiding principle.[92]

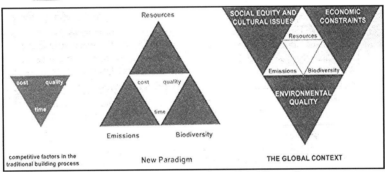

Figure 2.3:- The New Approach in a Global Context[93]

The above diagram is very significant in terms of the evolution of sustainable development, because it shows the rise of the concept from local, national and international levels to a global level of concern. This describes the

---

[92] International Council for Research and Innovation in Building and Construction (CIB), *Agenda 21 on Sustainable Construction*, CIB Report Publication 237, The Netherlands, 1999, pp.42
[93] ibid

human material well being as no longer a conflict between north and south, developed and developing countries, but it shows that the challenge is a global matter for one world and one environment. The diagram shows how sustainable development can only be achieved globally. It can not be done by one country or a group of countries in the developing world alone. The commitment has to be drawn from a global effort.

"Sustainable development emerges from a common purpose, that of re-valuating nature as an ethical principle and as a general condition for global sustainability of population and production."[94]

In general, sustainable development can achieve a better quality of life for everyone, now and for future generations, through four main strands. The first being the social progress which recognises the needs of everyone, the second is the maintenance of high and stable levels of economic growth and employment, whilst the third is protecting, and if possible enhancing, the environment, and finally, the fourth being the prudent use of natural resources.[95]

The United Nations Conference on Environment and Development (UNCED), held in Rio de Janeiro in 1992, was the first demonstration of this global context and world wide concern for the implementation of sustainable development. Taking into account the Rio principles and building on the achievements made since then, the eyes of the United Nations, as well as of the whole world, were focussed on the World Summit on Sustainable

---

[94] Enrique Leff, *Sustainable Development in Developing Countries: Cultural Diversity and Environmental Rationality*, Keekok Lee, Alan Holland and Desmond McNeil (Editors), *Global Sustainable Development In The Twenty-First Century*, Edinburgh University Press Ltd., Edinburgh,2000, pp.63
[95] Department of Trade and Industry (DTI), *What is Sustainable Development*, http://www.dti.gov.uk/sustainability/strategy/2.htm , Last accessed June 2003

Development, held in Johannesburg in August 2002 to push further the global efforts of implementation and allow each country and nation to reflect on their achievements so far towards a sustainable future.

The plan of implementation, published as one of the resulting document of the Johannesburg Summit, stated that; at the international as well as at national level, good policy governance is essential for achieving the level of sustainability first set as a goal. The plan also advised that the implementation should involve all relevant parties through partnerships, especially among governments and between governments and major groups to reach the wide goals of sustainability, where such partnerships are described as keys to pursuing SD in a globalizing world.[96]

As a result of globalization, external factors have become critical in determining the success or failure of countries in their national efforts; this is reflected in their policies towards sustainable development. At the domestic level, sound environmental, social and economic polices, democratic institutions responsive to the needs of the people, the rule of law, anti-corruption measures, gender equality and an environment enabling investment, are the basis for sustainable development.

Due to the importance given to international and domestic policies towards sustainable development and that in order to set the base of the research's hypothesis, it is essential at this point of the research to examine the European policy, as well as the UK local policy, in achieving sustainable development. This examination is set to highlight the efforts of

---

[96] World Summit on Sustainable Development (WSSD), *Plan of Implementation*, Johannesburg, United Nations Earth Summit 2002. www.johannesburgsummit.org last accessed June 2003

implementation of sustainable development and would therefore reflect on the local and the international agendas for sustainable construction.

2.4 European Policies for Sustainable Development

The EU and other signatories of the 1992 United Nations' `Rio Declaration` committed themselves, at the 19th Special Session of the United Nations' General Assembly in 1997, to draw up policies for `Sustainable Development` in time for the 2002 World Summit on Sustainable Development (WSSD). [97]

This commitment to sustainable development and its global agendas was the catalyst for the European Council to invite the European Commission at its meeting in Helsinki in December 1999 to prepare:-

"a proposal for a long term strategy dovetailing policies for economically, socially and ecologically sustainable development to be presented to the European Council in June 2001".[98]

In its long term vision, the European Commission envisaged sustainable development as a global objective, set to provide the European Council a new strategic goal, which would allow the EU to become the most competitive and dynamic knowledge-based economy in the world capable of sustainable economic growth with more and better jobs and greater social

---

[97] Commission of the European Communities, *A Sustainable Europe for a Better World: A European Union Strategy for Sustainable Development; Communication from the Commission to the Gothenburg European Council*, European Union, Brussels, 2001 (COM 2001, 264 final)
[98] http://europa.eu.int/comm/sustainable/index_en.htm , European Commission's official website, Sustainable Development section, last visited July2003

cohesion.[99]

The EU strategy for sustainable development offered a challenge for a positive long-term vision which recognises economic growth and social cohesion to go hand in hand with environmental protection. Achieving this in practice, requires that economic growth supports social progress and respects the environment, that social policy underpins economic performance, and that environmental policy would be cost-effective.[100]

2.4.1 Why a SD Strategy for the European Union is needed

The Commission, in its report on its strategy for sustainable development, calls on developed countries to take the lead in pursuing sustainable development. It specifically calls on them to also accept their responsibilities. Here, the EU wants to set the standard for commitment and is following up on its policies to enable sustainable development to have its effects on the everyday life of EU citizens.[101]

During the course of the 20th century, the standard of living rose higher than it had ever been for the countries of the EU, where growing interdependence of economies resulting from the single market, globalisation and new communication technologies provided a strong drive to EU efficiency and increased productivity, and offered new opportunities at all levels. But, in

---

[99] Commission of the European Communities, *A Sustainable Europe for a Better World: A European Union Strategy for Sustainable Development; Communication from the Commission to the Gothenburg European Council*, European Union, Brussels, 2001 (COM 2001, 264 final)
[100] ibid
[101] Official Journal of the European Union, *Opinion of the European Economic and Social Committee on "the Lisbon Strategy and Sustainable Development"*, The European Union Bulletin online http://europa.eu.int/abc/doc/off/bull/en/welcome.htm, April 2003

order to put sustainable development at the heart of the debate on the future of Europe, these positive developments should not overtake the potential threats that the EU faces. The commission acknowledges the growing awareness of the impact of human development activities which is putting increased pressure on the carrying capacity of our planet.[102]

From this perspective, the challenges facing the EU for sustainability go beyond current borders of each of the countries of the EU, where it is now a major challenge to secure the long term viability of its natural environment. Global warming is a clear example of these significant challenges facing the EU, and indeed the whole world, at present and in the future. Next to global warming and climate change, clean energy is a pressing matter as well as public health, management of natural resources, social exclusion, land use and territorial development, energy supply and environmental degradation.

In preparation for the WSSD, The European Commission created a short list of four closely linked sets of issues, which should be addressed in an integrated manner in order to design a balanced and forward-looking agenda of sustainable development. These four sets of issues are; protecting the natural resource base of economic development, integrating environment and poverty eradication, making globalisation sustainable and finally, enhancing good governance and participation.[103]

---

[102] Commission of the European Communities, *A Sustainable Europe for a Better World: A European Union Strategy for Sustainable Development; Communication from the Commission to the Gothenburg European Council*, European Union, Brussels, 2001 (COM 2001, 264 final)
[103] Commission of the European Communities, *Ten Years After Rio: Preparing for the World Summit on Sustainable Development (WSSD)*, Communication from the Commission to the Council and European Parliament, European Union, Brussels, 06 February 2001 (COM 2001, 53 final)

In May 2002, the European Union adopted and finalised its strategy for sustainable development, published under the name of `A Sustainable Europe for a Better Europe`[104]. In designing this European agenda for SD, which was also prepared before the WSSD, and in order to allow the EU to reach its goals; four strategic objectives were suggested to allow the EU to take the lead through the Summit and guide the world countries to a more sustainable approach to the future. The first of these four objectives is the increased global equity and an effective partnership for sustainable development, the second is a better integration and coherence at the international level, the third is the adoption of environment and development targets to revitalise and sharpen the political commitment and finally, the fourth objective is a more effective action plan at national level, and international monitoring.[105]

The role of these objectives and sets of issues is to ensure a balanced agenda for the EU to pursue a sustainable development commitment on the national level (within the EU) before committing to the international level, which emphasizes the importance of local agenda for the EU countries internally.

"These local agendas (i.e. local Agenda 21) have proven to be an effective means of building a consensus for change at local level."[106]

The Commission acknowledges that efforts to implement SD on the national level have so far had only limited success due to the difficulty of challenging established policies and patterns of behaviour and in bringing the responses

---

[104] The European Strategy for sustainable development can be accessed on the web http://europa.eu.int/comm/environment/eussd/ , last accessed July 2003
[105] ibid
[106] Commission of the European Communities, *Communication's proposal to the Gothenburg European Council*, European Union, Brussels, 2001,pp.4

71

together in a coordinated manner. Therefore, it suggests urgent actions, committed and far-sighted political leadership, a new approach to policy making, widespread participation and international responsibility which should originate from the national commitment level.[107] This emphasis on the importance of local agendas opens up the gate for the author to explore what has been achieved on the UK's level of commitment towards the implementation of sustainable development in terms of its policies before we highlight the efforts in integrating sustainable development to the construction industry.

2.5   Sustainable Development Policies in the UK

In May 1999, the UK Government published `A better quality of life, a strategy for sustainable development for the UK'[108] in a serious attempt to bring the environment, social progress and the economy alongside each other at the heart of policy making. This report marked the British commitment to ensure a better sustainable future for all its citizens. It also emphasised on the massive increase in wealth of the country and the well-being of its people which has been achieved in the past by focusing solely on economic growth risks ignoring the impact - both good and bad - on people and on the environment. The report acknowledges that if account had been taken of these links in previous decision making, it might have reduced or avoided costs such as contaminated land or social exclusion. In the past, success has been measured by economic growth (GDP) alone, but the British government acknowledges that it failed to see that the economy, the

---

[107] ibid.

[108] The UK Strategy for Sustainable Development can be accessed online, last visited July 2003 http://www.sustainable-development.gov.uk/uk_strategy/content.htm

environment and the society are all one, and that delivering the best possible quality of life, means more than concentrating exclusively on economic growth.[109]

Sustainable development is portrayed in the report as an important part of this government's programme to ensure that the economy thrives, and also as a guarantee that economic growth contributes to the quality of life, rather than degrades it. This will be achieved by making certain of keeping the balance between the three poles of the triple bottom line, while not forgetting that sustainability is only achieved by realising an economic, social and environmental balance.[110]

This strategy was only the beginning of the road towards a sustainable United Kingdom, providing a national focus which local and regional authorities should follow. Inline with the EU strategies that the international agendas originate from the national level of commitments to SD, the British government created a target for local authorities to prepare local sustainable development strategies; `Local Agenda 21` by the end of the year 2000.

These efforts represented significant steps for creating the UK's Agenda in preparation for its contribution to the WSSD. Therefore, special reviews were

---

[109] The British Prime Minister (Tony Blair), Forward by the Prime Minister for "A Strategy for Sustainable Development for the United Kingdom", Sustainable Development – the UK's government approach – Achieving a Better Quality of Life Website http://www.sustainable-development.gov.uk/index.htm , This website provides information on the activities within UK Government to improve the contribution that all Departments make to sustainable development through their policies and operations. Activities are divided into three main areas: Improving the performance of the Government Estate, Integrating sustainable development into decision making and Promoting understanding of sustainable development across Government.
[110] UK Government's Policy for SD, "A Better Quality of Life; Sustainable Development – the UK's Government Approach", The Stationery Office, London, 1999 www.sto.co.uk

necessary to go through the strategy and create an up-to-date version to help the UK put its commitments into action on the international scale.

This policy is aligned with the UK's priorities for the future, which starts with; more investment in people and equipment for a competitive economy, reducing the level of social exclusion, promoting a transport system which provides choice and also minimises environmental harm and reduces congestion, improving the larger towns and cities to make them better places to live and work, directing development and promoting agricultural practices to protect and enhance the countryside and wildlife, improving energy efficiency and tackling waste, and finally, working with others to achieve sustainable development internationally.[111]

These priorities have influenced the UK strategy for sustainable development in creating its four main aims; first, social progress which recognises the needs of everyone, second, effective protection of the environment, third, prudent use of natural resources and finally, the fourth aim is the maintenance of high and stable levels of economic growth and employment.[112]

These four aims are very similar to the European aims and sets of issues discussed earlier. In general, the levels of commitment of the EU Commission work within the same guidelines as those of the UK government. The UK government has set a list of ten principles to guide the implementation of SD policies. These principles are:-[113]

---

[111] ibid
[112] ibid.
[113] ibid

- putting people at the centre;

- taking a long term perspective;

- taking account of costs and benefits;

- creating an open and supportive economic system;

- combating poverty and social exclusion;

- respecting environmental limits;

- precautionary actions require assessment of costs and benefits of action;

- using scientific knowledge;

- transparency, information, participation and access to justice;

- making the polluter pay.

These principles and approaches give full weight to the economic, social and environmental aspects of sustainable development. The past discussions on sustainable development, particularly in richer countries, focused mainly on environmental limits. But this strategy acknowledges that economic and social boundaries must also be recognised. These principles target several levels of action, giving strength to the strategies in terms of their implementation.

"An economy in long term recession is not sustainable. Nor is a situation where many people are denied opportunity and face poverty and exclusion. Development which ignores the essential needs of the poorest people, whether in this country or abroad, is not sustainable development at all."[114]

Although these principles start from the individual level of action of the people concerned and also work on the business case of application to create penalties for the polluter, it is noticed in practice that the impact of these principles needs to be studied again and re-established in terms of practical

---

[114] ibid. Chapter 4, Section 4.2

application. This will be demonstrated later in chapter 5 when re-examining one of the existing governmental systems which acts as the guiding procurement system for governmental projects. The purpose of this re-examination is to identify the weakness of such principles in real-life processes where sustainability gaps (opportunities for more sustainable approaches) are identified.

2.5.1 Why a SD Strategy for the United Kingdom is needed

The UK strategy was developed with the Rio declaration in mind; it was based on the implications of the global commitment to sustainable development which took place at the Rio summit in 1992. Several reviews took place to manifest the new changes of the following decade and to allow a new level of implementation to be part of the action plan for the future.[115]

The WSSD in 2002 was calling for an up-to-date plan of action from all the countries taking part in the summit. It is now evident that the need for development is as great as ever, but future development cannot follow the model of the past. Therefore, sustainable development strategies have to represent the modified global interest in achieving a level of development that helps a social progress which recognises the needs of everyone, promotes effective protection of the environment, endorses prudent use of natural resources and finally, sponsors the maintenance of high and stable levels of economic growth and employment.

The UK among other developed countries acknowledges that it cannot stand aside from these issues, with concern that global prosperity must increase

---

[115] The first UK Strategy for Sustainable Development was published in 1994, by the Publications Centre for the UK Government in London.

while being more widely shared.[116]

From the early stages of preparing this strategy, the UK government published a report, `Opportunities for Change`[117], which laid down the basis for the current strategy. The report which was preceded by a consultation document, received general consensus from government, business and the wider society on the need for sustainable development to take a vital role in planning the future. Furthermore, there was now evident need to find a new way forward and to deal with the challenge of sustainable development.[118]

Aligned with the WSSD outcomes and commitments, and along with the efforts made on the international as well as national levels, there is now compelling evidence that the implementation of sustainable development might represent a challenge for governments' policies, businesses and society in general, but it also represents a challenge which provides an over-arching framework for more sector-specific initiatives. This demonstrates the need for change; the need for achieving economic, social and environmental objectives at the same time while considering the long term implications of decisions on all sectors.[119]

In order to attain the European and the UK objective of implementing sustainable development on all aspects of citizens' every day lives, there is now an urgent need to discuss the impact of sustainable development on the

[116] UK Government's Policy for SD, "*A Better Quality of Life; Sustainable Development – the UK's Government Approach*", The Stationery Office, London, 1999

[117] The UK Government, *Opportunities for Change*, the UK Government consultation document in preparation of the UK strategy for SD, (DETR), London, 1998

[118] Environmental Resources Management Ltd, *Analysis of the responses to the UK Government's consultation paper on Sustainable Development; Opportunities for Change*, the UK Government consultation document in preparation of the UK strategy for SD, London, 1999

[119] UK Government's Policy for SD, "*A Better Quality of Life; Sustainable Development – the UK's Government Approach*", The Stationery Office, London, 1999, chapter 1

main theme of this research; the construction industry sector.

2.6 The Sustainable Approach to the Construction Industry Sector

In order to achieve an effective implementation of sustainable development and face up to the challenge, putting these strategies into action demands the response of different sectors in society. More sector-specific initiatives are needed to allow the sustainable development framework to touch on the everyday aspects of life. They must provide environments in which people live and work enjoyably and efficiently and which encourage working and social communities to flourish.

The construction industry is the largest employment sector in the EU and in the UK. It is the largest consuming sector of natural resources and the biggest provider of man made waste and it is one of the major sectors affecting economies. Therefore, all sectors of the construction industry can make an important contribution to achieving progress on all the key strands of sustainable development. The goal is to achieve a sustainable construction industry. The challenge is to put the strategies into action to take part in the framework of the opportunities for change.

The construction industry stands a great potential for change because 'Sustainable Construction' is about much more than the fabric of the built environment. Housing and the social, commercial and transport infrastructures around them must all be built in ways that are sustainable in environmental and economic as well as in social terms. They must add value to the quality of life for the individual and the community.

More importantly, everyone associated with this sector has a part to play in making sustainable construction happen, where clients, financiers, developers and planners are key players in determining what is built, where and when, and which buildings are re-used and which are redeveloped. More frequent demands could be made for construction solutions where consumption and the use of other resources can be minimised over their lifetime. The early involvement of tenants, residents and businesses in project design can lead to significantly better quality capital investment decisions in housing and construction generally. Project managers and designers, with the project team, help develop and then interpret clients' and users' requirements. The team determines and influences the solutions adopted. Constructors can plan the construction process more efficiently to eliminate wastage, and select sustainable products to use. Materials producers and product manufacturers influence the quality of products, whether they are produced cleanly and efficiently, and whether they are easily maintained and have minimum impact on the environment over their whole life cycle including re-use and final disposal. Occupiers and managers of buildings make important contributions to sustainability through their purchasing decisions, and by ensuring that buildings are used and operated efficiently for the benefit of their occupants and in terms of the quality of the environment, the use of energy and water and waste minimisation.[120]

The adoption of sustainable approaches to different aspects and sectors of societies in the European Union and in the UK was not explicit to the

---

[120] The UK Government, Department of Environment, Trade and the Regions (DETR), *Opportunities for Change, Sustainable Construction*, (DETR), London, 1998.
http://www.sustainable-development.gov.uk/consult/construction/index.htm The report was last accessed online, July 2003

construction sector but more widely spread among all other sectors which hold within their systems good potential for change.

European and UK initiatives describe the construction industry as a sector on which to consult in greater depth because of the important impact it has on society and on the environment.

The relationship between the construction industry and sustainable development shows great potential for implementation with a wide and strong impact on the quality of life for societies. This strong bond empathises with the significant efforts done by the UK government as well as concerned construction authorities, on the integration of sustainable development guidelines into the construction process. It is an integral part of this research to demonstrate that more can be done, through the greater potential proposed in terms of more efficient integration and identifying the sustainability gaps in the existing processes as shown later in the research.

2.7 Sustainable Construction in the UK

The construction industry in the UK has gone through several stages of implementing changes to its sustainable performance. The government has put a lot of effort and extensive consultation into the sector following its belief that the built environment provides the context for most human activities and has a huge impact on the quality of life in the communities. Construction also provides the delivery mechanisms for many aspects of government policy aimed at the provision and modernisation of the nation's infrastructure like transport, housing, schools, and hospitals. The government recognises that the benefits which could flow from a more efficient and sustainable construction industry are potentially immense;

"The construction process lends itself to detailed measurement and sustainable construction can therefore act as a case study for developing a quantified framework for sustainable development more generally."[121]

The efforts of the UK government to implement change within the construction industry practices started even before sustainable development was the objective of any new policy initiatives. These efforts were manifested by several reports being published that promote the current manner in which construction practices are taking place and the need for change. These reports are pioneered by the Egan Report `Rethinking Construction` (chapter 1, section 1.5), which despite being criticised for not dealing explicitly with sustainability, it was still considered a significant milestone towards the road to change. The Building Research Establishment (BRE), in response to the government's consultation document on sustainable construction[122], describes the implications of `Rethinking Construction` as a significant attribute to completing the whole strategy into a new set of sustainable goals.

"The Egan initiative will bring about significant changes in the industry. It already deals with some important aspects of sustainability (efficiency, waste reductions, quality etc.). However, it does not deal explicitly with sustainability which needs to be included as an explicit Egan goal."[123]

---

[121] Department of Environment, Trade and the Regions (DETR), *Opportunities for Change, Sustainable Construction*, (DETR), London, 1998, Introduction Section 4

[122] The UK Government, *Opportunities for Change; Sustainable Construction* , the UK Government consultation document in preparation of the UK strategy for SD, (DETR), London, 1998

[123] The Building Research Establishment (BRE), quoted on the implications of "Sustainable Construction" for "Rethinking Construction", Section 5.3 in the Analysis of the responses to the UK Government's Consultation Paper on Sustainable Construction. The analysis http://www.sustainable-development.gov.uk/consult/construction/response/index.htm last accessed July2003

In the year 2000, the Department of the Environment, Transport and the Regions (DETR), published its report entitled 'Building a better quality of Life; a strategy for more sustainable construction'. This strategy is considered yet another significant milestone on the road to sustainability. It guides the industry through the challenge of a more socially and environmentally responsible, better regarded construction industry. This strategy, examined in chapter 1 section (1.4), is an active agenda which contributes positively to, the quality of buildings and structures and therefore to the quality of life.

One of the main issues emphasised in this strategy, and also within the European reports on general sustainable development, is the important role which 'businesses' play in the wide implementation of the sustainability guidelines. Not only in the construction sector but in all other sectors, one major milestone remains to challenge the sustainability road towards change. Change is unlikely to happen unless industries are convinced that there is a 'Business Case' for more sustainable performance.

2.8   The Business Case for Sustainable Development

"Business is as much a part of society as fish are part of the sea. We cannot swim too hard or for too long against prevailing currents. The prices of goods ought to reflect all the costs –financial, environmental, and social- involved in making them, using them, disposing of them or recycling them."[124]

If the whole society is leaning towards sustainable development, then business has to follow. The international community has long asked for the

---

[124] Charles O. Holliday, Stephen Schmidheiny and Philip Watts, *Walking the Talk; the Business Case for Sustainable Development*, Greenleaf Publishing Limited, part of the WBCSD publications, Sheffield, UK, 2002,pp.17

implementation of sustainable development through world conferences and research reports, but also acknowledges that full implementation will not happen only with governments' regulations and civil society commitment, but also with business' dedication to follow the same road.

The `Business Case` for sustainable development stands as a major challenge for businesses to accept and embrace sustainability into their financial planning and economic development. [125]

In general, sustainable development calls for more efficiency, higher standards of quality in delivering social progress, protecting the environment and ensuring economic growth. In order to achieve these targets, this will require a stable and competitive economy on the national economy level as well as the international one. In our fast changing world, the performance of the economy relies mainly on firms, corporations, market indexes, political decisions and the economic environment in which business perform and achieve their goals.

The ultimate goal of sustainability is achieved not only by creating regulations and guidelines but by implementing these guidelines into the development activities which are mainly controlled by businesses.

There are many cases that can be made for sustainable development such as moral, ethical and business. But, promoting or marketing the concept and guidelines of sustainable development to businesses, corporations, firms and

---

[125] World Business Council for Sustainable Development (WBCSD), *The Business Case for Sustainable Development; Making a difference toward the Johannesburg Summit 2002 and beyond*, World Business Council for Sustainable Development, Switzerland, 2002

financial markets is partially triggered by individuals' belief in either the moral and/or ethical case or evidently the business case for sustainable development.

The ethical and/or moral case for sustainable development cannot be discussed in specific terms because it generally relies on the beliefs of individuals in ensuring that present generations meet their needs without compromising the ability of future generations to meet their own. On the other hand, the business case for sustainable development can be explained and discussed because pursuing a mission of sustainable development can make firms more competitive, more resilient to financial risks, more unified in purpose, more likely to attract and hold customers and the best employees and make them more at ease with regulators, banks, insurers and financial markets.[126]

This competitive advantage represents a momentous leverage point to the sustainability agenda. Competitiveness represents vital criteria to the implementation of sustainable development into business practices with special focus on construction cases.

The relationship between businesses and sustainable development was and still is so strongly manifested in the financial markets that in 1999, the Dow Jones Sustainability Indexes (DJSI)[127] were launched as the first global indexes tracking the financial performance of the leading sustainability-

---

[126] Charles O. Holliday, Stephen Schmidheiny and Philip Watts, *Walking the Talk; the Business Case for Sustainable Development*, Greenleaf Publishing Limited, part of the WBCSD publications, Sheffield, UK, 2002

[127] www.sustainability-index.com DJSI: Based on the cooperation of Dow Jones Indexes, STOXX Limited and SAM they provide asset managers with reliable and objective benchmarks to manage sustainability portfolios. The DJSI are based on the world's first systematic methodology to identify the sustainability driven companies on a global basis.

driven companies worldwide.

"The business case for sustainable development is an entrepreneurial position; it looks to the next point on the business curve, the point at which business can be more competitive by being more sustainability driven."[128]

Integrating sustainability into financial performance gives businesses a significant competitive edge over other firms; it would attract special customers who are aware of recent and future needs.

Business, being one of the three pillars of society, the other two being civil society and government, stands to have a good chance of creating for itself clear competitive advantages on financial, environmental and social levels of costs for its goods. This way, the market will reflect environmental and social as well as financial realities.

"Leadership companies would be happy with full-cost pricing because, being cleaner and more efficient than other companies; they would be producing goods and services for less"[129]

All these criteria create a vision of sustainable development as an opportunity rather than a burden and it is proving to be a source of competitive advantage.[130] The business case for sustainable development has a financial bottom line. Businesses are ultimately interested in making profits and if the implementation of sustainability allows them to have a competitive advantage which would secure profits, then the business case has proven

---

[128] World Business Council for Sustainable Development (WBCSD), *The Business Case for Sustainable Development; Making a difference toward the Johannesburg Summit 2002 and beyond*, World Business Council for Sustainable Development, Switzerland, 2002,pp.2

[129] Charles O. Holliday, Stephen Schmidheiny and Philip Watts, *Walking the Talk; the Business Case for Sustainable Development*, Greenleaf Publishing Limited, part of the WBCSD publications, Sheffield, UK, 2002, pp.18

[130] ibid.

itself to be valid.

Bill Ford, great-grandson of Henry Ford and now chairman of the namesake company, stated at a meeting that his company's participation in environmental programs has confirmed his strong belief that, in addition to being the right thing to do, preserving the environment is a competitive advantage and a major business opportunity.[131]

When businesses take advantage of these opportunities for change, companies stand to gain customer success, brand strength, first mover advantage, motivated employees and potentially more profits. This would also contribute to the new paradigm of sustainable progress which has changed the ways companies now think about doing business.

Companies are now moving from seeing only costs and difficulties in the concept of sustainable development to seeing savings and opportunities. They are evolving from using environmentally unfriendly approaches to pollution to using cleaner, more efficient technologies throughout entire production systems and, further, seeking to make sustainable development integral to business development. Firms are changing from linear approaches to systems to holistic approaches and considering the long term impact of change rather than the short term. They are moving from seeing environmental and social issues as the responsibilities of technical departments or experts to seeing these issues as company wide responsibilities. Finally, companies and firms are changing premises of confidentiality to ones of openness and transparency to allow narrow

---

[131] Meg Mitchell Moore, *Green is Good*, Darwin Magazine, Massachusetts, USA, September 2001, http://www.darwinmag.com/read/090101/green.html

lobbying to move toward open discussions with stakeholders.[132]

The new paradigm of sustainable progress and acceptance of businesses to the concept of more involvement of sustainable development into their financial planning and core commitment has provided a significant opportunity for government sectors to follow suit. But this has proven yet as challenging as it was for general businesses to concur. For the construction industry, the challenge for construction businesses to embrace sustainable practices is still in its early phase and more needs to be done.

From the previous analysis of the interconnections between business and sustainability, it emerges that the concept of sustainable development is closely linked to efficiency and competitiveness.[133]

"Sustainable development is not incompatible – and can be mutually supportive- with competitiveness. Business has many `win-win` opportunities to create and/or social improvement whilst increasing profits and market share."[134]

The competitiveness of sustainability needs to be examined before reaching the integration part of the research. The competitive advantages of sustainability will certainly add to the qualities of the existing competitiveness of the construction industry, which should therefore provide sustainable construction with an even more competitive edge and advantage.

---

[132] Charles O. Holliday, Stephen Schmidheiny and Philip Watts, *Walking the Talk; the Business Case for Sustainable Development*, Greenleaf Publishing Limited, Sheffield, UK, 2002

[133] The UK Government, *Sustainable Development Fact sheets; The UK Government's Policy for SD for UK Businesses*, Her Majesty's Stationery Office (DETR), London, 1999 http://www.sustainable-development.gov.uk/uk_strategy/factsheets/ukbus/index.htm Last accessed July 2003

[134] Peter James, *Business, Eco-Efficiency and Sustainable Development*, report done for the European Commission, Lisbon, 2000,pp.5

2.9 Eco-Efficiency

"Business has reconciled the need for sustainable development with the demands of competitiveness through the concept of `eco-efficiency`".[135]

Eco-efficiency is a management strategy that links financial and environmental performance to create more value with less ecological impact. It is a philosophy that encourages business to search for environmental improvements which yield parallel economic benefits. It focuses on business opportunities and allows companies to become more environmentally responsible and more profitable while fostering innovation and therefore growth and competitiveness.[136]

Eco-efficiency is achieved by the delivery of competitively priced goods, and services that satisfy human needs and bring quality of life while reducing ecological impacts and resource intensity.

"Eco-efficiency is concerned with creating more value with less impact"[137]

The concept of eco-efficiency has helped a lot of businesses to reconcile with joining the road to sustainability as it promotes more profits, a competitive edge over other businesses, and an environmental awareness to guide the business practices to better performances. It stimulates creativity and innovation for new ways of practice while keeping the environmental and economic guidelines in perspective.

The concept of promoting better value of goods with less harmful impact on

---

[135] ibid pp.5
[136] World Business Council for Sustainable Development (WBCSD), *Eco-efficiency; creating more value with less impact*, WBCSD publications, Switzerland, October 2000
[137] ibid. pp.15

the environment while creating better profits touches only on the economic and environmental poles of sustainability. Eco-efficiency has been criticised for missing out or neglecting the social side of sustainability. The benefits of eco-efficiency cannot be denied but current businesses realise now that for the future and long term benefits of business, working on only two levels of sustainability's three elements is not sustainable. Less emphasis on the social pole will not deliver a sustainable development approach and in fact, will do more harm than good to the business case. [138]

Ignoring or disregarding the social aspect of sustainability will cause a significant imbalance to the sustainability triple bottom line. When the business case does not have in perspective the people and a social reflection, it can not serve its fundamental goals of serving customers and providing the service to them, nor does it serve the people working within its parameters; it becomes an unsustainable business case.

The European Commission is therefore calling upon businesses to move towards `responsible entrepreneurship` which incorporates the social level of sustainability. The European Union encourages companies to include social management tools into their environmental management plans because it envisages sustainable development as a good medium to incorporate not only social inclusion but also topics such as ethics and cultural diversity. It calls upon the need for eco-efficiency theories to include the social aspects of practices (i.e. employment) following a belief that governments' strategies and regulations should take that lead in understanding and speaking the

---

[138] Robert M. Day, Beyond Eco-Efficiency: Sustainability as a Driver for Innovation, Sustainable Enterprise Perspectives, part of the publications of the World Resources Institute (WRI), March, 1998 http://www.wri.org/wri/meb/sei/beyond.html

language of business.[139] As a result, businesses would be able to follow the lead and therefore the implementation of sustainable development policies would be more unified and at ease with social, economic and environmental goals insight.

The evidence strengthens the argument that good environmental and social performance is linked to good business performance where sound business objectives have shown great potential to innovate and make processes and products eco-efficient. This has been underpinned by the Dow Jones Sustainability Index outperforming the ordinary Dow Jones Index.[140]

Eco-efficiency plays an important role in our road to a better quality of life, because society now expects business to contribute to economic development and social progress.[141]

Sustainable business practice is the way forward and this will reflect on the different business sectors including the construction industry and its sustainable approach. Sustainable Development has established itself as the road to a better future and a better quality of life. With all the contributing factors to its current popularity, it highlights for governments, businesses and society the importance of not only future development on the economic level but also on the social and environmental levels.

---

[139] Peter James, *Business, Eco-Efficiency and Sustainable Development*, report done for the European Commission, Lisbon, 2000
[140] Claude Fussler, Director of Stakeholder Relations at the World Business Council for Sustainable Development, Proceedings of International Workshop organised by the European Commission, *The Role of Environmental Management Tools, Session 1: The contribution of Business to Sustainable Development; the Views from Stakeholders*, Lisbon, 2000
[141] World Business Council for Sustainable Development (WBCSD), *Eco-efficient Leadership; for Improved Economic and Environmental Performance*, WBCSD core publications, 1996

2.10 The Way Forward

In 1992, the United Nations organised the first Earth Summit in Rio de Janeiro, Brazil to help the world populations and societies understand the importance of sustainable development and the urgent need for integrating its guidelines into governments' policies, business practices and general development activities. The Summit was the first of its kind to gather the whole world to discuss the world of future generations. Environmental degradation was affecting the ecological balance of the planet and it was obvious that much needed to be done to ensure a better quality of life for current as well as future generations.

Ten years after the Rio Summit, 2002, was the time for the second Earth Summit; the United Nations held the World Summit on Sustainable Development in Johannesburg. The Rio Declaration called upon governments to create new policies and strategies to regulate, monitor and improve the economic, environmental and social sides of the quality of life offered to their societies.

At the Johannesburg Summit, it was the opportunity to review these strategies and identify the successful and less successful policies in order to create up-to-date initiatives which reflect the current global concerns as well as national issues. Sustainable Development was no longer just a national concern for developed countries but a global concern which needed to be dealt with urgently. The world is not only suffering from environmental degradation but economic downturns and deep social concerns. The UN now considers the agendas for sustainable development as the only way forward to a better quality of life.

The hypothesis of this research relies on the integration of sustainable development guidelines into the practices of the construction industry and more specifically into the project management aspects of construction projects. In this chapter, the concept of sustainable development and its involvement and impact on development activities in general, were explored. This introduction to sustainable development was necessary for the development of the research's hypothesis because it explores the general aspects of sustainability and how it evolved into its current status of global trend.

The reasons behind the emergence of sustainable development, its importance to and its impact on our lives, demonstrate that although future and continuous development is the aim of all nations, it cannot follow the same strategies of the past with no regard for the environmental, and social impacts. It has to be generated by the need for a change of attitude. National economies can no longer envisage development without considering the social and environmental aspects. Businesses have to integrate the sustainable development triple bottom line into the core of their financial plans.

The construction industry plays a major role in any nation's development and therefore, the potential it holds for sustainable approaches to a better performance is immense. This chapter highlighted the contributions which sustainable development offer to modern and future societies in general and more specifically the ways it affects the construction industry and its practices touching on the three pillars of any society; government, civil society and businesses. The sustainable approach to construction practices was examined on the European level with special focus on the UK experience to demonstrate that nations who work on this potential of integration are several steps ahead of other nations who are still lagging behind on the road to sustainability

Achieving more sustainability into the construction processes is possible by breaking down the existing system without losing perspective of the holistic nature of the construction processes. By breaking down the system, it is possible to identify where the sustainability gaps exist and work on better implementation for these gaps. Within the construction industry, project management stands as a significant stage of all projects and it is the role of the following chapter to introduce the functions of project management in general and more specifically within construction practices.

CHAPTER 3

PROJECT MANAGEMENT

"Project Management has grown from the early initiatives in the U.S. defense/aerospace sectors in the late 1950s and 1960s into a core competency that is recognized widely across most industry sectors." [142]

Peter W.G. Morris

Project Management (PM) represents a fundamental core element of the hypothesis of this research. As described in the introduction of this book, the main objective of this research is to introduce integrated processes of PM and sustainable development to construction practices. Generic project management for all industries and sectors does not differ in its core of basic knowledge to the application of project management to construction projects. It is therefore crucial to introduce the concepts of project management.

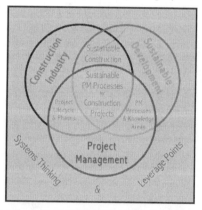

Figure 3.0: Project Management; the third of four pillars, in the research's hypothesis

---

[142] Peter W.G. Morris, *Updating the Project Management Bodies of Knowledge*, Project Management Journal Volume 32, Number 3, Pennsylvania-USA, The Professional Journal of the Project Management Institute (PMI), Publishing Division, Pennsylvania, USA, September 2001 pp.21

Figure (3.0) illustrates the hypothesis of the research with special emphasis on project management; the topic of this chapter.

3.1 Introduction

In this chapter, the core knowledge of PM is introduced starting with the definition of generic project management and followed by the application of PM knowledge for construction practices. The definition of project management relies on the definition of `project` and `management`, but the objective of this chapter is not to hide behind the long list of arguments and definitions in identifying them, but to introduce the core principles, processes and knowledge on which PM relies and to which it owns its definitions and applications. The history that underpins the importance of project management is introduced in the context of its application over the years and the significant importance that PM has acquired on the professional level as well as in research and development.

In the construction industry as well as in all other industries, project management applications have proved indispensable for the continuous progress of better performance along with the undeniable need for its existence among the early phases of projects. The effective involvement of project management processes in projects is shown as an essential factor of success in delivering/exceeding stakeholders'/clients' expectations and needs.

Among the numerous resources on project management a unique and significant body of knowledge is the one on which this chapter and this book are based. After a brief literature comparison among several project management bodies of knowledge, the research focuses on the creation of the

Project Management Institute [143] (PMI). It created a project management reference that is undeniably one of the most comprehensive bodies of knowledge for PM; the Guide to the Project Management Body of Knowledge (PMBOK). This chapter lays out how project management is presented in the PMBOK, identifies the main elements of the core processes, phases and the main knowledge areas which PMI considers as the core knowledge and practice of generic PM. More specifically for the construction industry, PMI has recently published `Construction Extension to PMBOK` which is also examined to highlight the differences as well as the common grounds between generic and construction oriented PM.

Projects are about change; the research discusses how project management techniques, processes and tools are equipped to deal with change and why it is argued that the solutions provided in PMBOK are not enough to enable a sustainable approach to better future performance.

Among the areas of knowledge set out in the PMBOK, risk management represents a very important threshold that threatens and/or strengthens all projects and therefore represents a major concern. The research examines the notions of risk management to demonstrate that it can not be responsible for all the blame that the industry's culture lays on it. When project fail or do not fulfil stakeholders' needs, the blame goes to the malfunction or even the lack of professional processes of risk management. This is demonstrated to be a failure of the industry to identify with risk management as part of a bigger

---

[143] Project Management Institute (PMI) www.pmi.org , Established in 1969 and headquartered outside Philadelphia, Pennsylvania USA, the Project Management Institute (PMI) is the world's leading not-for-profit project management professional association. For further details on the history of PMI as well as current performance, please refer to Appendix 2 Section1.

system; the project management processes. Risk management is argued to be part of the PM areas and can not stand on its own to ensure the successful completion of projects.

Stakeholders/clients demand more value for their investment from project management which is another argument that the research introduces and argues the lack of its role in the PMBOK. Value management is introduced as the one remaining knowledge area to complete the PMBOK areas and fulfil the expectancies of stakeholders from PM practices.

The chapter ends by introducing the final arguments on which the integration of sustainable development and project management in the construction industry is based. The research is set to describe the reasons behind the need for this integration and highlight the importance of introducing more committed project management processes and core knowledge to adding sustainable development indicators and constraints to their lists of tools and techniques illustrated in the PMBOK Guide and the new Construction Extension to PMBOK.

3.2 Introducing "Project Management" (PM)

A variety of literary resources, researchers and organisations looking into the history of project management have different interpretations of the evolution of PM. Some interpretations describe the existence of project management long before the pharaoh's time;

"Project Management started long before King Cheops planned the construction of his pyramid. For thousands of years, when this year's crops weren't ready for harvest in the "right" month, the Hebrews re-synchronized their calendar (based on the phases of the moon) with the annual seasons by the adding of an extra month,

thereby ensuring that everybody started planting next season at the right time (project start)." [144]

Other interpretations take their views with an interesting perspective demonstrating that project management and its processes were described by Shakespeare, Francis Bacon, Christopher Marlow and William Cowper.[145] These interpretations describing different aspects of project management process are very different to the processes currently used in the twenty first century.

Project management as known today began with military origins a few decades ago responding to the increasing complexities of the business and manufacturing worlds;

"The use of project management by the US Navy in the development of the Polaris program attracted considerable attention in the late 1950s. A few years later, NASA attracted similar attention from practitioners and academicians for the academicians that it made in project managing the large, complex Apollo program. Many are convinced that these programs could not have been successful without the use of project management"[146]

It was at this time that businesses and organisations began to see the benefit of organising work around projects and to understand the critical need to communicate and integrate work across multiple departments and professions, all working within the same time plan and allocated resources.

---

[144] Process Quality Associates Inc., *History of Project Management and CCPM*, http://www.pqa.net/ccpm/W05002001.html , website last accessed January 2003.

[145] Norman Sanders, *Article "and finally..."* , Project Manager Today, Issue October 2000, pp.52, an interesting article from a practitioner of PM into the history of Project Management, its processes and defining its scope into the manner it was perceived centuries before its current use and practices.

[146] R Max Wideman, *Criteria for a project management body of knowledge*, International Journal of Project Management, Volume 13, Number 2 , ELSEVIER Science publishing, Great Britain 1995, pp.71. Article can also be found at http://www.elsevier.com/locate/issn/02637863

3.2.1 Basic Definitions

In order to further research into the core processes and analysis of the project management body of knowledge, a vital clarification has to be made; the basic definitions and meanings of `project management`. As simple as it might seem, project management definitions have been subject to a wide range of studies on their applications, therefore highlighting the distinctions among the different uses and views of PM fundamentals.

The starting point in all such studies is the definition of the different characteristics of the work that organisations perform involving either operations or projects although the two may overlap. They both share many characteristics as they both are performed by people, constrained by limited resources and their processes are planned, executed, and controlled.[147]

Whilst `operations` tend to be ongoing and repetitive, `projects` are characteristically temporary and unique. In this case, `temporary` does not mean short in duration but of a finite duration with a defined beginning and end.[148] A project can, thus, be defined in terms of its distinctive characteristics:

"A project is a temporary endeavour undertaken to create a unique product or service."[149]

`Unique` means that the product or service is different in some distinguishing way from all similar products or services. Projects are

---

[147] Project Management Institute, *A Guide to the Project Management Body of Knowledge* (PMBOK Guide), Chapter 1 – Introduction, PMI Pennsylvania, USA, 2000 Edition, pp.4

[148] Paul D. Gardiner, Project Management, Heriot Watt University, Edinburgh, 1999, pp.1/3

[149] Project Management Institute, *A Guide to the Project Management Body of Knowledge* (PMBOK Guide), Chapter 1 – Introduction, PMI Pennsylvania, USA, 2000 Edition, pp.4

undertaken at all levels of the organisation and come in numerous shapes and sizes where the presence of repetitive elements or stages does not affect the fundamental uniqueness of the overall effort.

A project can also be defined as:

"A set of activities, linked over time, with a start and end point, carried out to produce a specific goal or goals."[150]

Projects involve a combination of goals, people, skills and achievements. When thinking about projects in general it has to be acknowledged that projects can be about learning where, at the end of a project, the knowledge and wisdom which were sought at the beginning have been reached. This knowledge can be radical, incremental, operational and strategic. For it to benefit others, it must be shared among the project's participants through a process of communication.[151] Projects also involve uncertainty where all their aspects are liable to change. A project will end safely and successfully by planning ahead, anticipating problems and opportunities and by structuring future work into discrete pieces with clear and measurable objectives; possibly called milestones or thresholds which eventually can reduce negative or positive risks. Projects are usually considered to be a collaborative effort. Even on a small project there is a need to blend complementary and often contrasting skills. There is tremendous awareness of the value of teamwork inside the process of any project;

"Transparency and openness nurture trust, which is a prerequisite of good teamwork

---

[150] Paul D. Gardiner, Project Management, Heriot Watt University, Edinburgh, 1999, pp.1/2
[151] Mohamed E.M. Eid, A review of "Project Management" & "Sustainable Development" for Construction Projects, Edinburgh Architecture Research Journal (EAR) Volume 27, University of Edinburgh, Architecture Department, September 2000, pp.39

and of a good understanding with the client."[152]

Projects involve investments in which people and organisations (client/stakeholder) pledge time and money. All resources on a project are in competition with alternative uses for those resources. Therefore, the investment must be continuously assessed against other priorities not just at the beginning and end of the project but also during its life cycle. Each project may represent a significant investment in time and energy for the project's sponsors or clients. Therefore, there is a continuous need to assess the return on the investment. This translates into a need to measure the efficiency of each project's use of resources during its life cycle so that good investment decisions can be made. Projects involve satisfying the need to introduce something new which the world or the client wants. Whatever their needs, they have to be accomplished by the project to meet the expectations of the client.

Finally, projects require focus and commitment; they concentrate means and energy in tightly focused, intense and deliberate effort, through the high use of resources to attain a defined target. Project methodologies stress the importance of assigning clear responsibility to tasks so that performance can be assessed and rewarded. Obviously, it is desirable to bring all projects to a successful conclusion where both the client and the project team are satisfied with the outcome.

The above descriptions of `projects` are clearly summed up by the following;

"Projects always require a mix of skills, organisation, people, processes and

---

[152] Paul D. Gardiner, Project Management, Heriot Watt University, Edinburgh, 1999, pp.1/10

technology: no single one of these aspects should be allowed to proceed at a greater pace then the others."[153]]

As a project moves on, management stages become more defined in their contribution to the achievement of the final objectives of the project. The `management` side deals mainly with the activities that contribute to the formation of the project and how these activities achieve the different stages of project work. These activities should be grouped into distinct processes according to the project work and thereafter included in the corresponding stages.

"Management encompasses the activities of planning and forecasting, organising, commanding, coordination and controlling."[154]

With the above analysis of `project` and `management`, the integration of both terms produces `Project Management`, where it is a tool that offers a way forward to improve outcomes and achieve successful conclusions. It is a way of structuring and organising change within projects that are, by their nature, all unique. Project Management is:

"The managerial task of accomplishing a project on time, within budget and to agreed technical and quality standards in order to meet or exceed stakeholder needs and expectations."[155]

Many definitions are given to describe the project management process, embodying the same general concept, but one significant definition gives PM

---

[153] Robert Buttrick, *Fundamentally Speaking (Part One)*, Project Manager Today, published by Larchdrift Projects Ltd., Volume XIII Issue 9, September 2001, pp. 22
[154] R Max Wideman, *Criteria for a project management body of knowledge*, International Journal of Project Management, Volume 13, Number 2 , ELSEVIER Science publishing, Great Britain 1995, pp.73. Article can also be found at http://www.elsevier.com/locate/issn/02637863
[155] ibid, pp.1/19

an extra dimension in its function that seems very obvious yet discreet in its significance, where PM is described as an art:

"...the ART of planning, executing and controlling a project from start to completion with the appropriate quality standards, in a given time, at a given cost, within given human and technical resources."[156]

It is an art in that it relies on the project manager's knowledge and grasp of the facts but also on his/her skills, talents and creativity in sustaining the coordination of all the aspects involved to reach the final goal.

"Astute project management requires at least as much art as science, as much human relations as management techniques"[157]

Another definition of project management is provided by: A Guide to the Project Management Body Of Knowledge (PMBOK® Guide), it revolves around similar concepts in defining it as:

"The application of knowledge, skills and techniques to project activities in order to meet or exceed stakeholder needs and expectations from a project."[158]

Meeting or exceeding stakeholder needs and expectations invariably involves balancing competing demands among scope, time, cost and quality. Also balancing between stakeholder with differing needs and expectations and finally between identified requirements (needs) and unidentified requirements (expectations).

The application of PM in different industries relies mainly on the same core

---

[156] Richard H. Clough, *Construction Project Management*, Wiley-Interscience, New York, 1985.
[157] Ibid. pp.5
[158] Project Management Institute, *A Guide to the Project Management Body of Knowledge* (PMBOK® Guide), Chapter 1 – Introduction, PMI Pennsylvania, USA, 2000 Edition, pp.6

of knowledge whatever the field of application, but it might differ in specific aspects only relevant to the industry in question. Project management is currently widely used in fields such as construction, IT, finance, insurance, consulting, education and general businesses.

3.3 Project Management (PM) in Construction

Project management in construction inherits its vital importance from the strengthening of general management definitions described earlier. Construction project management can be said to be:

"The planning, control and co-ordination of a project from conception to completion (including commissioning) on behalf of a client. It is concerned with the identification of the client's objectives in terms of utility, function, quality, time and cost, and the establishment of relationships between resources. The integration, monitoring and control of the contributors to the project and their output, and the evaluation and selection of alternatives in pursuit of the client's satisfaction with the project outcome are fundamental aspects of construction project management."[159]

Construction projects are complex undertakings where even a structure of modest proportions involves many skills, materials, and literally hundreds of different operations and overlapping activities. The construction team, which can include architects, engineers, tradesmen, contractors, subcontractors and merchants, changes from one job/activity to the next where the construction process is subject to the influence of highly variable and sometimes unpredictable factors. As a consequence of these circumstances, construction projects are typified by their complexity, diversity and by their non-standardised nature of production.

---

[159] Anthony Walker, Project Management in Construction, Granada Publishing, London, 1984, pp.5

104

In its report on UK post-war national development first published in 1944, the UK Institution of Civil Engineers recognised the need for a systematic approach to planning public works projects highlighting the importance of the role that project management could play in achieving best results in projects. In the report it stated that:

"In order to carry out work efficiently, it is essential that a scheme of operations be first decided by those directly responsible for the execution …With such planning, the work can be broken down into a series of operations and an orderly sequence or programme of execution evolved…Without a Programme the execution can only be haphazard and disorderly…The drawing-up of a Programme at the beginning of the work does not mean, of course, that it is drawn up once and for all and cannot be change. The exact reverse is the case…"[160]

The need for project management in the construction process is evident, not only in the planning of the different stages of the project but also from the earliest stages of initiation of any project. As technology has blossomed, projects have increased in complexity and as the construction process is not a self-regulating mechanism, project management has proved to be the essential and vital tool for managing such complexities and delivering more successful projects on target, time and budget.

"Projects are about change and, as the pace and complexity of change appears to be accelerating, so projects become more crucial. At the same time, resources appear to be scarcer. Therefore, those with project management skills are increasingly in demand"[161]

The involvement of Project management in projects in general and its evolution over the years has allowed especially construction projects to

---

[160] Institution of Civil Engineers, *The organisation of civil engineering work, post-war national development*, Report VI, UK (19 September 1944) pp. 38,39
[161] R Max Wideman, *Criteria for a project management body of knowledge*, International Journal of Project Management, Volume 13, Number 2, Great Britain 1995, pp.72

engage with the evident complexity which results from the numerous factors affecting the projects like the technological advances, the scale of the project as well as the growing standards of clients/stakeholders demands and expectations.

The Chairman of the Construction Industry Council (CIC)[162] describes comprehensive, informed and inclusive project management as the principal `means` to ensure the `ends`. In the same report on construction management skills, PM for construction is perceived as a process which runs throughout the construction life cycle and so touches all associated activities, recognising that the value added to a project by project management is unique; hence PM is an important component of the construction process.[163]

The purpose of project management described for the construction industry is to add significant and specific value to the process of delivering construction projects. PM adds significant opportunities for better and more efficient completion. Whether on small or large scale projects, they both share the same properties of `projects` described earlier, but the contribution of PM to the successful completion does not vary relatively to their sizes.

"The value added to the project by project management is unique: no other process or method can add similar value, either qualitatively or quantitatively."[164]

For construction and all other fields, projects are not only confined to major undertakings or large scale projects but they come in all sizes, varying in time plans, resources, goals and areas of applications.

---

[162] Construction Council Industry (CIC), *Construction Project Management Skills*, first published in 1996, UK.
[163] ibid. pp.3
[164] ibid. pp.2

"While it is true that major projects have provided the impetus for identifying and studying the principles of effective project management, these principles are nevertheless just as applicable to small projects as to larger projects."[165]

The importance of the project management's contribution remains the same whatever the scale or area of application. This contribution is underpinned by a core of knowledge and guidelines which generally remain the same but only vary in their applications according to the field of incorporation.

Due to the increasing demand on PM and since the skills required to manage projects successfully have multiple dimensions, models of the project management body of knowledge needed to be identified. Models which guide practitioners or academics working or researching on PM to identify the core basics of PM processes, stages and enable them to apply its basics to all fields and areas of application given that the management team is always responsible for determining what is appropriate for any specific project. The following is an analysis of these models defining the body of knowledge.

3.4 A Review of the PM Bodies of Knowledge

During the late 1980s and early 1990s, a significant increase of interest in knowledge management originated from a convergence of at least four interrelated trends: the first as described by Argyris & Schön[166] is the development of organisational learning, the second is an emphasis on re-engineering and re-invention of business processes as expressed by

---

[165] R Max Wideman, *Criteria for a project management body of knowledge*, International Journal of Project Management, Volume 13, Number 2 , ELSEVIER Science publishing, Great Britain 1995, pp.72

[166] C. Argyris & D. Schön, *Organizational Learning: A theory of action perspective*, Addison-Wesley Publication, Reading Massachusetts, 1978

Davenport[167] and Hammer & Champy[168]. The third trend is the total amount of advances in information technology such as computational speed and web applications as explained by Snider and Nissen[169] and the fourth trend being the associated development of information systems management theory and practise. These four trends have resulted, together, in an awareness of and attention to knowledge, particularly in the private sector, as an organisational asset or resource that may be leveraged for competitive advantage as illustrated in the work of Grant[170] & Spender[171].

["No concept so profoundly has affected the discipline of management in recent years as the idea of knowledge as the most critical ingredient in recipes for organisational success"[172]]

Such knowledge based research has extended into the field of project management as portrayed in the work of Busby[173], the research of Cooper, Lyneis & Bryant[174], and also the examination of Kamara, Anymba & Carillo[175]. The bodies of knowledge, in the case of project management, represent generally accepted sets of skills and tools that all certified

---

[167] T.H. Davenport, *Process Innovation: Reengineering work through information technology*, Harvard Publications, Boston, U.S.A, 1993

[168] M. Hammer & J Champy, Reengineering the corporation: A manifesto for business revolution, Harper Business School Press, New York, 1993

[169] Keith f. Sneider & Mark E. Nissen, *Beyond the Body of Knowledge: Knowledge-Flow approach to Project Management Theory and Practice*, Project Management Journal, PMI Publications, Volume 34, Number 2, Pennsylvania, 2003

[170] R.M. Grant, *Toward a knowledge based theory of the firm*, Strategic Management Journal, Volume 17, 1996

[171] J.C. Spender, *Making Knowledge the basis of a dynamic theory of the firm*, Strategic Management Journal, Volume 17, 1996

[172] P.F. Drucker, Managing in a time of great change, Truman Talley Ltd., New York, 1995

[173] J.S. Busby, *An assessment of post-project reviews*, Project Management Journal, PMI Publications, Volume 30, Number 3, 1999, pp.23-29

[174] G. Cooper, J. Lyneis & B. Bryant, *A clever approach to selecting a knowledge management strategy*, International Journal of Project Management, Volume 20, 2002, pp. 213-219

[175] J. Kamara, C. Anumba & P. Carillo, *Learning to learn, from past to future*, International Journal of Project Management, Volume 20, 2002, pp. 205-211

professionals should possess.[176] However, the studies mentioned above, deal with knowledge as something that is capable of being transferred, shared, or transformed in the context of any specific business sector.[177]

This fluid view of knowledge is at odds with the more static view implied by the bodies of knowledge of professional fields. This is tempered by recognition that none of the several project management bodies of knowledge describe themselves as complete and exhaustive repositories of all project management knowledge.[178]

"At least ten national or international organisations appear to be writing their own separate PMBOK documents. Five more organisations appear to be waiting for current efforts to mature before deciding whether to write their own documents or use someone else's."[179]

The following descriptions highlight the main publications of bodies of knowledge which describe the current state of project management bodies of knowledge in terms of their components and the level of details incorporated in their documentation.

First, the North American Project Management Institute (PMI)[180] last published in 2000 entitled `A Guide to the Project Management Body of Knowledge`, to reflect the PMI's new emphasis on generally accepted project management practices. This was followed by an application area extension to

---

[176] Keith f. Sneider & Mark E. Nissen, *Beyond the Body of Knowledge: Knowledge-Flow approach to Project Management Theory and Practice*, Project Management Journal, PMI Publications, Volume 34, Number 2, Pennsylvania, 2003, pp.5

[177] P. Berger, T. Luckman, *The social construction of reality*, Doubleday, Anchor Publications, New Jersey, U.S.A, 1967

[178] I. Wirth & D. Tryloff, *Preliminary comparison of six efforts to document the project management body of knowledge*, International Journal of Project Management, Volume 13, 1995, pp. 109-118

[179] ibid. pp.109

[180] Project Management Institute (PMI) official website www.pmi.org

construction practices in 2003 entitled `Construction Extension to the project management body of knowledge`.

The Australian Institute of Project Management (AIPM)[181] has produced a Reference Curriculum for Project Management Course which is essentially a draft Australian PMBOK. In addition to developing a project management knowledge classification system and a certification examination study guide, the AIPM is now working on generic project management competencies standards to improve its professional certification program and to support the Australian Government's interest in national competency standards for the professions.[182]

The Association of Project Managers (APM), the UK member of INTERNET[183] published its own Body of Knowledge[184], which tried to define key competencies of project managers. It is also leading an effort to introduce a European wide professional certification program based upon these competencies.

The Projektmanagement Austria Institut (PMA)[185] maintains a topical breakdown of selected reference books, periodicals and papers to assist

---

[181] Australian Institute for Project Management (AIPM) official website www.aipm.com.au
[182] A. Stretton, *Australian competency standards*, International Journal of Project Management, Volume 13, Issue 2, 1995
[183] INTERNET was the original name for the International Project Management Association until 1994 before it was changed to IPMA.
[184] *Body of Knowledge* Association of Project Managers, UK. First edition was published in 1992, latest edition was published in 2000. Association for Project Management (APM) official website www.apm.org.uk
[185] The Projektmanagement Austria Institut (PMA) official website www.p-m-a.at

project managers in their preparation for professional certification. It defines this bibliography as their Project Management-Body of Knowledge.[186]

The Norwegian Association of Project Management (NAPM -NFP)[187] published the `Fundamentals of Project Management` as the framework for the project management science on which harmonised education, training and certification programmes can be built.[188]

The International Standards of Project Management (ISO) is drafting ISO/CD 9004-6 entitled `Quality Management and quality system elements Part 6: Guidelines to quality in project management`, to provide a structure for the application of quality concepts in project management.[189]

Finally, the Federation of national project management associations (IPMA)[190] to which all European as well as many others societies belong (apart from PMI), produced a coordinated set of definitions which was published in English, French and German in 1998.[191]

It is now evident that several bodies of knowledge for project management exist, serving different purposes but in order to focus on one of these BOKs, it is necessary to have a closer look at the issues some discuss.

[186] I. Wirth & D. Tryloff, *Preliminary comparison of six efforts to document the project management body of knowledge*, International Journal of Project Management, Volume 13, 1995, pp. 110
[187] The Norwegian Association of Project Management (NAPM -NFP) official website www.prosjektledelse.com Norsk Forening for Prosjektledelse
[188] P.W. Hetland, *Education and training of project managers: developments in Norway*, Conference proceedings for the 11th World Congress Project Management conference in Florence, Italy, June 1992, pp. 665-670
[189] International Organisation for Standardisation, Switzerland, www.iso.org
[190] International Project Management Association (IPMA) www.ipma.ch
[191] G. Caupin, H. Knopfel, P.W.G. Morris, E. Motzel, & O. Pannenbacker, ICB IPMA competence baseline, Zurich, International Project Management Association, 1998

3.4.1 The APM, IPMA and PMI Bodies of Knowledge

In 1986, discussions in the UK led to the then Professional Standards Group (PSG) of the Association of Project Managers (APM) (now is the Association for Project Management) developing an outline of what was to become the APM's BOK. At this time, there was considerable debate both nationally and internationally about whether `certification` of project managers should be based on examination of knowledge or assessment of competence. The APM BOK was developed specifically for candidates to assess their level of PM knowledge for the certificated project manager (CPM) qualification then being introduced by APM.

The structure of the current APM BOK is organised into four `key competencies`: project management, organisation and people, processes and procedures, and general management (illustrated in Figure 3.1). Each of these competencies, in turn, is composed of 6 to 13 competency topics, there being 40 in all included. Under each of the competency topics, a definition can be found, examples of knowledge and experience levels as well as a list of references.[192]

---

[192] Peter W.G. Morris, *Updating the Project Management Bodies of Knowledge*, Project Management Journal Volume 32, Number 3, PA-USA, September 2001 pp.23

Project	Organization and People	Techniques and Procedures	General Management
▪ Systems Management	▪ Organization Design	▪ Work Definition	▪ Operational/Technical
▪ Program Management	▪ Control and Coordination	▪ Planning	▪ Management
▪ Project Management		▪ Scheduling	▪ Marketing and Sales
▪ Project Life Cycle	▪ Communication	▪ Estimating	▪ Finance
▪ Project Environment	▪ Leadership	▪ Cost Control	▪ Information Technology
▪ Project Strategy	▪ Delegation	▪ Performance Measurement	▪ Law Procurement
▪ Project Appraisal	▪ Team Building		▪ Quality
▪ Project Success/ Failure Criteria	▪ Conflict Management	▪ Risk Management	▪ Safety
	▪ Negotiation	▪ Value Management	▪ Industrial Relations
▪ Integration	▪ Management Development	▪ Change Control	
▪ Systems and Procedures		▪ Mobilization	
▪ Closeout			
▪ Post-project Appraisal			

Figure (3.1) the APM BOK Structure, Third Edition 1996

Work was initiated in mid 1997 by the University Of Manchester Institute Of Science and Technology (UMIST)'s CRMP (Center for Research in the Management of Projects) to conduct research aimed at providing empirical data upon which APM could decide how it wished to updates its BOK.

Figure (3.2), shows the updated structure of the CRMP/APM BOK, the remainder of the BOK contains definitions of the topics together with appropriate references. Also the final edition of the APM BOK is contains references which are more UK oriented and less wide ranging.[193]

This model shows the topics grouped into seven sections. The first section deals with a number of general and introductory items. The remaining six sections deal with topics to do with managing the project's strategic framework, the control issues, the definition of project's technical characteristics, the commercial features and the organisation structure.

---

[193] ibid. pp26

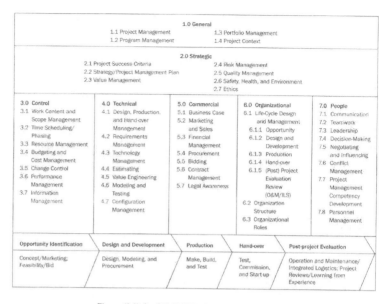

Figure (3.2) the CRMP/APM Structure model of BOK

For the European BOKs, it was following the launch in the UK, that several European countries became interested in providing their own versions of APM's CPM qualification. They translated the APM and CPM, making some changes as they did, though retaining the basic structure of the APM model. In the case of the French society (AFITEP)[194], they translated an abbreviated version of the BOK.[195]

---

[194] Association Francophone de Management de Project (AFITEP) www.afitep.fr
[195] Peter W.G. Morris, *Updating the Project Management Bodies of Knowledge*, Project Management Journal Volume 32, Number 3, PA-USA, September 2001 pp.23

By the mid 1990s, IPMA felt that it should attempt a coordination of the various national BOKs, so that those national associations what had not yet created their own version might have something to use.[196]

The IPMA BOK structure shown in figure (3.3) adopts the term `The Sunflower`, to describe its structure. This was specifically in recognition of the major issue that bedevils all attempts to produce a BOK: the structuring of the elements. The great advantage of the Sunflower is that the regular and symmetrical arrangements of the BOK elements minimize the difficulty of finding a structure that is acceptable to wide range of different national societies.[197]

For the Project Management Institute (PMI), it established its first project management BOK in 1976 on the premise that there were many management practices that were common to all projects and that codification of this BOK would be helpful not just to practicing project management staff, but also to teachers and certifiers of project management professionalism.

The revised edition of the PMI's standards resulted in a document entitled `A Guide to the Project Management Body of Knowledge` (PMBOK® Guide). Adding the word `guide` was to emphasise that even though the document defines the BOK as all those topics, subject areas, and intellectual processes that are involved in the application of sound management principles to

---

[196] G. Caupin, H. Knopfel, P.W.G. Morris, E. Motzel, & O. Pannenbacker, ICB IPMA competence baseline, Zurich, International Project Management Association, 1998
[197] Peter W.G. Morris, *Updating the Project Management Bodies of Knowledge*, Project Management Journal Volume 32, Number 3, PA-USA, September 2001 pp.25

projects, it will never be able to contain the entire project management BOK out there in the universe of PM.[198]

Figure (3.3) `The Sunflower` Structure of IPMA Competence Baseline (Version 1)

The structure of PMI's PMBOK® Guide document consists of `generally accepted project management practices` represented by 37 component processes shown in Figure (3.4). It also includes a description of pertinent

---

[198] ibid. pp.23

116

general management skills, and an introduction to the concept of a project management process model.[199]

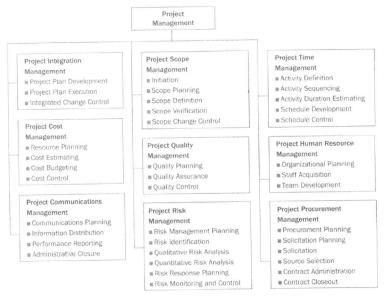

Figure (3.4) PMI PMBOK Structure (PMBOK® Guide 2000)

The US Project Management Institute (PMI) established in 1969[200], began the development of its project management body of knowledge with the objective of defining the scope and structure of project management as a prerequisite for the development of a distinct project management profession.[201] As acknowledged by Peter Morris[202], PMI was the first in the field of project management to create its own pioneering programs to test

---

[199] ibid.

[200] *Introduction to the Project Management Institute*, Project Management Institute (PMI) official website www.pmi.org , PA, USA. Website last visited March 2003.

[201] Warren E Allen, *Establishing some basic project management body of knowledge concepts*, International Journal of Project Management Vol. 13, No. 2, ELSEVIER Science Ltd., Great Britain, 1995, pp.77-82

[202] Peter W.G. Morris, *Updating the Project Management Bodies of Knowledge*, Project Management Journal Volume 32, Number 3, PA-USA, September 2001 pp.21

whether individuals practicing PM met their standards of project management professionalism, later followed by the UK based Association for Project Management (APM) and other project management organisations.[203]

From this brief review, the research acknowledges the several documentations of BOKs, each one presenting a new structure although mostly all of them revolve around the same parameters of project management. It is also now evident that each BOK is serving a specific purpose even when it is only a translation of an original BOK.

3.4.2 Focusing on the PMI's PMBOK

From the brief descriptive comparison of the previous BOKs, this book will narrow down the focus of the research to the first BOK for project management, published by PMI: the PMBOK® Guide 2000.

The main reasons behind choosing PMBOK for this research study are:

- In comparison to the previously mentioned BOKs of project management, the PMBOK® guide excels in its breakdown of application areas of project management and processes. The level of details provided in the PMBOK is not matched by any other BOK, specifically in the illustration of interactions between processes through the corresponding lists of inputs, tools & techniques and outputs.

---

[203] Project Management Organisations include:- Australian Institute of Project Management (http://www.aipm.com.au), The Engineering Project Management Forum (http://www.iee.org.uk/EPMF), the International Cost Engineering Council (http://www.icoste.org) and the International Project Management Association (http://www.ipma.ch)

- PMBOK allows a simple application to the circumstances of the construction industry and therefore an easy path to the successful completion of construction projects following the core knowledge of project management described in PMBOK.

- The new Construction Extension to PMBOK, is another demonstration of the important partnership between PM and construction practices, hence the new document details the additional knowledge areas which are more specific to construction.

- The practices and the project management of construction projects were one of the resources on which the original PMBOK was based. The involvement of construction from the early beginnings of PMBOK as an important body of PM knowledge makes the final document even more relevant to this research and touches on many sides of the industry.

- Unlike any of the international PM bodies of knowledge, no other PM initiatives had ventured in creating a PM document specific to construction as PMI pioneered in creating the Construction Extension to PMBOK.

- Due to the international exposure of PMBOK, it covers the practices of project management in many countries over the world including the UK, which makes its body of knowledge more applicable to more countries and industries than any other PM body of knowledge.

3.4.3 A Brief Look into the Evolution of the PMBOK® Guide

The journey to producing the current Project Management Body of Knowledge (PMBOK) started in the late 1960s to early 1970s where project management societies began to provide professional forums for communication on the discipline through journals, conferences and seminars. This continued until the mid 1980s when PMI as the first in this field[204] concluded that a body of reference was required to assess professionalism in this developing field. This professional testing curriculum was preceded by the establishment of the first project management body of knowledge (BOK) by PMI in 1976[205] and followed by the foundation of the original document PMBOK in 1987.

Over 25 years, it has gone through several revisions and rewriting stages to its latest version of the `Guide to the Project Management Body of Knowledge`[206] (A Guide to PMBOK) published by PMI in 2000. In September 2003, in a very clear acknowledgement of the importance of PM in general and PMBOK in particular to the construction industry, PMI published `Construction Extension to PMBOK Guide (2000 Edition)`[207]. This construction extension represents another attempt from PMI to provide a full service which covers present day PM practices found in the world wide construction industry.

PMI's PMBOK® Guide –hereafter referred to as PMBOK- is mainly focused on the generic processes required to accomplish projects `on time, in budget, to scope`.[208] For the Construction Extension to PMBOK, it aims to improve the efficiency and effectiveness of the management of construction projects and to include material specifically applicable to construction which is not

---

[204] D.L. Cook, *"Certification of project managers-Fantasy or reality?"*, Project Management Quarterly, Volume 8, No.2, PMI publishing, PA, USA, 1977, pp.32-34
[205] Peter W.G. Morris, *Updating the Project Management Bodies of Knowledge*, Project Management Journal Volume 32, Number 3, PA-USA, September 2001 pp.21
[206] Project Management Institute (PMI), *A Guide to the Project Management Body of Knowledge* (PMBOK Guide), PMI Pennsylvania, USA, 2000 Edition
[207] Project Management Institute (PMI), *Construction Extension to A Guide to the Project Management Body of Knowledge* (PMBOK® Guide – 2000 Edition), PMI Pennsylvania, USA, September 2003
[208] Peter W.G. Morris, *Updating the Project Management Bodies of Knowledge*, Project Management Journal Volume 32, Number 3, PA-USA, September 2001 pp.22

covered in the PMBOK 2000 Edition.

The PMBOK document represents itself as an authority in areas such as defining generally accepted practices of PM, the basis of certification testing for PM professionals and finally, also defining the basis for the accreditation of degree granting education programs in PM. [209]

Although the practices and project management of construction projects were one of the foundations of the original 1987 document PMBOK, and much of the PMBOK Guide 2000 Edition is directly applicable to construction projects, PMI felt the need for creating a more specific authority document to construction:

"Since the original 1987 document of PMBOK, a growing awareness of the values of project management to all kinds of projects and industries has led to a broadening of concepts and an inclusiveness that, because of its more universal nature, does not, in some respects; fully cover present day project management practices found in the world wide construction industry."[210]

Although PMI describes the changes and differences between the construction extension to PMBOK and PMBOK 2000 Edition itself as `not substantial`, PMI illustrates that they are different enough from other industries and applications to warrant an extension. Later in this chapter, the research examines both documents and highlights the differences between them as well as the common grounds among them.

---

[209] Warren E Allen, *Establishing some basic project management body of knowledge concepts*, International Journal of Project Management Vol. 13, No. 2, ELSEVIER Science Ltd., Great Britain, 1995, pp.77-82

[210] Project Management Institute (PMI), *Construction Extension to A Guide to the Project Management Body of Knowledge* (PMBOK® Guide – 2000 Edition), PMI Pennsylvania, USA, September 2003, pp. 4

This new construction extension as well as the anticipated new Edition of PMBOK due to be published in 2004 are simply demonstrations of the importance of PMI as an authority reference in the field of PM:

"PMBOK has shifted from the creation of an information structure reference to a professionalism authority reference"[211]

But obviously, it is unthinkable to believe that the whole body of knowledge of project management- or any other field for that matter- could be entirely described and included in one document. Therefore PMI has added the word `guide` to the title of its PMBOK. This does not undermine at any level the significant importance and role that the Project Management Institute's PMBOK plays in establishing the core generic processes for PM. Not only does it provide an outline description of the scope of project management knowledge, but it also establishes a glossary of frequently used project management terms, and it suggests a logical information classification structure that may be used by PM practitioners in the preparation, storage and retrieval of project management information.[212]

The following section of this chapter demonstrates the way PMBOK lays out the project management framework and more importantly the project management knowledge areas. These criteria are examined to demonstrate that there can be a sustainable agenda for project management which is not reflected in the PMBOK. Projects are required to have sustainable goals and processes. Despite of the great contribution of PMBOK to general project management, this book is examining the opportunities to provide more and contribute positively to sustainable project management practices. Although

---

[211] Warren E Allen, *Establishing some basic project management body of knowledge concepts*, International Journal of Project Management Vol. 13, No. 2, ELSEVIER Science Ltd., Great Britain, 1995
[212] ibid.

PMBOK Guide (2000 Edition) and the new Construction Extension do not mirror a serious commitment to any sustainable agenda, there is a vast potential for a sustainable set of processes; a dimension of sustainability needs to be added to the art of project management.

3.5   PMBOK & the Project Management Knowledge Areas

It is important at this stage to point out that the following examination is mainly focused on the contents of the PMBOK (2000 Edition), but because of the recent publication of the Construction Extension to the PMBOK (released in September 2003), the research will also highlight the additional information illustrated in the construction extension and therefore adds to the PMBOK original contents.

In the case of the PMBOK, it is in twelve chapters, and has two major sections; the first is the PM Framework and the second is the PM Knowledge areas.[213]

In the case of the construction extension to PMBOK, it also works within the previous two major sections but provides four additional knowledge areas to the nine original areas in PMBOK, which brings the total of knowledge areas to thirteen (numbered from four to sixteen in both documents and in this research as well to avoid confusion).

---

[213] Project Management Institute (PMI), *A Guide to the Project Management Body of Knowledge (PMBOK® Guide)*, Newtown Square, Pennsylvania USA, 2000 Edition, pp.7

3.5.1 The Project Management Framework

This section provides a basic structure for understanding project management. Starting with an introduction to the definition of key terms and providing an overview of the PMBOK, project management context is then introduced describing the environment in which projects operate where the team must understand the broader context of the necessity of managing the day to day issues. It is followed by the project management processes, describing a generic view of the manner in which project management processes commonly interact. Understanding these interactions is essential to understanding the second section of the PMBOK where the project management knowledge areas are introduced.

Figure (3.5) provides an illustration of the breakdown of this section into three distinctive parts.

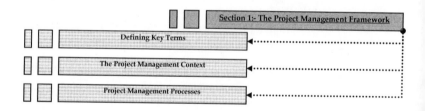

Figure 3.5:- Illustration of Section (I) of the PMBOK

3.5.2 The Project Management Knowledge Areas

The Project Management Knowledge Areas (Section II) describes the core knowledge of project management and practice in terms of their component processes which have been organised into nine knowledge areas in the PMBOK as illustrated earlier in figure (3.4) and additional four knowledge areas from the Construction Extension to PMBOK illustrated in figure (3.6).

124

The nine areas of knowledge in PMBOK are:-

- **Project Integration Management**; describes the processes required to ensure that the various elements of the project are properly coordinated.

- **Project Scope Management**; to achieve the successful completion of the project, it describes the processes needed to ensure the inclusion of all the required work into the project activities.

- **Project Time Management**; includes the processes required to ensure the project completion on time.

- **Project Cost Management**; describes the processes needed to ensure the project completion within the approved budget limits.

- **Project Quality Management**; describes the processes required to ensure that the project will satisfy the needs for which it was undertaken.

- **Project Human Resource Management**; includes the processes needed to make the most effective use of the people involved with the project.

- **Project Communication Management**; describes the processes needed to manage all aspects of project information including generation, collection, dissemination, storage and disposition.

- **Project Risk Management**; includes the processes working on identifying, analysing and responding to project risk.

- **Project Procurement Management**; describes the processes needed to acquire goods and services from outside the performing organisation.

The four additional knowledge areas from the construction Extension are:-

- **Project Safety Management**; describes the processes required to assure that the construction project is executed with appropriate care to prevent accidents that cause or have the potential to cause injury or property damage.

- **Project Environmental Management;** describes the processes required to ensure that the impact of the project execution to the surrounding environment will remain within the limits stated on legal permits.

- **Project Financial Management;** describes the processes to acquire and manage the financial resources and is more concerned with revenue source and net cash flows for construction projects than is cost management.

- **Project Claim Management;** describes the processes required to eliminate or prevent construction claims from arising and handling if they do occur.

Appendix 2 Section II presents the details of each knowledge area and the corresponding PM processes (lists of Inputs – Tools & Techniques – Outputs) as provided in the PMBOK illustrating the general PM knowledge areas as illustrated in figure (3.4) as well as the PM Knowledge areas specific to the construction industry as shown in figure (3.6).

The core knowledge presented in the PMBOK, has significant sustainable dimension in constraints and tools and techniques although very briefly mentioned in the project management context section, it is still not enough to embark the project management odyssey on a sustainable future performance.

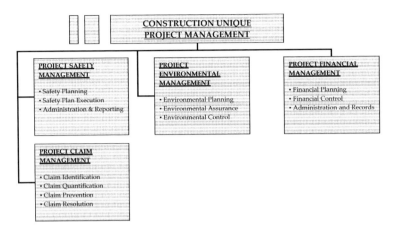

Figure 3.6:- Overview of Construction Unique Project Management Knowledge Areas and Processes - extracted from the Construction Extension to PMBOK Guide (2000 Edition)[214]

The same criticism is valid to the additional knowledge areas from the Construction Extension (figure 3.6); although the environmental side of PM seemed to be identified as individual knowledge area, it is still used to only describe the impact of the project execution on the surrounding environment due to legal commitments. The full potential of sustainable PM processes has not yet been fulfilled.

3.6   The Project Management Context

As a part of the project management framework, the project management context describes how both projects and project management operate in a

[214] Project Management Institute (PMI), Construction Extension to *A Guide to the Project Management Body of Knowledge (PMBOK® Guide- 2000 Edition)*, Newtown Square, Pennsylvania USA, 2000, pp.7 (Figure 1-2)

broader environment than that of the project itself;

"The Project management team must understand this broader context-managing the day to day activities if the project is necessary for success but not sufficient"[215]

The Project Management Context includes five aspects which describe key aspects of project management through project phases, project life cycle and their characteristics. These five aspects are: -

- **Project Phases and the Project Life Cycle:** They are usually marked by completion of one or more deliverables, where the conclusion of a phase is finalised by a review of both key deliverables and project performance to date. This review allows the beginning of the next phase in plan, as well as detects and corrects errors if any, in a cost effective manner. On the other hand, project life cycle serves to define the beginning and the end of a project where its definition determines the different phases of the project allowing the identification of the different activities to be included in the work plan. For construction projects, figure (3.7) shows an example illustration of a construction project life cycle.

---

[215] ibid. pp.11

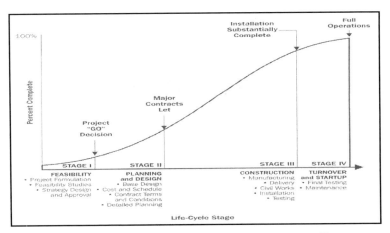

Figure 3.7:- An Illustration of a typical Construction Project Life Cycle[216]

- **Project Stakeholders:** The project management team identifies the requirements of the stakeholders and ensures successful completion of the project which meets or exceeds these requirements. In general terms, key stakeholders on projects could be used to describe project managers, customers, performing organisations, project team members and sponsors.[217]

- **Organisational Influences:** PMBOK describes that the project management context is always influenced by the organisation's maturity with respect to its PM systems, culture, style, organisational structure and its responsibility for and commitment to the results of the project.

- **Key General Management Skills:** The PM context also relies on `Key

[216] Peter W.G. Morris, *Managing Project Interfaces: Key Points for Project Success*, Project Management Handbook, 2nd ed., Englewood Cliffs, N.J: Prentice-Hall, 1988.
[217] Project Management Institute (PMI), *A Guide to the Project Management Body of Knowledge (PMBOK® Guide)*, Newtown Square, Pennsylvania USA, 2000 Edition, pp.16

General Management Skills` which represents a wide and broad subject including finance and accounting, sales and marketing, research and development (R&D), manufacturing and distribution, different types of planning (i.e. strategic, operational), organisational structure and behaviour including personnel, work relationships and finally managing the team as well as oneself.[218]

- **Social-Economic-Environmental Influences**: It is the fifth and last aspect of PM context which is the only direct reference to sustainability that exists in the entire PMBOK. Although the construction extension also mentions the same fifth aspect, the triple bottom line constraints (Social, Economic and Environmental) are referred to very briefly without making explicit reference to the common ground and essential points of connection between sustainable development and the project management context which the research envisage as critical to a sustainable agenda. This fifth aspect of PM Context is a direct and simple definition of SD guidelines for the triple bottom line.[219]

This brief mention of social, economic and environmental influences on the project management context does not describe the real potential for improving PM performance and commitment to sustainable future performance and processes. Although in the construction extension to PMBOK, the additional knowledge areas include environmental and

---

[218] ibid. pp.21
[219] Mohamed Eid, *Sustainable Management Systems; Embedding Sustainable Development into Project Management Processes*, Sustainable Development Forum, Alexandria-Egypt, Conference proceedings, January 2003

financial management, the context in which they are displayed does not embrace any complete sustainable approach.

"Virtually all projects are planned and implemented in a social, economic and environmental (sustainability) context... Organisations are increasingly accountable for impacts resulting from a project, as well as for the effects of a project on people, the economy, and the environment long after it has been completed..."[220]

The above quote is the only reference to sustainability that exists in the PMBOK, but a greater potential exists for integrating sustainable development into the core of PM, not only into the Project Management Processes but also into the heart essential knowledge of PM; the Project Management Knowledge Areas.

3.7 The Project Management Processes

"Project Management is an integrative endeavour-an action, or failure to take action, in one area will usually affect other areas"[221]

Successful project management is achieved by managing the interactions between the different areas of the project. To help understand the integrative nature of project management and highlight the importance of these interactions, PMBOK describes project management in terms of its component processes and their interactions.

PM is introduced as a number of interlinked processes which include the following five major sections described by the PMBOK as project processes, processes groups, processes interactions, customizing process interactions

[220] Project Management Institute (PMI), *A Guide to the Project Management Body of Knowledge (PMBOK® Guide)*, Newtown Square, Pennsylvania USA, 2000 Edition, pp.27
[221] ibid. pp.29

and mapping of project management processes.[222]

In general, a process is `a series of actions or steps towards achieving a particular end`[223] and projects are composed of processes commonly performed by people to either describe, organise and complete the work of the project or specify and create the project's product.[224]

The PMBOK organises the overall project processes into five groups of processes:-[225]

- Initiating Processes
- Planning Processes
- Executing Processes
- Controlling Processes
- Closing Processes

The process groups are normally linked by the results they produce where the results or outcome of one often becomes an input to another. The following figure (3.8) illustrates the links among the process groups in a phase of the project as presented in PMBOK.

---

[222] ibid.

[223] The Oxford Dictionary, Tenth Edition.

[224] Project Management Institute (PMI), *A Guide to the Project Management Body of Knowledge (PMBOK® Guide)*, PMI publications, Pennsylvania USA, 2000 Edition, pp.30

[225] ibid.

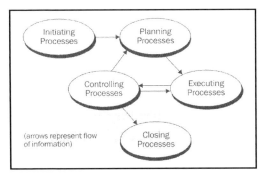

Figure 3.8:- An Illustration of a typical Project Life Cycle (PMBOK, pp.31)

The process groups may be repeated over the time span of the project in different phases and therefore may also overlap on each other in one given phase. This overlapping is shown in figure (3.9) as an example yet may be in different intensity depending on the nature and the objective of the phase in question.

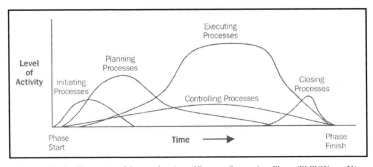

Figure 3.9:- An Illustration of the overlapping of Process Groups in a Phase (PMBOK, pp.31)

Since the process groups are normally linked by their results, their interactions also may cross phases since the output of one group represent the input to another. This interaction is illustrated in figure (3.10) to give an example of the interaction between phases. It is a continuous cycle among all the phases defining the whole project work.

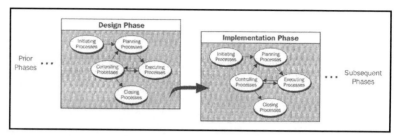

Figure 3.10:- An Illustration of the interaction between Phases (PMBOK, pp.31)

The manner in which these interactions are linked on the time span of the project is through their inputs and outputs, thus each process is described in terms of: -

- **Inputs:** documents or documentable items that will be acted upon.
- **Tools and Techniques:** mechanisms applied to the inputs to create the outputs.
- **Outputs:** documents or documentable items that are a result of the process

This is a simple breakdown of the project management processes to Inputs, Tools and Techniques, and Outputs, which also represent the main foundation on which the PM Knowledge Areas are based.

The five groups of processes which make up the overall project management process -illustrated in figure (3.8) - rely basically on the interaction between the short list processes defining the different knowledge areas including the thirty nine generic processes –illustrated in figure (3.4) – as well as the four construction processes of the construction extension –illustrated in figure (3.6)- where each knowledge area has its own defined list of components processes also broken-down and described in terms of inputs, tools & techniques and outputs.

The project management processes (total of fifty two) represent the common ground between the five project management process groups of initiating, planning, executing, controlling, and closing and the thirteen knowledge areas as illustrated in `Table (3.1)` below. The list of processes as described in PMBOK is not meant to be exclusive but it indicates generally where the project management processes fit into both the project management process groups and the knowledge areas.[226] The list of processes varies from one project to another depending on its nature and the decision of the management team to either include or exclude any of the processes.

---

[226] ibid. pp.38

Process Groups / Knowledge Area	Initiating	Planning	Executing	Controlling	Closing
Project Integration Management		• Project Plan Development	• Project Plan Execution	• Integrated Change Control	
Project Scope Management	• Initiation	• Scope Planning • Scope Definition		• Scope Verification • Scope Change Control	
Project Time Management		• Activity Definition • Activity Sequencing • Activity Duration Estimating • Schedule Development	• Activity Weights Definition	• Schedule Control • Progress Curves Development • Progress Monitoring	
Project Cost Management		• Resource Planning • Cost Estimating • Cost Budgeting		• Cost Control	
Project Quality Management		• Quality Planning	• Quality Assurance	• Quality Control	
Project Human Resource Management		• Organisational Planning • Staff Acquisition	• Team Development		• Project Completion
Project Communications Management		• Communication Planning	• Information Distribution	• Performance Reporting	• Administrative Closure
Risk Project Management		• Risk Management Planning • Risk Identification • Qualitative Risk Analysis • Quantitative Risk Analysis • Risk Response Planning		• Risk Monitoring & Control	
Project Procurement Management		• Procurement Planning • Solicitation Planning	• Solicitation • Source Selection • Contract Administration		• Contract Closeout
Project Safety Management		• Safety Planning	• Safety Plan Execution		• Administration & Reporting
Project Environmental Management		• Environmental Planning	• Environmental Assurance	• Environmental Control	
Project Financial Management		• Financial Planning		• Financial Control	• Administration & Records
Project Claim Management		• Claim Identification • Claim Quantification		• Claim Prevention	• Claim Resolution

Table 3.1:- Mapping of Project Management Processes and Construction Management Processes to the

Process Groups and Knowledge Areas[227]

---

[227] Management Institute (PMI), Construction Extension to *A Guide to the Project Management Body of Knowledge (PMBOK® Guide- 2000 Edition)*, PMI publications, Pennsylvania USA, 2003, pp.18

136

3.8 Completing the PMBOK Knowledge Areas

The knowledge areas describe project management knowledge and practice in terms of their component processes. The component processes function on the basis of their list of inputs, tools & techniques and outputs. In Appendix 2 Section II, the nine knowledge areas from the PMBOK (2000 Edition) are examined, and then followed by the examination of the four additional knowledge areas provided by the construction extension to PMBOK.

Despite of the recent publication efforts, and although the additional knowledge areas address environmental and financial management, they still do not directly address the issues of sustainable construction performance.

This research acknowledges that there is also one knowledge area which is missing from the PMBOK lists; Value Management. Although it has been discretely mentioned in several knowledge areas and for certain process of the knowledge area (i.e. Procurement Management) it is completely reliant on its involvement, Value Management is not described in the PMBOK as one its component processes.

The following section of this book, explains the reasons why Value Management is a necessary addition to the PM knowledge areas to ensure the maintenance of value standards which fulfil clients/stakeholders needs.

3.8.1 Value Management (VM)

"Value Management is a tool that has application at all stages in a project life cycle, from strategies planning, concept development, design review, through to

implementation and operation."[228]

Value Management studies, as well as Earned Value Management practices, are briefly listed among the component processes of the PMBOK knowledge areas in several places in the project management life cycle.

Value management is such an important tool and application that most of the knowledge areas rely on its presence within its inputs, tools and techniques or outputs. Although, mostly used within procurement phases and processes, it is also commonly available within cost management, quality management and risk management.

"There is growing, global acceptance of earned value management as a methodology for the planning, controlling, and integration of project scope, schedule, and resources. Consequently, Earned Value Management (EVM) is becoming an essential technique (or tool) for managing projects."[229]

Value Management should be explored and analysed to complement the PMBOK version of Project Management Knowledge Areas. The use of Value Management (VM) is increasing as clients seek better outcomes from their investment in buildings and structures. In some cases, the project is an outcome of strategic value management processes used in client organisations. By bringing together the widest possible range of project stakeholders in VM workshops, where different views and perspectives can be openly debated, many of the problems that typically arise in building

---

[228] Gerard De Valence and Rick Best (Editors), *Building in Value* (Pre-design Issues), University of Technology, Sydney, Australia, 1999.
[229] Project Management Institute (PMI) Website, *Practice Standard for Earned Value Management*,
http://www.pmi.org/prod/groups/public/documents/info/pp_practicestandardforevm.asp

projects can be avoided.[230]

There are two particular advantages of VM; first is the co-operative and inclusive nature of the workshops where people talk to each other and move in the same direction. The second is the establishment of a formal process for considering and weighing up the options available to a client for a building project.

Although the origins of VM lie in the manufacturing industry of the 1950s it is widely applied, in various forms, within most industries these days. For the building industry, VM offers a technique to counter the public perception of the industry as being essentially unconcerned about the client's business requirements or goals because it is basically about clarifying what these goals are and how they can be met.[231]

The concept of Value Management (VM) and its application across all stages of the project life cycle relies on challenge. A challenge in the case of the construction industry would be to determine how the client can achieve best value from an investment in a building and how better buildings can result from a process that is based on good decision–making procedures being put in place before the design work actually commences.[232]

A working definition of VM from the Australian and New Zealand Standards:

---

[230] Mohamed E.M. Eid, A review of "Project Management" & "Sustainable Development" for Construction Projects, Edinburgh Architecture Research Journal (EAR) Volume 27, University of Edinburgh, Architecture Department, September 2000, pp.43
[231] Shen, L.Y., Building in Value (Pre-design Issues), New York, 1999.
[232] L.D. Miles, Techniques in Value Analysis and Engineering (Value Foundations USA), 1989

"Value Management is a structured, systematic and analytical process, which seeks to achieve value for money by providing all the necessary functions at the lowest total cost consistent with the required levels of quality and performance."

(AS/NZS 4183, 1994)[233]

The structure is provided by the methodology, which comprises a five-stage creative problem-solving process known as the 'Job Plan'. The approach is systematic in that all five stages of the job plan are addressed in sequence. The process involves the identification and analysis of function which makes clear the objective, or purpose, as well as the means of achieving it. This analysis leads to the generation of creative ideas about achieving the function or purpose by alternative means at a lowest total cost whilst achieving specified levels of performance and quality.[234]

The Value Management Study (VMS)

VMS is part of the procurement process; it commences with the decision to build and ends just prior to the preparation of sketch drawings. It is comprised of three separate stages each with its own purpose and objectives:- [235]

Stage 1: - The Pre-workshop Stage

Involving the facilitator and the sponsor of the study to establish a VM timetable, objectives, participants, brief them and circulate information.

---

[233] The Australian Standards website , Last accessed January 2003, Documents found at :- http://www.standards.com.au/catalogue/script/Details.asp?DocN=stds000011255
[234] Mohamed E.M. Eid, A review of "Project Management" & "Sustainable Development" for Construction Projects, Edinburgh Architecture Research Journal (EAR) Volume 27, University of Edinburgh, Architecture Department, September 2000, pp.44
[235] Adam E., Value Management Cost Reduction Strategies for the 1990s, Melbourne: Longman Professional, 1993.

Stage 2: - The Workshop Stage

Involving a facilitated workshop comprising key stakeholders, in which the facilitator leads the group through the five phases of the job plan; information, analysis, creativity, judgement and development phases. The outcome of the last of these phases - the development phase - may take several forms and can be expressed in an action plan, workshops for findings and recommendations or formal presentations.

Stage 3: - The Post-workshop Stage

It includes the implementation of the action plan, de-briefing stakeholder, distributing study report and evaluating the study performance.

3.8.2 Why is VM Important to PM?

Value Management facilitates identifying and meeting the needs and interests of all the groups involved (i.e. Stakeholders). Generally, the client is most concerned with achieving value for money from the investment. Users are most concerned that the project meets their needs as closely and effectively as possible. Designers are keen to meet the expectations of both client and users and to comply with relevant standards and performance criteria. Project managers are keen to ensure that the project is managed within the constraints of time, quality and budget and finally, contractors are keen to provide services at an adequate profit.[236]

Value management enhances both an understanding of the project and the communication processes. It clarifies stakeholders' needs; separates needs from wants, with a refined definition of user requirements, defines the

---

[236] Akiyama, K., *Function Analysis: Systematic Improvement of Quality and Performance*, Cambridge, MA, Productivity Press, 1991.

project's objectives and improves client brief.

The complexity of a project increases with the number of disciplines involved in the design, with the number of stakeholders, with competing interests and if priorities amongst a number of contentious items are not established. Value Management provides a methodology for addressing such complexities and for providing a range of potential solutions same in the case of construction projects or more generally, in the management of all projects.

Such studies can be used to accelerate projects and also to audit capital works procurement programmes which can be utilised to achieve continuous improvement of standard products and used to check a project rigorously. Thus, Value Management is used to ensure that value for money is being achieved throughout the client's capital works programme.[237]

Value Management provides the users with a tool which can ensure a project is cost effective, resolve a complex problem, identify a number of options and select a preferred one and, identify the means by which a service maybe provided. VM is also a tool which can review a brief, identify the means by which a project may be delivered, identify ways of providing functions at a lower total cost, and improve the standard of performance or quality of the project outcomes. Finally, VM generates commitment to outcomes through structured participation of stakeholders.[238]

The relationship between Value Management and Project Management is

---

[237] Gerard De Valence and Rick Best (Editors), *Building in Value* (Pre-design Issues), University of Technology, Sydney, Australia, 1999.
[238] Department of Trade and Industry (DTI), *A Quick Guide to Value Management*, http://www.dti.gov.uk/mbp/bpgt/m9bd13001/m9bd130011.html

directly oriented towards the benefit to the client and the general outcome of the designated project. Value management can be included in the processes of the Project Management as described in PMBOK knowledge areas as an important and vital element that ensures the expectations of the client are achieved.

3.9 The Way Forward

Project management is the third element of the integration proposed in this research. The relationship which has already been established firmly between the construction practices and project management has been demonstrated in this chapter and proven to have strong mutual interactions. In past years, the practices of the construction industry, and indeed most of other industries, have shown significant reliance on the incorporation of project management processes to their performance activities. Project management processes and guidelines have endorsed construction projects with better performance, better delivery and better benchmarking standards.

Since its emergence in the 1950s until now, PM has undergone many changes and developments in concepts, targets and guidelines. PMBOK is now providing the business world and most importantly the construction industry with a reliable, reputable and extensive guide to its core of knowledge. But the world is always changing and the global commitment to sustainable development agendas has created a significant gap in the 2000 Edition PMBOK; a gap which needs to be filled with a clear commitment to sustainable future performance for project management practices. The publication of the Construction Extension to PMBOK (2000 Edition) in September 2003, did not fulfil the sustainable agendas for construction projects led by the industry which is following serious government initiatives in sustainable development.

It was essential for the purpose of this research, to demonstrate in this chapter the manner in which PMBOK describes project management processes in order to identify where sustainability is needed and where the changes could be implemented. Project management is described in terms of its Framework (including its context and processes) and its Knowledge Areas (including component processes and lists of inputs, tools and techniques and outputs). The way PMBOK describes and analyses project management processes lead the reader to its core knowledge where it mainly relies on the interaction between the different lists from one process to another and from one stage to the other. This interaction feeds the different stages of a project with continuous information on which progress to the following stage relies.

The essence of project management has been identified by PMBOK; the project management knowledge areas, their component processes along with their inputs, tools and techniques and outputs. These component processes and lists represent the initial information which project management processes deal with, to incorporate them into the PM life cycle.

The construction industry holds within its practices significant opportunities that allow project management processes to contribute more sustainably into its framework. But after displaying all the knowledge areas from the PMBOK and adding the new areas from the Construction Extension, the combined knowledge areas from both publications do not portray any serious commitment to sustainable construction. This book demonstrates that a PM

144

commitment which honours the government's initiatives for sustainable construction industry is needed and indeed possible to achieve.

Integrating sustainability strategies into the PM life cycle has to start from within the core of project management processes, following the theory of systems thinking. The sooner sustainability changes are integrated into project management, the more significant and stronger the impact we can expect. The following chapter examines `Systems Thinking` as the tool which will facilitate the integration as the vehicle to assist the integration of sustainable development into the project management processes for construction projects.

CHAPTER 4

SYSTEMS THINKING & LEVERAGE POINTS

"The approach of systems thinking is fundamentally different from that of traditional forms of analysis . . . Systems thinking, focuses on how the thing being studied interacts with other constituents of the system- a set of elements that interact to produce behaviour- of which it is a part".

Daniel Aronson host of the "Thinking Page"[239]

In the last few years, a new understanding of the process of organisational change has emerged. It is not top-down or bottom-up, but participative at all levels- aligned through common understanding of systems.[240] This way of thinking has significant and direct impacts on the way complex systems are professed. Beyond the change in organisational structures, the manner in which any process or system functions is now perceived in a new understanding of the way `change` in existing systems can be introduced.

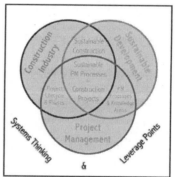

Figure 4.0: Systems Thinking & Leverage Points; the fourth pillar in the research's hypothesis

---

[239] Daniel Aronson, *Introduction to Systems Thinking,* The Thinking Page (www.thinking.net), 1999. Article accessed at http://www.thinking.net/Systems_Thinking/systems_thinking.html Last visited February 2003

[240] Peter Senge, *The Fifth Discipline Field book; Strategies and Tools for building a Learning Organization,* London, Nicholas Brealey Publishing Limited, 1999, pp.89

146

Figure (4.0) illustrates the hypothesis of the research with special emphasis on systems thinking and leverage points; the topic of this chapter.

4.1 Introduction

It is not the intent of this chapter to propose a new definition for `systems` as many definitions already exist. The existing definitions rely on categorising `systems` according to their nature, components, coherence, and boundary, or their activity description. A brief literature review is introduced to portray the general aspects of `systems thinking` as well as the leading researchers in the field. This research mainly focuses on the work of two significant researchers in systems thinking and leverage points.

Starting with a general definition used by Peter Senge[241] in his significant work on building learning organisations, the chapter begins to lay the ground for identifying the way people relate to systems and the perceptions of existing complex systems, such as project management processes and the construction industry. A brief look at the work of Peter Senge in identifying the `Fifth Discipline` and how his research work would help in explaining the manner in which systems work and function. Senge examines the factors that affect the state of systems as well as the `leverage points`.

When discussing the state of systems in general, it appears useful to demonstrate a research on `places to intervene in a system` to explore the potential for embedding `change` and what modifications to expect from the

---

[241] Peter M. Senge (1947-) was awarded his PhD on Management from MIT as well as his masters' degree on social systems modelling; he is currently the director of the Centre for Organizational Learning at the Sloan School of Management, Massachusetts Institute of Technology (MIT)

workings of systems. Identifying the places to intervene in existing and complex systems represents a major strand in this book' hypothesis. It explains the method of integrating the main three pillars of this research; Project Management, Sustainable Development and Construction Practices.

The chapter then goes to explore a new area of UK government research on what is called `The Sigma Project`; suggested guidelines to create sustainable management systems. A highlight of the differences between EMS (Environmental Management Systems) and SMS (Sustainable Management Systems) is explored to demonstrate the future for sustainable approaches.

Finally, the chapter looks at the way forward from this stage of the research where it would now be possible to explore the benefits of analysing complexes systems using `Systems Thinking` and `Leverage Points` to integrate sustainability and project management for construction practices.

4.2 A Review of `Systems Thinking`

General systems theory was introduced in the 1940s by Ludwig Von Berttalanffy, but has been vastly expanded since its inception.[242] It developed as a response to rapid technological complexities that confronted engineering and science. It was a radical departure from traditional science which dealt with cause and effect explanations. [243]

Systems thinking viewed an organization and its respective environment, as

---

[242] T.G. Cummings, *Systems theory of organizational development*, Wiley Publications Ltd, New York, 1980
[243] B.H. Gardner & S. Demello, Systems thinking in action, Healthcare Forum Journal, Volume 36, issue 4, 1993

a complex whole of interrelating, interdependent parts. It stressed the relationships and the processes that make up the organizational contact, rather than the separate entities or the sum of the parts.[244]

In 1960s Jay Forrester[245] developed a branch of systems thinking which focused on organizational change. Hence, the field of system dynamics emerged with the very term implying that constant change with sociotechnical systems is a given. It is this aspect of systems thinking that is so relevant to contemporary organizations struggling to maintain their competitive edge.[246]

Peter Checkland's[247] classification system described the purposeful activity of human beings as human activity systems; this classification includes organizations, industrial activity, and political systems and is the one which is of most interest to managers and employees.[248] A human activity system will be part of a systems hierarchy, it will be a subsystem within a greater system, or it will be a larger system incorporating smaller subsystems within itself.[249] These original thoughts triggered the interest of several researchers

---

[244] T.G. Cummings, *Systems theory of organizational development*, Wiley Publications Ltd, New York, 1980

[245] Jay W. Forrester Senior Lecture and Professor at the Sloan School of Management, MIT, Author of *World Dynamics*, Portland, Productivity Press, 1971, and *Urban Dynamics*, Portland, Productivity Press, 1969

[246] S.A. Cavaleri & D.S. Fearon, *Systems integration through concurrent learning*, Industrial Management Journal, Volume 36, issue 4, 1994

[247] Professor Peter Checkland is a professor of systems and management science at the Management School of Lancaster University; he is the creator of Soft Systems Methodology and the writer of several significant books in the field of systems thinking and its relation to the creation of information systems.

[248] G.P. Richardson, *Feedback thought in social science and systems theory*, University of Pennsylvania Press, Philadelphia, 1991

[249] B. Wilson, *Systems: Concepts, Methodologies and Applications*, Wiley Publications Ltd., New York, 1984

to highlight the importance of systems thinking within organizations and to demonstrate how feedback processes can generate the patterns of behaviour seen in large organizations and their frameworks which Jay Forrester's work was credited with.[250]

A very significant contributor to the theory of systems thinking and organizational learning is Chris Argyris[251]. Agyris's early research focused on the unintended consequences for individuals of formal organizational structures, executive leadership, control systems, and management information systems, and on how individuals adapted to change those consequences. He then turned his attention to ways of changing organizations, especially the behaviour of executives at the upper management levels.[252]

But for the vision of the learning organization and its perception as an effective playground for introducing the theories of systems thinking, Peter Senge's[253] research on the analysis of complex systems highlighted a major way of understanding reality that emphasises the relationships among a system's part, rather than the parts themselves. It was his 1990 book entitled the `Fifth Discipline` that firmly established his reputation as an expert in

---

[250] E. Wolstenholme & R. Stevenson, *Systems thinking & systems modelling; New perspectives on business strategy & process design*, Management Services Journal, Volume 39, issue 2, 1994
[251] Chris Argyris, a director of the Monitor Group in Cambridge, Massachusetts and also is the James Bryant Conant Professor of Education and Organizational Behaviour at Harvard Business School. He has a distinguished career at M.I.T., Kansas University, was awarded his PhD from Cornell University in 1951 and was also part a faculty member at Yale University.
[252] C. Argyris & D. Schön, *Organizational Learning: A theory of action perspective*, Addison-Wesley Publication, Reading Massachusetts, 1978
[253] Peter M. Senge was named a `Strategist of the Century` by the Journal of Business Strategy, one of the 24 men and women who have `had the greatest impact on the way we conduct business today` (September/October 1999)

systems thinking and disseminating the concept of 'learning organization'.[254]

It is the intention of this research to focus on the work of Peter Senge on the theory of learning organization to discuss the importance of his research and its impact on the perception of complex systems. Senge's work has influenced many researchers but this chapter focuses on the impact his work had on the theories of learning, systems thinking and leverage points.

4.3   The Five Disciplines and the Learning Organization

The structure of a system includes the quality of perception with which the observer gives it functionality, therefore 'a system is a perceived whole whose elements 'hang together' because they continually affect each other over time and operate toward a common purpose'.[255]

The old theories about single leadership and successful organisations relying on one 'grand strategist' are discredited in this era of globalisation, corporate joint ventures, interdependences of industries and interrelatedness of public and private sectors. It is now the idea of creating 'Learning Organisations' described by the major corporate head of planning for Royal Dutch/Shell (Arie De Geus) as 'the ability to learn faster than your competitors may be the only sustainable competitive advantage'[256], which will enable organisations to excel in their long term planning, in terms of sustaining and maintaining their market edge.

---

[254] M.K. Smith, *Peter Senge and the learning organization*, the encyclopaedia of informal education, www.infed.org./thinkers.senge.htm , 2001

[255] Peter Senge, *The Fifth Discipline Field book; Strategies and Tools for building a Learning Organization*, London, Nicholas Brealey Publishing Limited, 1999, pp.90

[256] Peter Senge, *The Fifth Discipline; the Art & Practice of the Learning Organization*, London, Random House Business Books, 1999, pp.4

Senge's research argues that the world we live in is not created of separate, unrelated forces but it has become far more complex and far less certain. Therefore, traditional management strategies that seemed sufficient as recently as a generation ago are found wanting today. To survive and/or to improve in the current era requires up-to-date knowledge of contemporary management strategies as well as the skills and competencies needed to work with them.[257]

According to Senge, learning organisations are 'organisations where people continually expand their capacity to create the results they truly desire, where new and expansive patterns of thinking are nurtured, where collective aspiration is set free, and where people are continually learning to see the whole together'.[258]

Understandably, when dealing with problems or disadvantages facing the organisation or even the system of how this organisation performs, it is not only about breaking down the system into its elements and components but it is primarily about understanding the system as a whole, 'the big picture', in order to tackle the failures or gaps in the system. This point of view is echoed by the fact that the act of expanding an existing system is successful and reaches its long planned target, only when the organisation/system is able to continually expand its inner capacity and therefore create its own future.

---

[257] Robert Louis Flood, *Rethinking The Fifth Discipline; Learning within the unknowable*, London, Routledge – Taylor and Francis Group, 1999, pp.1
[258] Peter Senge, *The Fifth Discipline; the Art & Practice of the Learning Organization*, London, Random House Business Books, 1999, pp.3

152

For a learning organization it is not enough to survive. `Survival learning` or what is more often termed `adaptive learning` is important – indeed it is essential. For a learning organization, `adaptive learning` must be coupled with `generative learning`, learning that enhances our capacity to create.[259] Five basic disciplines are identified by Senge in his research as component technologies which must converge to innovate in learning organisations.

These five disciplines are concerned with a shift of mind from seeing parts to seeing wholes, from seeing people as helpless reactors to seeing them as active participants in shaping their reality, from reacting to the present to creating the future[260]. These disciplines consist of: -

1. **Systems Thinking**

2. **Personal Mastery**

3. **Mental Models**

4. **Building Shared Vision**

5. **Team Learning**

Before analysing the importance and significance of each discipline, it is vitally important to understand that `Systems Thinking`, although it is the fifth discipline in Senge's list of five disciplines for innovating in learning organisations, it represents the cornerstone of his theory and acts as the facilitator for each of the remaining four disciplines to function as an individual discipline as well as a discipline or a `part` of the `whole` of the

---

[259] Smith, M. K., *Peter Senge and the learning organization, the encyclopaedia of informal education,* 2001, www.infed.org/thinkers/senge.htm Last accessed January 2003
[260] Peter Senge, *The Fifth Discipline; the Art & Practice of the Learning Organization,* London, Random House Business Books, 1999, pp.69

153

converging component technologies.

In his research, Senge refers to systems thinking as a conceptual cornerstone of the learning organisation[261]. He calls it `The Fifth Discipline`.

In order to simplify the analysis of systems thinking, the breakdown of the theory begins with ranking `systems thinking` as the first discipline rather than the fifth as laid out by Senge. It necessary to understand the significance of the fifth discipline; not so much in its order in relation to the remaining four disciplines, but in its functions and interconnections with the other four disciplines. Therefore, it is important to explore the remaining four disciplines in order to highlight the significance `systems thinking` which underlies all of the five learning disciplines and their interconnections. `Systems thinking` acts as the catalyst for systems' theory, while being a part of Senge's five disciplines.

4.3.1 Systems Thinking

A great virtue of Peter Senge's work is the way in which he puts systems theory to work. The Fifth Discipline provides a good introduction to the basics and uses of such theory and the way in which it can be brought together with other theoretical devices in order to make sense of organizational questions and issues. `Systems Thinking` is the conceptual cornerstone of his approach. It is the discipline that integrates the others, fusing them into a coherent body of theory and practice. Systems theory's ability to comprehend and address the whole and to examine the interrelationship between the parts provides both the incentive and the

---

[261] ibid

means to integrate the disciplines.

It is necessary at this stage to highlight one or two elements of Senge's presentation of Systems Theory. First, while the basic tools of systems theory are fairly straightforward they can build into sophisticated models. Peter Senge argues that one of the key problems with much that is written about, and done in the name of management, is that rather simplistic frameworks are applied to what are complex systems. People tend to focus on the parts rather than seeing the whole, and to fail to see organization as a dynamic process. Thus, the argument runs, a better appreciation of systems will lead to more appropriate action.[262]

When viewed in systems terms, short-term improvements often involve very significant long-term costs. A key challenge is the nature of the feedback received where some of the feedback will be reinforcing, or amplifying, with small changes building on themselves.

"Whatever movement occurs is amplified, producing more movement in the same direction".[263]

A further key aspect of systems is the extent to which they inevitably involve delays; interruptions in the flow of influence which make the consequences of an action occur gradually.[264]
Senge advocates the use of 'systems maps'; diagrams that show the key elements of systems and how they interact to formulate the working system.

---

[262] Smith, M. K., *Peter Senge and the learning organization, the encyclopaedia of informal education,* 2001, www.infed.org/thinkers/senge.htm Last accessed January 2003
[263] Peter Senge, *The Fifth Discipline; the Art & Practice of the Learning Organization,* London, Random House Business Books, 1999, pp.81
[264] ibid. pp.90

155

These diagrams make it a lot easier to grasp the interrelatedness of the system's components and highlight the different kinds of existing relationships.

Alongside systems thinking, stand four other 'component technologies' or disciplines. A 'discipline' is viewed by Peter Senge as a series of principles and practices that are studied, mastered and integrated into our lives. He considers systems thinking to be the cornerstone while acknowledging that each discipline provides a vital dimension and must be used in combination with the other four if organizations are to 'learn'. It is considered to be the discipline that integrates all five disciplines into a combined theory for the learning organisation.[265]

4.3.2 Personal Mastery

"Organizations learn only through individuals who learn. Individual learning does not guarantee organizational learning. But without it no organizational learning occurs".[266]

Personal mastery is the discipline of continually clarifying and deepening our personal vision, of focusing our energies, of developing patience, and of seeing reality objectively.[267]

It means developing one's own proficiency, not by achieving dominance over people or things, but rather it is a journey whereby a person continually

---

[265] Robert Louis Flood, *Rethinking The Fifth Discipline; Learning within the unknowable*, London, Routledge – Taylor and Francis Group, 1999, pp.22
[266] Peter Senge, *The Fifth Discipline; the Art & Practice of the Learning Organization*, London, Random House Business Books, 1999, pp.139
[267] ibid. pp.7

clarifies and deepens personal vision, focuses energy on it and develops patience in seeking it, thus leads people to produce positive actions towards achieving the personal vision.[268] Personal mastery as a part of the combined theory for the learning organisation, helps to clarify the dynamic nature of structures in our lives where `systems thinking` illustrates the interrelated nature of creative and emotional tensions, and how to better achieve our basic desires by amplifying creative tension and soothing emotional tension.[269]

The fifth discipline allows manifesting `personal mastery` skills in understanding the interconnectedness between actions and the reality of the surrounding world.

4.3.3 Mental Models

"Mental models are the images, assumptions, and stories which we carry in our minds of ourselves, other people, institutions and every aspect of the world."[270]

They are also explained as conceptual structures in the mind that drive cognitive processes of understanding. They influence people's actions because they mould people's appreciation of what they see, therefore observe selectively. They define our relationship with each other and with the world in which we find ourselves.[271]

---

[268] Robert Louis Flood, *Rethinking The Fifth Discipline; Learning within the unknowable*, London, Routledge – Taylor and Francis Group, 1999, pp.20
[269] ibid. pp.22
[270] Peter Senge, *The Fifth Discipline Field book; Strategies and Tools for building a Learning Organization*, London, Nicholas Brealey Publishing Limited, 1999, pp.235
[271] Robert Louis Flood, *Rethinking The Fifth Discipline; Learning within the unknowable*, London, Routledge – Taylor and Francis Group, 1999, pp.22

The discipline of mental models starts with turning the mirror inward; learning to unearth our internal pictures of the world, to bring them to the surface and hold them rigorously to scrutiny. It also includes the ability to carry on 'learningful' conversations that balance inquiry and advocacy, where people expose their own thinking effectively and make that thinking open to the influence of others.[272]

Systems thinking helps to expose assumptions that mental models are making about the dynamic nature of reality and to evaluate the validity of the assumptions. The aim is to better understand and indeed to improve our mental models of the world, not to draw elaborate systemic diagrams of the world.[273]

4.3.4 Building Shared Vision

"Creating a sense of purpose that binds people together and propels them to fulfil their deepest aspirations." [274]

This is Senge's definition of this discipline where catalysing people's aspirations doesn't happen by accident; it requires time, care and strategy. Thus, the discipline of building shared vision is centered on a never-ending process whereby people in an organisation articulate their common stories; around vision, purpose, values, why their work matters and how it fits in the larger world.

---

[272] Peter Senge, *The Fifth Discipline; the Art & Practice of the Learning Organization,* London, Random House Business Books, 1999, pp.9
[273] Robert Louis Flood, *Rethinking The Fifth Discipline; Learning within the unknowable,* London, Routledge – Taylor and Francis Group, 1999, pp.23
[274] Peter Senge, *The Fifth Discipline Field book; Strategies and Tools for building a Learning Organization,* London, Nicholas Brealey Publishing Limited, 1999, pp.298

It is argued that it can also foster a sense of the long-term, something that is fundamental to the fifth discipline.[275] The practice of shared vision involves the skills of detecting shared 'pictures of the future' that foster genuine commitment and enrolment rather than compliance. In mastering this discipline, leaders learn the counter-productiveness of trying to dictate a vision, no matter how heartfelt.[276] Where organizations can go beyond linear thinking and seize system thinking, there is the possibility of bringing vision to fruition.[277]

The fifth discipline explains the spread of shared vision in generative learning as a reinforcing process; it will be an essential tool for making any shared visions a reality with the help of strategies and the vision of finding leverage points[278].

4.3.5 Team Learning

Such learning is defined by Senge as 'the process of aligning and developing the capacities of a team to create the results its members truly desire. It builds on the discipline of developing shared vision. It also builds on personal mastery...'[279] but building on personal mastery and shared vision are not enough. Where individuals are able to act together, the teams will

---

[275] Smith, M. K., *Peter Senge and the learning organization, the encyclopaedia of informal education,* 2001, www.infed.org/thinkers/senge.htm Last accessed January 2003
[276] Peter Senge, *The Fifth Discipline; the Art & Practice of the Learning Organization,* London, Random House Business Books, 1999, pp.9
[277] ibid. pp.227
[278] Peter Senge, *The Fifth Discipline Field book; Strategies and Tools for building a Learning Organization,* London, Nicholas Brealey Publishing Limited, 1999
[279] Peter Senge, *The Fifth Discipline; the Art & Practice of the Learning Organization,* London, Random House Business Books, 1999, pp.236

learn together therefore, as Senge suggests, individuals will grow more rapidly than could have occurred otherwise.

Team learning is vital because teams, not individuals, are the fundamental learning unit in modern organisations.

"There has never been a greater need for mastering team learning in organisations than there is today."[280]

The reason behind that is explained by Senge as all important decisions are now made in teams, either directly or through the need for teams to translate individual decisions into actions.

The discipline of team learning starts with 'dialogue', the capacity of members of a team to suspend assumptions and enter into a genuine 'thinking together', where a stream of meaning flows allowing individuals to make a genuine attempt to appreciate matters of concern through the eyes of people who raise the concerns.

Within organisations, team learning has three critical dimensions; first, there is the need to think insightfully about complex issues. Second, there is the need for innovative, coordinated action and finally, there is the role of team members on other teams.[281] Team Learning offers a language that helps individuals get to grips with dynamic complexity; it helps to bring together people's mental models in a shared systemic language, generating team

---

[280] ibid.
[281] ibid.

learning and understanding, and a shared sense of purpose.[282]

4.3.6 The Interrelatedness of the Five Disciplines

After this short description of each of the five disciplines, and a general look at systems theory, a simple definition arises which describes `systems thinking`, while being the fifth on the list of five disciplines, as the discipline that brings together all five of Senge's disciplines in pursuit of a combined body of theory and a mode of practise for the learning organisation.

For the discipline of personal mastery, `Systems Thinking` highlights the connectedness of individuals to the world, and brings to light the interdependencies between actions and reality.

Systems thinking in mental models, exposes assumptions and tests if they are systematically flawed as well as helping individuals and organisations to tackle the facts and gaps in their existing systems and not to be affected by pre-conceptual ideas.

In Shared vision, "it clarifies how vision radiates through collaborative feedback processes and fades through conflictual feedback processes."[283] Finally, systems thinking in the discipline of team learning identifies positive and negative synergy in discussion and dialogue where, the whole becomes greater than or less than the sum of its parts.

"All (The five disciplines) are concerned with a shift of mind from seeing parts to

---

[282] Robert Louis Flood, *Rethinking The Fifth Discipline; Learning within the unknowable*, London, Routledge – Taylor and Francis Group, 1999, pp.25
[283] Robert Louis Flood, *Rethinking The Fifth Discipline; Learning within the unknowable*, London, Routledge – Taylor and Francis Group, 1999, pp.27

seeing whole...from reacting to the present to creating the future."[284]

The five disciplines work together and develop as an ensemble[285], mainly to lead the individuals to what Senge describes as the leverage points.

4.4 Defining "Leverage Points"

Leverage points allow individuals to identify the opportunities in existing systems/organisations where `change` could be implemented to lead the system to the long planned goals and objectives. Senge describes them as places to pursue the goals in a way that takes advantage of, instead of working against, the systemic structures around them. [286]

"Leverage points are places where actions and changes in structures can lead to significant, enduring improvements...the best results come not from large scale efforts but from small well-focused actions"[287]

Identification of these opportunities for improvement of performance and changes are guided by the implementation of the five disciplines described above. As Senge illustrates, the bottom line of systems thinking is leverage. [288] In order to discuss leverage points in details, an introduction to the proposed argument of this research is essential. Working on leverage points will realise focused action that is normally less obvious to individuals working on existing systems.

---

[284] ibid. pp.69
[285] Peter Senge, *The Fifth Discipline; the Art & Practice of the Learning Organization*, London, Random House Business Books, 1999, pp.12
[286] Peter Senge, *The Fifth Discipline Field book; Strategies and Tools for building a Learning Organization*, London, Nicholas Brealey Publishing Limited, 1999, pp.347
[287] Peter Senge, *The Fifth Discipline; the Art & Practice of the Learning Organization*, London, Random House Business Books, 1999, pp.114
[288] ibid

Building on the significant work of Peter Senge and trying to deepen the research on leverage points; the research of Donella Meadows[289] arises to demonstrate yet the same concepts of the art of systems thinking. The art that lies in being able to recognise increasingly complex and subtle structures, the wealth of details, pressures and potential opportunities for improvement (leverage points) that attend all real management settings.[290] The behaviour of all systems follows certain common principles, the nature of which are being discovered and articulated;

"At its broadest level, Systems Thinking encompasses a large and fairly amorphous body of methods, tools and principles, all oriented to looking to the interrelatedness of forces, and seeing them as part of a common process."[291]

This analysis underpins the categorisation made earlier with the five disciplines working on the components of the system without loosing perspective of the whole process and the manner in which it functions. Therefore it is also necessary to demonstrate how `systems` work in general and follow up on the work of Meadows in identifying `leverage points` in systems.

4.4.1 Leverage Points; Places to Intervene in a System

Leverage points are seen as opportunities in existing systems where

---

[289] Dr. Donella H. Meadows (1941-2001) the founder of the Sustainability Institute, was awarded her PhD in biophysics, Harvard University, is a systems analyst, journalist, college professor, international coordinator of resource management institutions, farmer and writer of several books as well as weekly newspaper column "The Global Citizen" commenting on world events from a systems point of view as well as involved in several studies on Sustainability.

[290] Peter Senge, *The Fifth Discipline; the Art & Practice of the Learning Organization,* London, Random House Business Books, 1999, pp.126

[291] Peter Senge, *The Fifth Discipline Field book; Strategies and Tools for building a Learning Organization,* London, Nicholas Brealey Publishing Limited, 1999, pp.89

embedded actions and changes can lead to significant, enduring improvements. Donella Meadows describes Leverage points as;

"Places within a complex system where a small shift in one thing can produce big changes in everything."[292]

Meadows describes them as points of power because individuals know `intuitively/instinctively where leverage points are` but the problem is that `everyone is trying very hard to push them in the wrong direction`. Complex systems are `counter-intuitive` -as described by Jay Forrester- and since leverage points are intuitive, people tend to use them backwards, systematically worsening whatever problems they are trying to solve or overcome. This backward intuition is clearly demonstrated in the world's leader's commitment to economic growth where they disregard the costs and concentrate on the benefits.

The costs of economic growth are more likely to cause environmental degradation, social inequalities, poverty and hunger and therefore, it becomes exposed as a backward intuition. People tend to think instinctively that `growth` is always a good point of leverage where sometimes what is really needed is a slower growth or even negative growth (e.g. population growth)

Donella Meadows describes her list of leverage points as an invitation to think more broadly about the many ways there might be to get systems to change; therefore it is not a simple, sure-fire recipe for finding leverage

---

[292] Donella Meadows, *Leverage Points: Places to Intervene in a System,* The Sustainability Institute, 1999, pp. 1 , The article can be accessed at http://sustainer.org/resources.html

points.[293]

It is necessary to describe the way in which `systems` function in general. This will allow the identification of the general aspects and functionalities of systems and help understand where and how leverage points exist and react within systems.

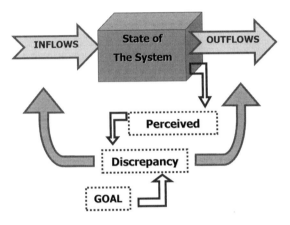

Figure 4.1: The State of the System Diagram[294]

In this diagram, the `state of the system` is whatever standing stock is of importance, which is usually physical stocks, but they could be nonmaterial ones as well. The state of the system is also the condition of the matter in question, the way the system operates, individuals function within its boundaries, the actions and interactions that happens within it. There are usually inflows which increase the stock and outflows which decrease it. The

---

[293] Donella Meadows, *Leverage Points: Places to Intervene in a System*, The Sustainability Institute, 1999, pp. 3 , The article can be accessed at http://sustainer.org/resources.html
[294] ibid. pp.4

165

change caused by inflows and outflows is inevitable; there is no system that does not deal with continuous change. These flows could be representing information flows, activities, decisions, or events. The rest of the diagram shows the information that causes the stock to change. The difference between the way the state of the system is perceived and its actual condition (Perceived) and the objective to be reached (Goal), define the discrepancy in the diagram.

Peter Senge's List of `Systems Archetypes` (Opportunities for Improvement – Leverage)	Donella Meadows' List of `Places to Intervene in a System` (Leverage points)
• Balancing process with delay	• Constants, parameters, numbers
• Eroding goals	• Regulation negative feedback loops
• Limits to growth	• Driving positive loops
• Tragedy of the commons	• Material flows & nodes of material intersection
• Growth and under-investment	• Information flows
• Shifting the burden	• The rules of the system
• Corrective actions that fail	• The distribution of power over the rules of the system
• Escalation	• The goals of the system
• Success to the successful	• The mindset out of which the system arises

Table 4.1: Senge's and Meadows' Lists of Leverage Points

This table is a representation of Peter Senge's work on systems archetypes and Donella Meadows' list of leverage points. Senge's archetypes are elaborate patterns of systems' structure which recur repeatedly. Senge refers to them as the opportunities for improvement and therefore considers them as leverage, while Meadows identifies her list of leverage points as places to intervene and implement `change` in existing systems.

First, Senge argues that extending one's knowledge of systems archetypes expands one's ability to get to grips with management issues and thereby identifies the opportunities that exist for improvement[295]. His list of leverage points demonstrates the places where it is possible to realise focused action that is normally less than obvious to most people operating solely from intuition.

Second, Meadows' list of leverage points represents her initial thoughts about the identification of leverage, she describes this list as `not exactly tightly reasoned`[296], as it is not a simple, sure-fire recipe for finding leverage points. Therefore, after more research and collaboration with other systems analysts, Meadows rethought the initial list, added and deleted items, changed the order and added caveats to bring out her modified list of leverage points, which she called `Places to Intervene in a System`.

The following part of the research is based on Meadows' list of leverage points because of its elaborative contents and extensive analysis yet rich simplicity and also because it includes more detailed representation of general systems' processes and procedures with detailed highlights of the interrelatedness between the parts and the whole of the system in question.

4.4.2 The Places to Intervene in a System (Leverage Points)

Meadows chose in her research to display the leverage points in an increasing order of effectiveness. This increasing order has also been used in this analysis of her list of leverage points in order to allow the reader's

---

[295] Peter Senge, *The Fifth Discipline; the Art & Practice of the Learning Organization*, London, Random House Business Books, 1999, pp.114-126
[296] Donella Meadows, *Leverage Points: Places to Intervene in a System*, The Sustainability Institute, 1999, pp. 3

judgement to evolve with the list from the less effective to the more effective points. It also ensures the maintenance of the reader's interest in finding out the most effective leverage point. It was also important to maintain the order of effectiveness in a list format as it facilitates the referral to each leverage point later in this research.

Meadows' list of leverage points comprises[297]: -

12. Constants, Parameters, and Numbers:

Parameters in systems jargon are the numbers/values which determine how much of a discrepancy affects the quantity and value of the inflows or the outflows at a determinate time. In her research, Meadows describes `Parameters` as the points of least leverage on the list of interventions. Although ninety nine percent of the attention goes to parameters, she argues that there is not a lot of leverage in them. Meadows yet disputes that this does not mean that they are not important, but in fact, they can be of relative importance, especially in the short term and particularly, to the individual who is directly dealing with the impact of any flow.

"People care deeply about parameters and fight fierce battles over them, but they rarely change behaviour"[298]

The numbers in this point of leverage, represent the time of the event and the significance. These considerations as a matter of numbers, some of which represent a physical part of the event/flow are unchangeable, but are mostly popular interventions points.

"Systems goals are parameters that can make significant differences, especially when

---

[297] ibid. pp.5
[298] ibid

the smallest change in a number can drive the system from order to disorder, but fortunately most systems have evolved or are designed to stay clear of critical parameter ranges."[299]

If the system is chronically stagnant, parameters' changes rarely make a difference. If the system is variable, they don't usually stabilise it and it is going out of control, they cannot stop the growth, but they become leverage points with significant impact when they go into ranges that control items such as interest rates in banking systems or birth rates in population growth.

11. The sizes of buffers and other stabilising stocks, relative to their flows:

A large, stabilising stock/ inventory is known as `buffer`. Stocks that are big, relative to their flows, are more stable than small ones.

"The stabilising power of buffers is why we keep money in the bank rather than living from the flow of change through our pocket. It's why stores hold inventory instead of calling for new stock just as customers carry the old stock out the door."[300]

This is why individuals rely on maintaining more than the minimum they need on which they base their actions. A system can often be stabilised by increasing the capacity of a buffer, but if a buffer is too big; the system becomes inflexible because it reacts too slowly and also because some big buffers have high build or maintenance costs.

"The reason why buffers are at the less influential end of the list of leverage points is because they are usually physical entities, not easy to change."[301]

---

[299] ibid. pp.6
[300] ibid. pp.7
[301] ibid.

10. The structure of material stocks and flows and nodes of intersection:

The process of building stock or inventory, their flows and their physical arrangements can have an enormous effect on the way systems operate. Some are just not possible to change or control and in some cases the only way to fix a system that is poorly laid out is to rebuild it where possible.

"Physical structure is crucial in a system but rarely a leverage point; because changing it is rarely simple."[302]

The leverage point is in the proper design in the first place because after the structure is built, the leverage is in understanding its limitations and bottlenecks and refraining from fluctuations or expansions which could strain its capacity.

9. The lengths of delays, relative to the rate of system changes:

"Delays in feedback loops are common causes of oscillations. If you're trying to adjust a system state to your goal, but you only receive delayed information about what the system state is, you will overshoot and undershoot."[303]

A system cannot respond to short term changes when it has long term delays.

"A delay in a feedback process is critical relative to rates of changes in the system state that the feedback loop is trying to control."[304]

Delays that are too short cause overreaction, oscillations which are amplified by the jumpiness of the response. Delays which are too long, cause

---

[302] ibid. pp.8
[303] ibid.
[304] ibid.

dampened, sustained or exploding oscillations, depending on the value of the prolongation or excess but, at the extreme, they might cause chaos.

"Overlong delays in a system with a threshold, a danger point, ranges past which, irreversible damage can occur, cause overshoot and collapse."[305]

8. The strength of negative feedback loops, relative to the impacts they are trying to correct against:

From this leverage point onwards the list of interventions is beginning to move from the physical part of the system to the information and control parts, where more leverage can be found.

"Negative feedback loops are found everywhere (ubiquitous) in systems. Nature evolves them and humans invent them as controls to keep important system states within safe bounds."[306]

Any negative feedback loop needs a goal, a monitoring and signalling device to detect excursions from the goal and a response mechanism. A complex system usually has numerous negative feedback loops that it can bring into play, so it can self-correct under different conditions and impacts. These negative feedback loops may not be visible but their presence is critical to the long-term welfare of the system. The strength of a negative loop can be determined by its ability to keep its appointed stock at or near its goal. It depends on the combination of all its parameters and links; the accuracy and rapidity of monitoring, the quickness and power of response, the directness and size of corrective flows.

The strength of a negative feedback loop is important relatively to the impact

---

[305] ibid. pp.9
[306] ibid.

it is designed to correct. If the impact increases in strength, the feedbacks have to be strengthened too.

7. The gain around driving positive feedback loops:

"A negative feedback loop is self-correcting; a positive feedback loop is self-reinforcing. The more it works, the more it gains power to work some more."[307]

Positive feedback loops are sources of growth, explosion, erosion and collapse in systems. Positive loops have to be continuously checked to prevent the system from destroying itself. Reducing the gain around a positive loop is usually a more powerful leverage point in systems than strengthening negative loops, and much preferable to letting the positive loop run.

6. The structure of information flows:

"It's not a parameter adjustment, not a strengthening or weakening of an existing loop. It's a new loop, delivering information to a place where it wasn't going before and therefore causing people to behave differently."[308]

Missing feedback is one of the most common causes of system malfunction. Adding or restoring information can be a powerful intervention, usually much easier and cheaper than rebuilding physical infrastructure. It is important that the missing feedback be restored to the right place and in compelling form.

"Because humans have a systematic tendency to avoid accountability for our decisions; so many feedback loops are missing. This is the reason why this kind of

---

[307] ibid.
[308] ibid. pp.13

leverage point is so often popular with the masses, unpopular with the powers that be, and effective, if you can get the powers that be to permit it to happen."[309]

5. The rules of the system:

"They are high leverage points. Power over the rules is real power."[310]

The rules of the system define its scope, its boundaries, and its degrees of freedom. Donella Meadows describes that as individuals try to imagine restructured rules and what their behaviour would be under them, they come to understand the power of rules. Whether the rules that form the reality of the existing system are strict or weak, it is the interaction of the users with these rules that controls the point of leverage.

4. The power to add, change, evolve, or self-organise system structure:

"The most stunning thing living systems and social systems can do is to change themselves utterly by creating whole new structures and behaviours."[311]

Meadows describes `Self-organisation` saying that it means changing any aspect of a system lower on this list: adding completely new physical structures, such as brains or wings or computers; adding new negative or positive loops: making new rules.

"The ability to self-organise is the strongest form of system resilience."[312]

Self-organisation is basically the combination of an evolutionary raw

---

[309] ibid.
[310] ibid. pp.14
[311] ibid.
[312] ibid. pp.15

material and a means of experimentation, for selecting and testing new patterns. This raw material could also be seen as a highly variable stock of information from which to select possible patterns.

"Any system, biological, economic, or social that becomes so encrusted that it cannot self-evolve, a system that systematically scorns experimentation and wipes out the raw material of innovation, is doomed over the long term on this highly variable planet."[313]

3. The goals of the system:

"The goal of a system is a leverage point superior to the self-organising ability of a system. If the goal is to bring more and more of the world under the control of one particular central planning system, then everything further down the list, physical stocks and flows, feedback loops, information flows, even self-organising behaviour, will be twisted to conform to that goal."[314]

It is not easy for individuals within a system to identify whole systems goals, nor is it easy to argue whether these goals are good or bad, because it always depends on the person controlling the goals. Corporate power and dominance in competitive markets among the competitors is a goal that has to be overtaken by the whole system goal of maintaining a competitive market. The same struggle exists between corporate power and government policies, dominance and power could be the ultimate goals for existing systems.

2. The mindset or paradigm out of which the system arises:

"The shared idea in the minds of society, the great big unstated assumptions- unstated because unnecessary to state; everyone already knows them- constitute that

---

[313] ibid. pp.16
[314] ibid.

society's paradigm, or deepest set of beliefs about how the world works."[315]

Meadows argues that paradigms are the sources of systems, where from them, from shared social agreements about the nature of reality, come system goals and information flows, feedbacks, stocks, flows and everything else about systems. Whether by social consensus or scientific consent, some paradigms do not need any rules or evidence to support their existence as described by Thomas Kuhn in defining the structure of scientific revolutions;

"The existence of a paradigm need not even imply that any full set of rules exists"[316]

Kuhn argues that societies' and scientists' success depends upon knowledge that is acquired through practise and which cannot be articulated explicitly, this demonstrating a strong belief in this kind of paradigm that is usually transferred from one generation to the next.

Changing paradigms takes individuals outside the system and forces them to see it as a whole. When implementing the changes to the whole, the core of the system must first change and therefore the impact is significant because this change happened in the roots of the system no matter how small the change may have been.

1. The power to transcend paradigms:

In her research, Donella Meadows argues that there is yet one leverage point that is even higher than changing a paradigm and that is to keep oneself

---

[315] ibid. pp.17
[316] Thomas S. Kuhn, The Structures of Scientific Revolutions; International Encyclopaedia of Unified Science, Volume 2-Number 2, The University of Chicago Press, USA, 1970,pp.44

unattached in the arena of paradigms, to stay flexible, to realise that no paradigm is true, that every one, including the one that sweetly shapes our own worldview, is a tremendously limited understanding of an immense and amazing universe that is far beyond human comprehension.

"If no paradigm is right, you can choose whatever one will help to achieve your purpose. It is in this space of mastery over paradigms that people throw off addictions, live in constant joy, bring down empires, found religions... and have impacts that last for millennia."[317]

This point of view on the power of paradigms is shared by Thomas Kuhn in describing paradigms when dealing with challenging puzzles and supplying clues to their solutions and it is all embedded in the belief that succeeding in solving them is sometimes in believing that paradigms exist within our own knowledge and perception of clues to these puzzles.

"Only those who have taken courage from observing that their own field (or school) has paradigms are likely to feel that something important is sacrificed by the change"[318]

The reason behind the identification of leverage points and places to intervene in a system, is mostly because individuals and participants in systems need to study where changes can be implemented and the manner in which these changes should be introduced as well as the nature of these changes. Senge and Meadows, both argue that small changes and well focused actions can produce significant, enduring improvements if they are introduced to the system in the right place, with the right value needed and

---

[317] Donella Meadows, *Leverage Points: Places to Intervene in a System*, The Sustainability Institute, 1999, pp.19
[318] Thomas S. Kuhn, The Structures of Scientific Revolutions; International Encyclopaedia of Unified Science, Volume 2-Number 2, The University of Chicago Press, USA, 1970,pp.179

at the right time.[319]

A final crucial lesson that needs to be retained from this analysis of systems thinking and leverage points is the conclusion that both Meadows and Senge agree upon; the higher the leverage point in question is on this list, the higher and more effective the impact it has on the system. The choice from the list of interventions of leverage points should be based on the impact individuals want to reach in improving their system's performance. The earlier the change is introduced to the existing system, the more effective its impact on succeeding stages and processes. It is not by enforcing the change onto the system, but by identifying the potential gaps/opportunities (leverage points) within the existing framework that a conclusive opportunity arises to achieve a higher level of positive impact of change towards the targeted objective when introduced.

During the last decade, environmental management systems seemed to provide the right platform for better environmentally aware performance from institutions. But in recent years, following a global interest in sustainable development approaches, which reached its peak with the launch of the Earth Summit, held in South Africa in August 2002, sustainable management systems seem to be under the spotlight. The lead taken in sustainable development has changed the global reality and commitment to a better future, and has also affected the commitment of private and public sectors in pushing forward the application of a smooth transition from environmental management systems to sustainable management systems.

---

[319] Peter Senge, *The Fifth Discipline; the Art & Practice of the Learning Organization,* London, Random House Business Books, 1999, pp.64, also see Donella Meadows, *Leverage Points: Places to Intervene in a System,* The Sustainability Institute, 1999, pp. 1

4.5   From Environmental Management Systems to Sustainable Management Systems

4.5.1 Environmental Management Systems (EMS)

At the Rio Summit in 1992, a new challenge for the international community was laid down for a global commitment to a better future. It was the challenge of implementing 'Sustainable Development and the Triple Bottom Line'. The International Organisation for Standardization (ISO) had responded earlier to the environmental challenge by showing a concrete manifestation of the global commitment and introduced Environmental Management System (EMS)[320]. Although a structured approach to fortifying the environmental bottom line, yet this was still serving just one of the three sustainability factors.

In general terms, environmental management system represent a part of the overall management system which includes organisational structure, planning activities, responsibilities, practices, procedures, processes and resources for developing, implementing, achieving, reviewing and maintaining the environmental policy of organisations.[321]

EMS created a long list of international standards (e.g. ISO 14000), a family of standards that boosted the certification business and authorities. It includes an extensive list of tools and techniques to guide any organisation towards better environmental performance embracing tools for environmental life cycle assessment, auditing, environmental management, labels and declarations, vocabulary and guidance for environmental aspects in products

---

[320] International Organisation for Standardisation (ISO), www.iso.org visited January 2003
[321] ibid.

178

and services.

Environmental management systems are mostly concerned with the environmental side of management systems in support of the environmental bottom line representing only one of the triple bottom lines justifying the global awareness and commitment to sustainable development.

Environmental Management Systems (EMS) represent a vehicle for significant steps towards sustainability, along with the world commitment for a sustainable future. The natural step forward was to create sustainable management systems that would not only highlight the environmental aspects of organisational performance, as the tools and techniques of EMS provided, but also to place emphasis on the social as well as the economic sides of practice.

4.5.2 Sustainable Management Systems (SMS)

It is a management framework to help organisation in tackling the issue of sustainability, with a set of principles, tools and approaches that integrate sustainable development into the major processes of decision making and practice. SMS follows, of course, the main guidelines of sustainability in working on three parallel levels of economic, environmental and social constraints. The initiation of development of such management systems highlights the potential role and contribution of conventional business and public sector organisations in corporate and public environmental, social and economic management for all practices.

The conversion of environmental management systems to sustainable

179

management systems, represent a smooth transition to face the new global challenge, embracing sustainable business thinking, tools and techniques to identify, evaluate and improve social, economic and environmental organisational commitment.

A major challenge in implanting sustainable management systems in many organisations is to free the logjam that currently exists between `understanding` and `action` in many organisations.[322] Therefore, several British governmental organisations and standards institutes came forward with the SIGMA Project.

4.6 The SIGMA Project ($\sum$)

The SIGMA Project -which stands for **S**ustainability; **I**ntegrated **G**uidelines for **Ma**nagement- was launched in 1999 by the British Standards Institution, Forum for the Future, and Accountability, and is primarily funded by the UK Department of Trade and Industry (DTI).[323]

" *Many pioneering organisations world-wide now believe that if they do not address social and environmental issues as well as economic goals, they will not survive... they embrace the idea of the triple bottom line in their management system – accounting not just for their economic performance but also their environmental and social performance*"[324]

Therefore, the SIGMA Project created a set of Guidelines, based on a series of

---

[322] The SIGMA Project website http://www.projectsigma.com/Index.asp last accessed February 2003
[323] Full version of the SIGMA Guidelines and overview is found at http://www.projectsigma.com/SIGMAProject/Publications/IntroGuidelines.asp last visited February 2003
[324] *The SIGMA Project Guidelines*, The SIGMA Project website, Pilot Draft May 2001, Section 2.0 pp. 11 http://www.projectsigma.com/SIGMAProject/Publications/IntroGuidelines.asp

180

inter-linking and supporting components. These components comprise:[325]

- A set of principles that help an organisation to understand and navigate the parameters of sustainability.
- A management framework that integrates sustainability issues into core processes and mainstream decision-making.
- A series of tools and approaches which organisations can use to implement effective strategies, initiate culture change, promote learning, set objectives, and then achieve the goals.

While the tools can be applied flexibly according to the organisational needs, existing practices and culture, the SIGMA principles and management framework are core elements of the guidelines.

The project's objectives are to develop a management framework to help organisations tackle sustainability, develop practical guidance and tools that empower organisations to move towards a more sustainable way of doing business and to develop a management process that embeds sustainability into mainstream organisational policy, strategy, practice and procedures. It is also part of the objectives to establish and nurture learning communities that furthers the aims and objectives of sustainable development and finally to ensure the development of these objectives is achieved through a genuine dialogue with stakeholders.[326]

This short description of the SIGMA project shows how extensive sustainable management systems can get to help organisations on their road to attain the triple bottom line principles. Whether organising the SIGMA principles on

---

[325] ibid.
[326] http://www.projectsigma.com/SIGMAProject/SIGMAProjectOverview.pdf

two levels; firstly, underpinning concepts of accountability, capital enhancement and environment sustainability and secondly, by a series of questions that organisations should ask themselves about their performance and practices, or whether analysing the key phases contained in the management framework or whether using any of the tools in the SIGMA toolkit, it becomes obvious to business that sustainable systems are the way forward to survive and remain competitive.

4.7 The Way Forward

This Transition from EMS to SMS has shown that awareness of the critical importance of the environment is not enough, but that social and economic concerns are on the same level of significance for better performance. In this chapter, it was important to analyse `Systems Thinking` in general, and describe how the theory functions.

Peter Senge's work has provided the basics for systems thinking theory and the five disciplines. Donella Meadows built her research on this theory to analyse and demonstrate how to implement changes to existing systems by identifying the different leverage points in the system. Applying sustainable management systems, as in the case of the SIGMA Project, gives a better opportunity for sustainable performance. It is not only about environmental concerns, but it is about a better future on the three parallel strands of economic, social and environmental concerns.

Sustainable approach to management systems is proven to be a valid contribution to sustainable performance which aligns with the arguments for implementing sustainability into the project management process, from the early phases of any project, as advised by Meadows. Achieving a more effective impact is possible when the change is implemented from the early stages using the right leverage points.

The next stage of this thesis illustrates the interaction between the three pillars of this research (i.e. Project Management, Sustainable Development and Construction Industry's Practices) within a tri-dimensional framework to achieve a more sustainable project management process for construction practices starting from the earliest phases of projects. Systems thinking and its theory's basics and the identification of leverage points will act as the `milieu` which will allow the tri-dimensional integration to take place and will fortify their existing relationships.

PART II: Rethinking the Relationships; The Tri-Dimensional Integration

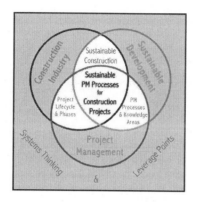
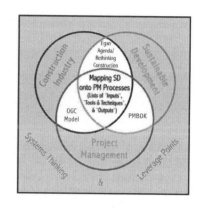

CHAPTER 5

THE INTEGRATION

"A systems approach...provides a multi-dimensional framework in which information from different disciplines and domains can be integrated without being forced into a one-dimensional mapping."

Clayton and Radcliffe "Sustainability: A Systems Approach"[327]

This chapter represents the beginning of the second part of the research; a systems thinking approach to the integration of sustainable development into project management processes for the construction industry.

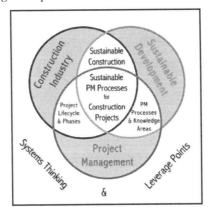

Figure 5.0: Illustrating the four pillars of the research's hypothesis with special emphasis on the outcome of the Tri-Dimensional Integration.

Figure (5.0) demonstrates the research's hypothesis which relies on using the guidelines of `systems thinking` theory and leverage points in bringing together the complex systems of construction, sustainable development and

---

[327] Anthony M H Clayton, Nicholas J Radcliffe, *Sustainability: A Systems Approach*, The Institute for Policy Analysis and Development and WWF-UK, Earthscan Publications Limited, UK, London, 1997, pp.12

185

project management. In this chapter, the `systems thinking` approach is argued to generate a tri-dimensional integration between Sustainable Development (SD) and Project Management (PM) processes for the construction industry.

The construction industry, the sustainable development guidelines, the project management processes and areas of knowledge and finally, the theory of systems thinking and leverage points have all been examined as an individual dimension with a limited standpoint on the potential for integrating them. This chapter is the transformation; taking the previous analysis to a synthesis of the arguments and demonstrate these elements working together in a multi-dimensional functioning agenda.

5.1 Introduction

This chapter is not only proposing a tri-dimensional integration between the complex systems of project management, sustainable development and construction practises but also a systems thinking approach to this integration through the identification of leverage points within the existing systems and processes. This is first justified in the chapter to demonstrate how systems thinking and leverage points would act as the best means or catalysts for allowing the synthesis between the three pillars. This is displayed through allowing the elements in question to interact within a systems thinking `milieu` enhancing this interaction, thus they are not forced into a one dimensional framework but rather a tri-dimensional structure that enhances information flow from one system to the other.

The main objective of this chapter and the research as a whole, is not only to propose a different approach or a new integration but mostly it is to recommend a contribution towards a solution as to how to translate such suggestions into real active actions in real practices. This is why; the body of the chapter relies on three distinctive case studies as a fundamental part of the methodology of the research. The first practical application of the hypothesis portrays the Egan Agenda's Drivers from a systems thinking point of view; integrating SD into construction practices generates a sustainable construction agenda.

The second case study is the identification of leverage points within one of the most important phases of all construction projects; the procurement stage. This is demonstrated as an example to the integration between PM and construction practices through a systems thinking approach. Project lifecycles and phases are demonstrated through the procurement stage to attain a more sustainable application to the project phase in question (i.e. procurement) through the identification of sustainability gaps within an existing Government model which should have been following Government's sustainable initiatives.

The final case study application withdraws the research into its fundamental conclusion; integrating SD into PM processes for construction projects. The case study examines the notions of a sustainable development approach to the PMBOK processes and knowledge areas and describes the way forward to implement the desired change into the core knowledge of PM to envisage an efficient implementation of SD guidelines into the PM standards of the PMBOK. The integration explores the potential of a holistic approach to strategic project management and show how a systems thinking approach to

PM processes would enhance PM's contribution to construction projects.

This chapter is an analysis of what the hypothesis of this research stands for in terms of integrating the previous elements of the research into a more coherent and active framework that would enhance sustainability performance within construction through the vital contribution that project management offers to construction practises.

5.2 Impelling Reasons for A Systems Thinking Approach

"...what is needed is not the continual search for the single method as the way to achieve better practice. We need new thinking, underpinned by a strong philosophy, to give us a coherent set of concepts that integrate and add value to the best of the existing ideas. Such an approach will help us clarify what needs to be done and what needs not to be done. It will allow us to focus on what is necessary and sufficient, and enable us to establish responsibilities and accountabilities. We are proposing the use of `Systems Thinking` to `Rethink Construction`."[328]

`Systems Thinking` can be used across a wider range than just construction because of its generic uses and analysis of leverage points which allows greater applications in many fields and working environments. However, this chapter puts forward new emphasis on its implementation in construction practices and processes through the analysis of the component parts of construction projects while keeping a perspective on the whole picture of practices. Furthermore, the research first presents the criteria for assessing the success of applying systems thinking to the proposed integration.

---

[328] David Blockley and Patrick Godfrey, *Doing it differently; systems for rethinking construction*, Thomas Telford Publishing, London, 2000, pp.11

The research's arguments can not develop the use of systems thinking as the governing milieu of this integration unless this is justified. The following list represents the justification of such proposition.

The views expressed by David Blockley and Patrick Godfrey in their recent publication `Doing it differently; Systems for rethinking construction`[329], endorse the research's approach to the use of systems thinking for the integration of sustainable development, construction and project management as the following list demonstrates.

This research argues that the use of systems thinking and leverage points theories will help the practice to produce a simple approach to the complexity of the construction processes. An integration underpinned by a systems thinking approach allows the break down of processes and systems to a simpler level of system description which makes interventions and changes easier to identify.

A systems thinking approach would demonstrate flexibility in embracing practical steps towards change. Applying new visions of systems thinking on practical projects is demonstrated to be efficient and generate a more positive impact because it originates from within the system and is not imposed on it from without.

It would acknowledge sustainability as part of the tools and techniques for the knowledge areas of PM. This integration makes use of sustainability tools to manage uncertainty and influences the transformation of Inputs to

---

[329] ibid. Part 1 "The need to do it differently – 1. Meeting the Challenge", pp.3-26

Outputs. This linear interaction will be analysed again but from a systems thinking point of view in terms of integrating sustainable development within its list of tools and techniques.

The theories of systems thinking would help the reader understand how complex systems function through the analysis of their diagrams of influence (systems maps/diagrams as Peter Senge called them). This representation of complex systems as diagrams, allows better identification of processes, stages and leverage points to simplify the complexity of the system in question.

As a governing milieu, systems thinking theories would allow the Integration of sustainable development guidelines more easily and clearly into construction processes starting with the core of its activities which are represented by the project management knowledge areas and processes. This would highlight the connections between and among sustainable development, construction and project management as presented in figure (5.2) below.

The theories embrace the current government's initiatives such as the Egan Report and Rethinking Construction agenda but from a holistic point of view rather than regulations enforced upon the industry. It helps understand the common ground and relationships between quality and value which underpins the necessity of adding project value management to the nine main areas of knowledge provided by the PMBOK as described in chapter 3.

The approach would recognise the need for radical change not only on the environmental strand but also the social as well as the economic levels because sustainability not only calls for environmental protection but also for adding value to the clients, users and employees while maintaining economic profitability.

A systems thinking approach would identify the great potential in implementing changes to the parts which will benefit the whole; this would help the industry accomplish the Egan agenda while benefiting from the sustainability approach. Not only on the construction side of projects, but particularly through the fundamental parts of projects, where project management processes and knowledge areas represent a crucial part of all current projects.

It would also help the reader realise that changing processes driven by compelling propositions of a sustainability approach would accomplish a stronger more creative vision which would enable and facilitate the connectivity with practicality. It is not only about introducing new initiatives but mainly about how to apply these strategies to current practices.

Finally, the proposed approach incorporates people and processes in order to transform the processes from a guiding procedure to a peg on which to hang all attributes. This incorporation allows the processes to maintain the vision of the whole while preserving the individuality of the parts. Therefore, the processes become the source of actions and the core base of knowledge for all projects.

From a systems thinking point of view, the process in which any system proceeds becomes the most important part of the framework. A systems thinking approach calls for more focus on the processes and therefore, it encourages systems' analysts to use creative thinking in representing the processes in diagrams of influences. This new interpretation of the importance of processes for all systems underpins the central role of processes in unifying ideas and techniques;

"Process is the core concept on which all other ideas are hung as attributes to represent what the process is...processes are used to integrate ideas and give us a way of seeing an essential simplicity in complexity." [330]

In the Current View, Process is:-	In Proposed New View, Process is:-
• a task or activity	• a way of getting from where you are to where you want to be
• can only be viewed from one perspective	• can be viewed from many perspective such as function, value, risk and change
• only useful in a restricted way	• the central idea on which ideas are `hung`
• only useful when condition are stable and repetitive	• useful to help manage risk when conditions are uncertain
• inflexible, difficult to accommodate change	• flexible and can be use to manage change
• only useful when condition are predictable with low uncertainty	• useful to manage high uncertainty
• not very dependent on teamwork	• totally dependent on teamwork
• not seen as being useful across organisational boundaries	• essential for work across organisational boundaries
• only to be used on a clear problem	• useful to clarify complicated problems
• a lot of work to produce a model	• to be used right from the start
• limited in the number of attributes used	• used to unify ideas with a rich set of attributes, particularly a clear purpose, definition of success and a process owner

Table 5.1: A New View of Process[331]

Table 5.1, describes the proposed view of `process` in comparison with the typical current view. This new view underpins the emphasis on focusing on

---

[330] David Blockley and Patrick Godfrey, *Doing it differently; systems for rethinking construction,* Thomas Telford Publishing, London, 2000, pp.55
[331] ibid. pp.30

the PM processes as well as general processes of construction discussed by the Egan drivers which will be analysed from a systems thinking point of view later in this chapter.

But first, the research now presents the body of the proposed integration in terms of components, interconnections and general characteristics governing the interactions.

5.3 The Framework for the Integration

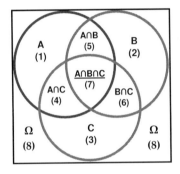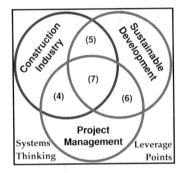

Figure 5.1:
Left hand side: Typical Venn diagram between A, B and C producing 7 Interior Regions (1) to (7) and 1 Exterior Region (8)
Right hand side: The Tri-Dimensional Integration between Construction Industry "A" (1), Sustainable Development "B" (2) and Project Management "C" (3) within the External `milieu` of Systems Thinking and Leverage Points (Ω)

Figure (5.1) is composed of 2 shapes; on the left, a diagram of a typical Venn diagram on 3-sets (A), (B) and (C) and the outside `milieu` of (Ω). On the right, is the illustration of the tri-dimensional integration between the construction industry, sustainable development and project management enhanced by the external `milieu` of systems thinking and leverage points.

193

On the left hand side of figure (5.1), the Venn diagram produces 7 interior regions (1) to (7) and one exterior region (8) which represents the region embracing the diagram. This illustration explores not only the relationships between the three intersecting circles (1), (2) and (3) but also the interconnections among them; represented by the regions (4) to (7). The regions (4) `A ∩ C`, (5) `A ∩ B` and (6) `B ∩ C` consist of common grounds among two sets but not the third, the region (7) `A ∩ B ∩ C` consists of common grounds which are simultaneously in all three.

On the right hand side, an illustration of the tri-dimensional integration proposed where the four pillars of the integration are: -

1. The Construction Industry (chapter 1) represented by the Blue Circle is the substitute of Region (1)

2. Sustainable Development (chapter 2) represented by the Green Circle is the substitute of Region (2)

3. Project Management (chapter 3) represented by the Red Circle is the substitute of Region (3)

4. Systems Thinking and Leverage Points (chapter 4) represented by the square surrounding the three circles; the substitute for Region (8) or (Ω). It acts as the tool proposed by the author to enhance this integration as its catalyst.

5.4 The Interconnections between the Three Dimensions

Figure (5.2) explores in greater detail the interconnections between the three dimensions explained earlier in the right hand shape of figure (5.1). Based on the previous analysis of the construction industry, sustainable development and project management in chapters 1, 2 and 3, figure (5.2) details the relationships between and among them.

Chapters 1 and 3 demonstrated the imperative role that project management plays in the successful completion of construction projects from the early phases of initiation through all the following project phases; this is represented in figure (5.2) below by Region (4) `Project Lifecycle and Phases`.

Chapters 1 and 2 explored the relationship between the sustainable development agenda and construction which produced a new approach to construction performances; `sustainable construction` represented in figure (5.2) by Region (5).

Chapters 2 and 3 demonstrated that the project management commitment to the sustainability agenda was vague and did not represent the great potential of possible integration within the PM processes and knowledge areas illustrated in the PMBOK. This potential which will be examined in further detail in this chapter is represented by Region (6) `PM Processes and Knowledge Areas`.

Finally, Region (7) illustrates in figure (5.2) the `Sustainable PM Processes for Construction Projects`; it is the common ground resulting from the interaction between the three dimensions.

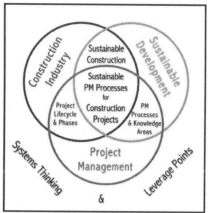

Figure 5.2:- A Venn diagram illustrating "The Tri-Dimensional Integration within a milieu of `Systems Thinking` theory and Leverage Points"

The context of `Systems Thinking` theory represents the milieu or setting which allows the identification of leverage points among the interconnections between the three dimensions of the framework; the external region (8) or (Ω).

While `systems thinking` enhances the interconnection between each of the three circles, representing a corresponding dimension of the integration, the identification of leverage points becomes a vital stage of this enhancement between the three dimensions without losing perspective of the whole framework of integration. Maintaining this vision of `the whole` while working on the components of the framework has been already explained but this chapter highlights, explains and analyses the interconnections between the three dimensions as well as identifies the leverage points among them.

196

5.5 CASE STUDY 1: Systems Thinking Approach to Sustainable Construction

This research discussed the current under performance of the construction industry in Europe and more specifically in the UK, by analysing some of the government initiatives to improve the industry's performance as well as the links between those initiatives and the need for sustainable development to be involved in dealing with the inevitable change. The Egan Report represented a significant milestone on the road to a better construction future but this book presented the case for criticising the report for its lack of commitment to sustainability. Sustainable construction is therefore a new agenda for dealing with change and it presents itself as the solution for integrating sustainable development guidelines into construction practices.

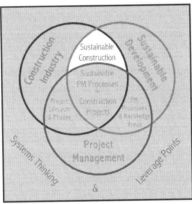

Figure 5.3: Illustrating the research's hypothesis with special highlight on the interaction between the `Construction Industry` and `Sustainable Development` to create `Sustainable Construction`.

This section discusses the sustainable construction agenda (highlighted in figure (5.3)) from a systems thinking point of view.

Government's initiatives were introduced to guide the industry towards sustainable construction with guidelines illustrated in (figure 5.4). The Egan report praised the performance of the industry but called for more to be done. `Rethinking Construction` was the answer to government's commitment to implement sustainability into construction practices. The inevitable change confronting the industry carried risks but also created opportunities for a better future for the industry.

Figure 5.4: The Road to Sustainable Construction[332]

Sustainability can be introduced to the Egan drivers and transform the Egan agenda to a more effective way of integrating sustainable development guidelines into the industry.

Following the impelling reasons for a systems thinking approach, looking at the Egan drivers from a systems thinking point of view could change `Rethinking Construction` significantly as it has been introduced in the

---

[332] The Construction Confederation and CIRIA, *The Towards Sustainable Construction Conference -Building a Better Way of Life*, Conference proceedings, Queen Elizabeth Conference Centre, London, July 2000.

research work done by David Blockley and Patrick Godfrey in `Systems for Rethinking Construction`[333]. This interpretation reflects on the analysis of the procurement processes as a significant part of all construction processes and furthermore, on the importance of `process` in the new view of a systems thinking approach.

5.5.1 The Egan Agenda from a Systems Thinking Point of View

Rethinking Construction – The Egan Drivers	From a Systems Thinking Point of View
• Committed leadership • Focus on the customer • Quality driven agenda • Integrating processes and teams • Commitment to people	• Focus on the customer to define purpose • Be clear about roles to deliver the purpose • Clear any differences of understandings of what makes up or forms the system • Make sure the system is appropriate for the purpose • Make sure the system is dependable and measurable • Be clear about systems value and ethics

Table 5.2: The Egan Drivers from a Systems thinking Point of View[334]

- **Committed Leadership**

Systems thinking emphasises the ideas of the leaders as team coaches whose role is to bring out the best in their team by encouraging and developing their skills. Success is about team behaviour as a whole and it is just as important to support the team leader by appropriate behaviour as it is to lead. Peter Senge described shared vision and team learning as crucial ideas in thinking through these ways of behaviour especially when senior managers are so involved in the day to day activities that these essential leadership qualities go absent.

---

[333] David Blockley and Patrick Godfrey, *Doing it differently; systems for rethinking construction*, Thomas Telford Publishing, London, 2000, pp.300-302
[334] ibid.

- **Focus on Customer**

Systems thinking helps to understand value and not just focus on cost. It helps acknowledge that bringing value to the project originates from the processes and that thinking about the whole life cycle of process identifies opportunities to deliver value to customers. Value originates from the clients and the individuals who are part of the general processes. A systems thinking approach makes that connection easier to grasp and calls for the process to include less of what is not needed and more of what adds real value.

- **Integrated Processes and Teams**

Systems thinking is all about the whole as an entity and the parts from which the whole derives. Maintaining this vision, allows the understanding of what makes the whole; the framework integrates, naturally, processes and teams where the latter deliver success for every process previously identified by the team leader. This displays a more serious commitment to shared vision, one of the five disciplines of Senge, and helps the team members to believe in the process they are working on, rather than just following the visions of senior management.

- **Quality Driven Agenda**

A systems thinking approach gives a much wider understanding of what quality is and its connections with value. A quality driven approach to existing processes delivers higher value through better effectiveness and efficiency embedded by systems thinking. A systems thinking understanding of what the process entails helps deliver quality to the agenda which fulfils the customer's expectations.

- **Commitment to People**

Systems thinking puts an emphasis on people whether as leaders or team members. It gives them empowerment both inwards in their personal development and outwards when taking roles and responsibilities within the process. Systems thinking presents and helps identify opportunities for improvements at all levels and self fulfilment for individuals as it highlights the prospects for change within the existing process in order to improve performance.

This analysis of the Egan drivers from a systems thinking point of view, highlights the importance of a systems thinking approach to the agenda and demonstrates the importance of involving systems thinking when tackling sustainable construction.

Environmental responsibility, social awareness and economic profitability are the key strands for sustainable construction identified by most of the previously analysed initiatives. Sustainable construction presents itself as the new agenda, but the major question is how to introduce this sustainability agenda to the existing frameworks of construction practices? The integration of sustainable development into construction, when considered as an inevitable and required change to current practices, has to start from within project management processes through the methods and theories of systems thinking and leverage points.

The answer to better integration of sustainable development into construction projects and their processes is a systems thinking approach to sustainable construction.

5.6 CASE STUDY 2: The OGC Generic Procurement Process Model

"The development of new procurement strategies is an approach increasingly being adopted by construction clients to achieve improvements in quality and value and to allocate risk where it can be managed."[335]

Procurement processes represent a vital stage of PM as one of its knowledge areas and also a major phase for all construction projects. The delivering of sustainable construction is dependent upon adopting an appropriate procurement strategy and this places responsibility on the client/stakeholders to play a key leadership role during the pre-design stages of construction projects.

In general, procurement processes stand for the acquisition stage of all project related goods and personnel (i.e. consultants and contractors), it is mainly about balancing quality and price. This emphasises the importance of procurement processes as an essential part of the PM areas discussed earlier in chapter 3. Procurement processes have a direct impact on all other areas of construction management. More specifically, for sustainable construction, procurement issues should be one of the main stepping stones into the sustainability route.

Since government's initiatives, which discuss sustainable construction, are calling for better integration of sustainability guidelines into their practices, it is now the research's intention to examine whether government's models of practice follow the recommendations of these initiatives.

---

[335] B. Addis & R. Talbot, *Sustainable Construction Procurement; A guide to delivering environmentally responsible projects*, CIRIA publications C571, London, 2001

202

This is why; the following OGC model is an illustrated example to demonstrate the possibility of applying the previous analysis on a practical process by identifying the best way for integrating sustainability into the existing process that does not have sustainable development within its objectives.

The Office of Government Commerce (OGC)[336] is an independent Office of the Treasury reporting to the Chief Secretary created by the government in 1999. It is responsible for a wide ranging programme which focuses on improving the efficiency and effectiveness of central civil Government procurement. From 2003-04 it has a key role in assisting departments set up project and programme management centres of excellence in all departments including construction where it also provides construction procurement training and technical assistance covering the `Essential Requirements for Construction Procurement`[337].

Since January 2001, the OGC agreed that new procurement projects in civil Central Government will be subject to a new process which has been titled `Gateway Reviews`. This new process applies equally to those organisations which already have strategic partnering arrangements in place.[338]

[336] The Office of Government Commerce (OGC), Website www.ogc.gov.uk last accessed October 2003
[337] ibid. "Construction Procurement Training"
[338] ibid www.ogc.gov.uk

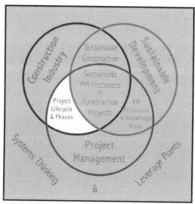

Figure 5.5: Illustrating the research's hypothesis with special highlight on the interaction between the `Construction Industry` and `Project Management` throughout the `Project Lifecycle and Phases`.

This section discusses `Procurement Processes` as an example of one of the phases of projects as shown in figure (5.5). Indeed, the procurement phase is one of the most important stages of any project's lifecycle. Therefore the OGC procurement Gateway Reviews model was chosen as a platform for illustrating a systems thinking approach to construction projects lifecycle.

The Gateway Review is a review of a procurement project carried out at a key decision point (gate) by an experienced team, independent of the project team where procurements are any finite activity designed to deliver a government requirement and involving government expenditure. It examines any project at the critical stage in its lifecycle to provide assurance that it can progress successfully to the next stage.

The Gateway Review is designed to be applied to all projects that procure services, construction or property, IT enabled business change projects and procurements utilising framework contracts. It also meets the requirements of the Gershon Report[339] and is consistent with `Achieving Excellence in Construction`[340]. The Gateway Process is based on well proven techniques that lead to more effective delivery of benefits together with more predictable costs and outcomes.

Figure (5.6) shows the critical points at which the Gateway Process considers the project in its development, they are identified as Gateways. There are six Gateways during the life cycle of a project, four before contract award and two looking at service implementation and confirmation of the operational benefits; Gateway Review 0 to Gateway Review 5. At this point, it is necessary to point out that the current OGC Gateway process Model (published in July 2003) has gone through few amendments since it was first introduced and published on the OGC website in June 2000.

There are minor differences between the two versions. In the early version there were only five Gateways, named Gateway Review 1 to 5 preceded by a `Start Up` phase of information gathering and developing of project brief. In the latest version, this is called Gateway Review 0 (Strategic Assessment).

---

[339] The Gershon Report is a report titled `REVIEW OF CIVIL PROCUREMENT IN CENTRAL GOVERNMENT` written by Peter Gershon who was appointed to head the review team by the Paymaster General and the Parliamentary Secretary to the Cabinet Office in November 1998 and following Ministerial changes that took place in December 1998, the Chief Secretary to the Treasury became responsible for procurement matters. The report can be accessed at www.hm-treasury.gov.uk
[340] "Achieving Excellence in Construction" is a ministerially endorsed Office of Government Commerce (OGC) strategy that central departments, agencies and Non Departmental Public Bodies (NDPBs) are required to adopt on all new construction, refurbishment and maintenance projects. Latest version published by the Government Construction Clients' Panel (GCCP) and the Office of Government Commerce (OGC) in February 2003. It is based on a government initiative "Achieving Excellence" which started 1999 to improve the performance of governmental clients of the construction industry. The report discusses the strategy for sustained improvement in construction procurement performance and in the value for money achieved by government on construction projects. The report can be accessed at http://www.ogc.gov.uk/sdtoolkit/reference/achieving/achievin.html

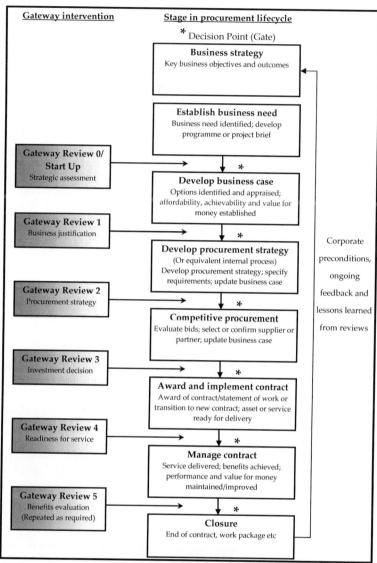

Figure 5.6: Overview of the Gateway Process[341]

[341] The Office of Government Commerce (OGC), *Gateway Review; Leadership Guide*, OGC Best Practise, Published by the OGC, UK, 2003, pp.5

5.6.1 The OGC Gateway Reviews

Figure (5.7) shows the latest version of the OGC Generic Procurement Project Process Model with the start up phase renamed into `Gateway Review 0/ Start Up`. The remaining five Gateways have minor changes in wording. The arguments of this illustration are based on the early version of the model but having reviewed the latest published Gateway Reviews Model, it is clear that the changes do not affect the perspective of the following analysis nor the general arguments.

Appendix 3 portrays a detailed examination of the existing model and its Gateway Reviews from Start Up (Gateway Review 0) to Benefits Evaluation (Gateway Review 5). It shows the OGC's description of the model which highlights the obvious lack of sustainable development guidelines which are, in fact, non existent in the description of any of the Gateways.

Although the model represents the government initiative for better procurement performance, including construction projects, it does not echo government initiatives for sustainable performance throughout the range of its different activities. The OGC model does not address any sustainable agenda and falls short of any mention of sustainable development as an objective or guideline for the Gateway reviews process.

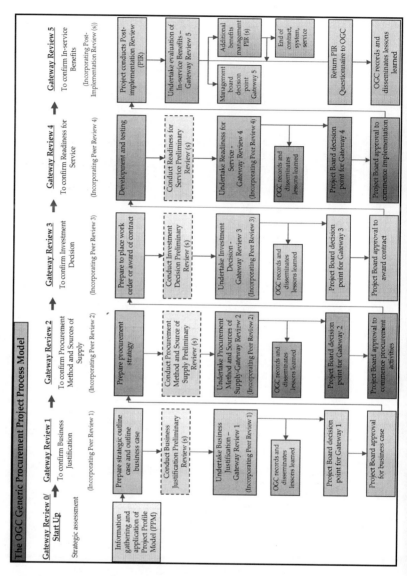

Figure 5.7: The OGC Generic Procurement Project Process Model[342]

Although, the OGC Gateway Reviews Process represents a positive initiative

[342] The Office of Government Commerce (OGC), The Gateway Reviews Procurement Model, website www.ogc.gov.uk last accessed October 2003

for procurement and a significant step forward towards better future performance, it clearly falls short of showing any clear commitment to the incorporation of a sustainable development agenda in the processes. It has been mentioned in the OGC reports that this model follows all the governmental initiatives including those for the construction industry. But this research has now proved that the model requires a serious implementation of `change` to its process. The model mentions neither sustainability guidelines nor makes any serious attempts to address sustainability within its objectives or guidelines. Sustainable development is the `change` which needs to be introduced to the process.

5.6.2 A Sustainable Approach to the OGC Procurement Model

For each of the reviews, the OGC provided in the corresponding reports long lists of questions discussing `the areas to probe` for each Gateway Review. These questions did not put any stress on the importance of sustainable development for such an important process such as the procurement process.

Thus, the research suggests an additional list of `areas to probe` which query the sustainability issues of the process, by proposing additional purposes for the Gateways that would help the whole Review process to benefit from the proposed integration between sustainable development and the procurement process. These additional purposes comprise:-

- Initiate a sustainable development agenda which would serve the business case and the client's needs and expectations.
- Ensure that sustainable development is discussed from the early stages as a fundamental objective for the process. It has to start from within a high level of decision making to ensure proper implementation in each

Gateway.

- Establish a list of sustainable development goals and guidelines to ensure the proper feasibility of each of the Gateways.

- Identify the benefits of integrating sustainable development and clarify the potential of a sustainable approach to the clients, stakeholders, team leaders and team players.

- Identify the social, environmental and economic benefits and guidelines in terms of the overall of the process. The Key strands of sustainable development are not viewed as restrictions to the process but opportunities to proceed with the Gateways Reviews in a sustainable approach.

- Ensure that the proposed strategy for sustainable development for the process meets the guidelines of the governmental agenda of making the industry more sustainable.

- Ensure at every stage and Gateway that the proposed sustainable development strategy complies with the goals and objectives of the corresponding stage.

- Restrict the list of suppliers or bidders to authorities which favour sustainable acquisitions and sustainable chain management procedures.

- Identify a sustainable approach to assess, monitor, anticipate and deal with risks.

- Assess the sustainability strategy before and after each Gateway to monitor and weigh up the achievement of the goals on each level of the process.

- Ensure the documentation of all phases of the strategy to guarantee the recording of all findings, benefits, risks and lessons learned in implementing the integration.

210

A new model for the procurement process which serves the purposes listed above is now presented as a model which addresses the sustainability questions and benefits the whole process.

The focus of the research now is to put these arguments into practice by demonstrating how to introduce sustainable development as a factor of change to the existing system of the OGC procurement process. This new model illustrates how the previous analysis of systems thinking and leverage points helps integrate change in more efficient and effective ways.

The new proposed model shown in figure (5.8) identifies the sustainability gaps which are recognised as opportunities for creating a sustainable procurement process. The new version of the model addresses sustainability as a fundamental part of the process and the criteria for creating the business case unlike the original version shown in figure (5.7).

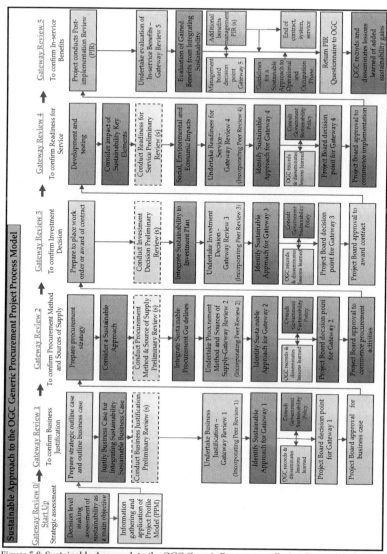

Figure 5.8: Sustainable Approach to the OGC Generic Procurement Project Process Model[343]
Boxes shaded in grey = original OGC procurement model shown in figure (5.7)
Boxes shaded in green = proposed leverage points for integrating the sustainable approach

---

[343] Mohamed Eid, *A Sustainable Approach to the Project Management Odyssey*, Proceedings of PMI Research Conference, Seattle, Washington, USA, 2002, pp. 214

5.6.3 The Leverage Points for the Sustainable OGC Model

In the original procurement process proposed by the OGC, the six Gateways Reviews discuss matters such as business case, teams, reports, lessons learned, procurement strategies, supply methods, development of service, evaluation of benefits and general management benefits. Despite all the implications of these matters on the social, environmental and of course the economic sides of the process, the reviews do not include sustainable development as a major objective in their plans.

Sustainable Development seems vital to the completion of such processes, especially when providing a procurement process for construction projects in order to achieve a better level of social service, protect the environment and of course complete a successful business case.

The sustainability gaps within the OGC process should be addressed as opportunities and most importantly as points of leverage for introducing the new sustainable approach. Figure (5.8) is the proposal for a new sustainable approach to the original OGC procurement model. The leverage points which were identified within the process following systems thinking theories are now put forward through the proposed model as an enhanced version of the original. No additional Gateways have been added but a new approach to the existing Gateways, with sustainable development in perspective, identifies the places to intervene in the model with efficiency and stronger impact.

Donella Meadows' list of leverage points will be the basis of the following analysis. Although, the twelve points of leverage represents major opportunities to intervene in any system, it seems very unlikely that all would be identified in one system; therefore only few of them will be used in this analysis as they are identified as the most obvious opportunities for change.

In general, clear leverage points for the whole system would be through `the goals of the system` (leverage point 3) as well as `the mindset or paradigm out of which the system arises` (leverage point 2). Integrating sustainability using these two points of leverage of high order of effectiveness aims at assuring that sustainability is firmly embedded into the purposes and deliverables of the model. This approach follows the idea that sustainable development has to present its case from the early stages of setting the goals to be achieved by the system so it would affect, and introduce sustainable impacts on every other deliverable that follows in later stages.

The mindset from which the system arises is based on delivering a high level of service while minimizing the risk of procurement for a better social, environmental and economic performance and clearly, this is where sustainable development fits into the main framework of the system.

Gateway Review 0 / Start Up: Strategic Assessment

Ultimately, when introducing change to a system, an effective leverage point would introduce the change to the core objectives and sources of the system; leverage point 2 `the mindset or paradigm out of which the system arises`. Hence, the change becomes a fundamental catalyst of the process and therefore influences the deliverables of the system. As explained earlier, the aim of this review is to produce a preliminary justification for the project

214

based on a strategic assessment of business needs through an extensive phase of information gathering and data collection. The start up review is the most significant opportunity to introduce sustainability to the process and expect the most positive impact towards a sustainable process from the whole model.

When sustainable development is integrated within the project start up phase, it comes in through a high level of decision making with a clear assessment from all stakeholders. A decision making level assessment of sustainability is to be introduced to the start up review (the mindset from which the process arises).

Gateway Review 1: Business Justification

The review focuses on the project's business justification, providing assurance to the project board that the proposed approach to meeting the business requirement has been adequately researched and can be delivered.

Justifying the business case is fundamental to the scope of the model and the continuity of the whole project, therefore integrating sustainability into this Gateway Review through `the rules of the system` (leverage point 5) seems to accomplish the target. Through this highly efficient point, sustainability can be part of defining the scope, boundaries and constraints/opportunities for this stage. A sustainable approach to the business case, especially on the strategic level of making primary decisions, provides evidence that no conflict exists between the economic benefits and the goal of achieving sustainable development.

Gateway Review 2: Procurement Strategy

This review assesses the project's viability and potential for success and whether it is ready to invite proposals or tenders from the market. It reassures the project board that the selected procurement approach is appropriate for the proposed acquisition.

Considering a sustainable procurement method and a sustainable approach to the whole Gateway would help establish the embodiment of SD into the system strategy. This identifies with 'the power of adding, evolving and self-organizing the system structure' (leverage point 4). This means introducing new sustainable rules/guidelines to the procurement process including adding positive or negative loops to the method. In this case, the guidelines represent the opportunities of doing the process differently. It is an enhancement of the previous system towards sustainable efficient performance.

Gateway Review 3: Investment Decision

This Gateway confirms that the recommended contract decision is appropriate before a contract is signed with a supplier or partner. It provides assurances on the processes used to select a supplier and it also assesses whether the process has been well managed; whether the business needs are being met. The author introduces a new approach to the investment plan is introduced through a sustainability approach which would confirm the need for sustainability to be integrated and which would have significant impacts on the whole Gateway as well as the following Reviews.

In this Gateway, two possible leverage points exist to intervene and integrate sustainable into the system; 'the strength of negative feedback loops' (leverage point 8) as well as 'the gain around driving positive feedback loops' (leverage point 7). Whether the need is to have a self-correcting or self-reinforcing feedback loop, the investment plan can be integrated with both, depending on the circumstances of each stage of the investment plan. Maintaining the monitoring authority for the Gateway is vital to ensure the proper feedback of sustainable development of the investment decision making. Whether the Gateway is experiencing a positive or negative feedback loop, the important step is to consider the triple bottom lines guidelines and their impact on the decision making level.

Gateway Review 4: Readiness for service

This review focuses on whether the solution is robust prior to delivery; how ready the organization is to implement the business changes that occur before and after delivery, and whether there is a system for evaluating ongoing performance.

Leverage point 9 'the length of delays, relative to the rate of system changes' is introduced as the critical point to integrate and consider the impact of sustainability key elements on the service and the degree of readiness to proceed with it. Social, environmental and economic impacts represent guideline opportunities to the rate of changes of the system and allow longer or shorter delays in the feedback loops. The Gateway can only proceed when the triple bottom lines are justified and fulfilled.

Gateway Review 5: Benefits Evaluation

This focuses on ensuring that the project delivers the benefits and value for money identified in the business and benefits plans, as there should be periodic reviews in accordance with planned project reviews and the contract administration arrangements.

For this final stage of reviews, the structure is already built and the real Leverage point is in understanding its limitations and bottlenecks and refraining from fluctuations or expansions that strain its capacity. Leverage Point 10 `the structure of material stocks and flows and nodes of intersection` allows the evaluation of the gains and benefits from integrating the sustainability approach into the system from the start as well as establishing the guidelines for a sustainable approach to the operational and occupation phase.

5.6.4 The Strength of the Leverage Points' Impact on Gateways

Going through the six Gateway Reviews, trying to identify the most efficient leverage point for each stage, it is apparent that the further we go into the model; moving from Gateway 0 to Gateway 5, the leverage points identified seem to lean more towards the less efficient points on Meadows' list of places to intervene in a system identified in chapter 4.

As explained for Meadows' list, the leverage points were displayed in an increasing order of effectiveness (leverage point 12 to 1), where the most effective and higher desired impact of change on the whole system is leverage point 1. Meadows argued in her publication, that the desired impact from introducing change is ultimately achieved when the change is

218

incorporated within the early phases of the system, hence, it would have significant desired impacts on the following stages. For the OGC model, the research identified the sustainability gaps within the original model as critical places/points to introduce the sustainability agenda to the process.

Gateway Review 0 represents the most efficient opportunity to introduce the change as it deals with the fundamentals of the whole procurement model. But as the Gateway Reviews progress, the change could still be implemented. Change can be introduced to any of the Gateway although the impact becomes less efficient the closer the process comes to an end. Understandably, when sustainable development is embedded from the early stages of the strategic level of decision making of the project, the more anticipated impact we can expect.

5.6.5 Identifying the Right Questions

Reaching the potential of success desired from implementing that change, affects the purposes of each Gateway as well as their potential. When sustainable development is integrated into the system, the purposes of each Gateway would include: -

- Ensuring that SD is implemented and achieved within this stage and thereafter.
- Establishing a list of SD goals and ensuring their feasibility.
- Clarifying the benefits of integrating SD for the initial business case.
- Ensuring that the goals meet/exceed stakeholders' needs and expectations.

The potential for success would include: -

- The social, environmental and economic benefits.
- Confirmation that the SD plans meet the government SD strategy.
- Assurance that SD strategies proposed comply with the overall guidelines for success.

While reviewing each Gateway, these questions will be added to the review list: -

- Has the working frame of achieving SD been complying with the goals of this phase?
- Have the social, environment and economic outcomes been considered in the overall management process?

Finally, when studying the readiness for each successive Gateway Review, from the strategic assessment stage to the In-service benefits Gateway, the following points have to be considered: -

- Are there any social, environmental or economic requirements that need to be achieved before the next Gateway Review?
- Have all sustainable goals for this current Gateway Review been successfully attained?
- Is there a clear plan for achieving, monitoring and controlling embedded sustainability goals and targets?
- Are there documentations and records of all lessons learned in each Gateway and for the overall process of the model?

The most important aspect of this implementation is always to keep a perspective on the whole process. While implementing the changes on parts of the process (phase/Gateway Reviews), the impact affects not only the parts but, more importantly, it affects the whole process. This has been a fundamental part of the proposal as shown in figure (5.8), but while the changes, introduced at the critical points (leverage points) of each Gateway, are important, one must keep an eye on the bigger picture and consider how the model as a whole would react to the sustainable approach. The sustainable approach to the whole of the process has to start from within its parts.

The OGC procurement model that sustainable development can be integrated into the model's Gateways Reviews to give the overall process a new sustainable approach. Keeping an even bigger picture in perspective; the procurement processes for construction projects represent only a part of the bigger framework of processes and knowledge areas of project management listed in the Project Management Body of Knowledge (PMBOK). The theories of systems thinking and leverage points have been followed in implementing the change on the procurement model, but from a wider perspective. The research now examines the possibilities of using systems thinking to integrate sustainable development into the project management processes and knowledge areas listed in the PMBOK.

5.7 CASE STUDY 3: Systems Thinking Approach to Project Management

"Comprehensive, informed and inclusive project management is the principle `means` to ensure the `ends`...The Value added to a project by project management is unique: no other process or method can add similar value, either qualitatively or quantitatively."[344]

This part of the research presents the case for better construction performance when sustainable development is introduced to the project management practices within construction. It is now evident that, starting with project management, to implement the desired change would have greater impact on the overall performance of construction because of the crucial importance of PM to construction projects.

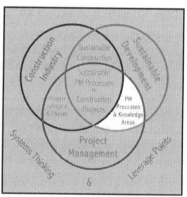

Figure 5.9: Illustrating the research's hypothesis with special highlight on the interaction between the `Project Management` and `Sustainable Development` within the `PM Processes and Knowledge Areas`.

---

[344] Construction Industry Council (CIC), *Construction Project Management Skills*, CIC publications, London, 2000,pp. 2

222

Figure (5.9) discusses a systems thinking approach to the PM processes and knowledge areas which are identified to be significant opportunities for integrating sustainable development into PM practices.

Having explained the reasons for a systems thinking approach to all of the three dimensions of this research, then discussed the connections between the same approach and sustainable construction, the research now introduces systems thinking to project management; the third and final dimension of the research.

Project management breaks down to the interactions between the inputs and outputs taking place within each process group. Examining project management from a holistic point of view, the framework of the system relies mainly on the interaction between its fundamental parts (i.e. Inputs – Tools and Techniques – Outputs). These fundamental parts constitute and ensure the functionality of the whole system, hence when monitoring the PM process, it is vital to observe closely these interactions while keeping the end result of each phase in perspective. When any of the project activities fail to proceed according to the planned schedule, project managers have to breakdown the process of the activity in question to its fundamental components to reveal where and when the failure took place and therefore be able to remedy the failure from its origins. In that case, the failure is considered as an undesired `change` which manipulated the structure and affected the whole process of the system. A similar procedure is proposed but to introduce a desired `change`; integrate sustainable development into project management processes.

Following the guidelines of systems thinking, introducing sustainable development to the existing framework of project management has to take place through the identification of leverage points within the system. This takes the analysis back to the components of project management as a functioning system, to the fundamental parts out of which it is formed; the processes and their interactions which rely on their inputs and outputs. Implementing a significant change such as `sustainable development` into project management has to take place from within its core of knowledge or paradigm out of which the project management process arises.

The hypothesis of this research relies on changing the interactions between the lists of inputs and the lists of outputs through embedding sustainable development guidelines, indicators and measuring tools into the list of tools and techniques of all the PM processes and their knowledge areas listed in the PMBOK. Leverage point 2 (the mindset or paradigm out of which the system arises) is a very high point on Meadows list in terms of the effectiveness of the implementation of the desired change. This point of leverage allows the change to take place from within the sources of the system. However small this change could be, its effectiveness is expected to be of very high significance because the change is introduced to the core of the system. This will mean therefore that all subsequent activities, knowledge areas, process groups, project processes, project management practices and ultimately, the construction projects would be affected by the impact of this change.

Project Management (PM) in this case, not only ensures the proper completion of construction projects on time, on budget and within quality standards but also becomes the driver for delivering a Sustainable

Development (SD) approach to the project. Systems thinking and leverage points allow this integration to happen while ensuring that the end result of sustainable PM process for construction is achieved.

5.7.1 Integrating SD into PM Processes

The PMBOK was criticized in this research for its lack of commitment to sustainable development and failure to address sustainability issues more seriously and direct practitioners' interest towards the global pressure for a better sustainable future. PMBOK holds, within its knowledge areas, significant opportunities to embrace sustainability; the following analysis represents the main hypothesis for integrating sustainable development within project management processes. The hypothesis will be demonstrated by introducing a new sustainable approach to the interactions between the groups of process and their lists of inputs and outputs as the origin of the continuity of the whole PM functioning system.

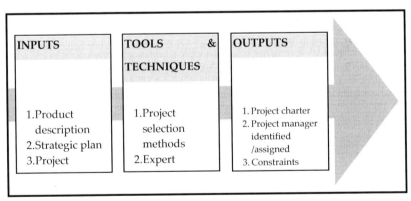

Figure 5.10: Interactions between Inputs and Outputs for Initiation Process (PMBOK)[345]

Appendix 2 Section II displays the PMBOK's illustration of the knowledge

[345] Project Management Institute (PMI), *A Guide to the Project Management Body of Knowledge (PMBOK® Guide)*, PMI publications, Pennsylvania USA, 2000 Edition, pp.53

areas and their corresponding lists of inputs, tools & techniques and outputs. As shown in figure (5.10), when analyzing each process, the PMBOK displays the interactions between the list of inputs and outputs by listing the suggested tools & techniques which facilitate the transformation of inputs to outputs. For all combined fifty two processes, PMBOK uses the format shown in figure (5.10) to display the linear interconnections among the lists of inputs, tools and techniques and outputs for each process. The example shown in the figure is for the first process of `Initiation` which is part of the knowledge area of `Project Scope Management` and the Process Group of `Initiation`.

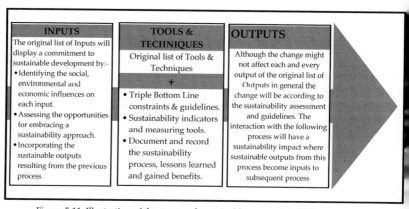

Figure 5.11: Illustration of the proposed sustainable approach to PM processes

The argument is based on adding sustainable development guidelines, indicators and measuring tools to the original list of tools and techniques for each corresponding process. Clearly, it is not an attempt to substitute the existing list but to add sustainability drivers to its content to enhance and direct all of the interactions towards sustainable development.

Figure (5.11) above illustrates the new proposed sustainable approach to all of the PM processes. The illustration demonstrates the changes which will affect the interaction between inputs and outputs on the level of the process in question and more importantly on the subsequent process where the outputs of the first become the inputs for the latter.

- **For the lists of `Tools & Techniques`: -** Each process should maintain its original lists portrayed in the PMBOK. These are not alternative tools or techniques but add-ons; constraints of sustainability guidelines. Tools and techniques should include triple bottom line constraints and rules where sustainability indicators have been agreed upon by a high level decision making assessment and choice of sustainability measuring tools.

- **For the lists of `Inputs`: -** The original list of inputs should display a clear commitment to sustainable development because it originates from the projects objectives, business case and resources. A commitment to sustainability should allow the process to identify the social, environmental and economic influences on inputs. The main goal of this approach is to assess the opportunities for embracing sustainability through the identification of the need for change from within. The assessment should also incorporate the sustainable outputs from the previous process to ensure the continuity of the interactions.

- **For the lists of `Outputs`: -** they should be representative of the outcome of the interactions between `Inputs` and `Tools & Techniques`. Sustainable development is embraced by the lists of inputs and integrated within the lists of tools and techniques. Therefore, sustainability as an outcome might have a different effect on each output, generally, the list of outputs changes dramatically towards the sustainable agenda. The new sustainable outputs in one process become the new sustainable inputs to

227

the subsequent process, hence the whole process benefits from the sustainability approach while preserving its continuity.

The above briefing defines the hypothesis in terms of general applications on all the processes, another example now demonstrates how that approach would be applied to the `Initiation` process shown earlier in figure (5.10) as illustrated by the PMBOK.

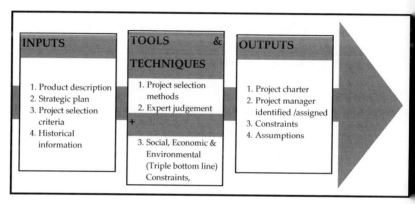

Figure 5.12: A Sustainable Approach to the Initiation Process

Figure (5.12) illustrates the examination of integrating sustainable development into the Initiation process. The following is a detailed demonstration of the proposed changes.

- **For the list of Tools and Techniques for Initiation:** - Sustainable development is added to the list and becomes an integral part of the transformation of inputs to outputs. The primary concern of the new approach is to generate further opportunities for the social, environmental and economic guidelines to be involved in the interactions as well as to reassure that the triple bottom line constraints have been

228

followed and therefore the business case is still robust, the social impact is being monitored and is under control and finally, that no environmental violations are occurring.

1. `Project selection methods`: It would also be affected by the sustainable approach in terms of changing the decision criteria for measuring value or attractiveness to the project owner following not only the economic value, but also the social and environmental values. While the project selection methods rely on the benefits measurement methods and constrained optimization methods, sustainability becomes fundamental to the selection by way of enhancing the benefits and integrating the triple bottom line into the general techniques.

2. `Expert Judgement`: when required to assess the inputs to this process, sustainable development expertise may be provided by means of specialised knowledge or training.

- **For the list of Inputs to Initiation:** - For the initiation process, the inputs represent the authorisation to start a new project, since the process itself is the first on the list of PM processes. Including sustainability within the first documents of the projects on decision making level fortifies the approach.

1. `Product description`: The product description documents the characteristics of the product or service that the project was undertaken to create. It also documents the relationship between the product being created and the business need or any other incentive that gave rise to the project; which is the leverage point (the mindset or paradigm out of which the system arises). The early involvement of

sustainable development catalysts in such documents illustrates the opportunity for a more effective impact on the succeeding processes. In this case, sustainable criteria become associated with the project goals and the business case and more importantly the sustainable approach rules the relationship between the end product and the business need.

2. `Strategic goals`: the strategic plan of the organization performing the project should be considered as a factor in project selection decisions. When sustainable development becomes an integral part of the organisation's general policies and project strategies, not only does it affect the current project but it grows to be a future scheme for all tasks.

3. `Project Selection criteria`: they cover the full range of possible management concerns such as financial return, market share, public perceptions, environmental rules, social impacts and maintaining the economic profits for the business case.

4. `Historical Information`: when initiation involves approval for the next phase of a project or even the start of a new project, information about the results of the previous phases and/or previous similar projects is often critical. Therefore, documentation of sustainable historical performance is vital not only for the current project but also for future assignments.

- **For the list of Outputs from Initiation:** - The outputs test whether sustainable development has successfully been part of the tools and techniques and also if it has been effectively considered within the list of inputs.

230

1. `Project charter`: this is the document that formally authorises a project. The authorisation includes the product description (from the list of inputs) and the business need addressed earlier. The sustainable approach proposed can now be identified within the business need as explained earlier in the business case for sustainability. The characteristics of the end product are expected to be in line with the environmental rules and social impact guidelines. Most importantly, in the bigger perspective, the whole charter should also be in line with the governmental initiatives for sustainable development.

2. `Project manager identified/assigned`: the project's team leader, process owners and team players should all be aware of the new approach and following Senge's discipline for the learning organisation, they should all share the sustainable vision while working in a team learning scheme. When identifying and assigning the project manager, it is obvious that his/her role as a team leader is important in demonstrating personal mastery in terms of sustainable approach while allowing the team to be involved with the same vision and willingness to exercise shared visions and sustain the team learning.

3. `Constraints`: Although constraints are factors which limit the project management team's options, they can also be defined as challenges to perform activities differently while preserving/enhancing the environment, monitoring the social aspects and sustaining the economic profits.

4. `Assumptions`: generally involve a certain degree of risk because they are factors that, for planning purposes, are considered/assumed to be true, real or certain. Since they affect all aspects of project planning,

they are part of the progressive elaboration of the project. The sustainable approach should not necessarily change the nature of these assumptions especially if they describe technical related information, but for the planning process in general, the new approach should be clearly identified within its processes and criteria.

The analysis of the initiation process is demonstrated as an example of integrating sustainable development to its processes. The remaining processes found in the PMBOK® Guide (2000 Edition) are illustrated in a special questionnaire attached in Appendix 4[346].

From the previous analysis, it is now obvious that the approach is applicable to the processes and relies on adding sustainable development guidelines, indicators and tools to the lists of tools and techniques and also assesses the opportunities for change starting from the inputs.

In order to move forward with the hypothesis of the research, it is vital at this stage to map the opportunities for integrating sustainable development to the general as well as the specific elementary origin of construction PM processes; the knowledge areas.

---

[346] The questionnaire in Appendix 4 is a detailed analysis, launched by the author in June 2003, of identifying the opportunities for a sustainable development involvement in the PM process. It only includes the processes listed in the PMBOK® Guide 2000 Edition. The Construction Extension for the PMBOK Guide displays new processes specifically for the construction industry (13 new processes) but because it was published at the end of September 2003 therefore it is not included in the questionnaire analysis.

232

5.8 Mapping the Opportunities for SD to PM Processes and Knowledge Areas

In the PMBOK, the fifty two processes and their descriptions are listed in detail and mapped to the process groups and knowledge area in the matrix shown in chapter 3 (Table 3.1). When analysing these processes, the opportunities for integrating the sustainable approach within the lists of inputs of each process were identified. As explained in the analysis of the sustainable approach to the initiation process (figure 5.11, 5.12), the potential for adopting a sustainable agenda is significant.

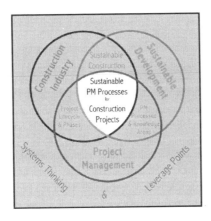

Figure 5.13: Illustrating the research's hypothesis with special emphasis on the outcome of all the elements of the integration working together and interacting to create 'Sustainable PM Processes for Construction Projects'.

As shown in figure (5.13), this section discusses the outcome of the research's hypothesis. After discussing the four pillars of the research, their interactions and the outcomes of these interactions, the research now examines the overall final result of the integration by mapping the opportunities for creating a sustainable approach to all PM processes.

A strong potential is identified and illustrated below in figure (5.14). The knowledge areas, as the origin of PM processes, hold within them the core catalyst for change in performance. This also represents a very efficient leverage point on Meadows' efficiency scale to introduce sustainable development to the whole process and guarantee significant positive impact.

Figure (5.14), maps the identified opportunities for integrating sustainability to the PM process groups based on the generic knowledge areas provided in the PMBOK (2000 Edition) and the construction knowledge areas listed in the Construction Extension to the PMBOK in terms of their relevance to the Sustainable Development (SD) Triple Bottom Line (TBL) criteria (i.e. Social, Economic and Environmental).

The matrix shown in the figure below demonstrates that the relevance of each knowledge area to sustainable development is not necessarily the same among its own processes (e.g. for 6- Project Time Management; `6.1 Activity Definition`, `6.4 Schedule Development` and `6.8 Progress Curve Development`) nor is the relevance constant among the three elements of sustainability when compared for one process (e.g. `7.2 Cost Estimating`: relevance of `* *` `medium relevance` to the Social element, relevance of `* * *` `high relevance` to the Economic element and finally, relevance of `*` `low relevance` to the Environmental element). This, of course, does not rule out the possibility of similarities in relevance among the processes nor does it rule out the `None` relevant option (e.g. Claim Identification). The matrix is not meant to be exclusive, but to demonstrate how the PM processes can be integrated with sustainability and to identify the potential areas of knowledge, which lead to a more sustainable approach.

234

PM Process Groups	SOCIAL PM Processes	Relevance	ECONOMIC PM Processes	Relevance	ENVIRONMENTAL PM Processes	Relevance
1- INITIATING	5.1 Initiation	***	5.1 Initiation	***	5.1 Initiation	***
2- PLANNING	4.1 Project Plan Development	***	4.1 Project Plan Development	***	4.1 Project Plan Development	***
	5.2 Scope Planning	***	5.2 Scope Planning	***	5.2 Scope Planning	***
	5.3 Scope Definition	***	5.3 Scope Definition	***	5.3 Scope Definition	***
	6.1 Activity Definition	***	6.1 Activity Definition	***	6.1 Activity Definition	***
	6.2 Activity Sequencing	**	6.2 Activity Sequencing	***	6.2 Activity Sequencing	**
	6.3 Activity Duration Estimating	**	6.3 Activity Duration Estimating	**	6.3 Activity Duration Estimating	**
	6.4 Schedule Development	**	6.4 Schedule Development	**	6.4 Schedule Development	**
	7.1 Resource Planning	***	7.1 Resource Planning	***	7.1 Resource Planning	***
	7.2 Cost Estimating	**	7.2 Cost Estimating	***	7.2 Cost Estimating	*
	7.3 Cost Budgeting	None	7.3 Cost Budgeting	***	7.3 Cost Budgeting	None
	8.1 Quality Planning	**	8.1 Quality Planning	**	8.1 Quality Planning	**
	9.1 Organisational Planning	***	9.1 Organisational Planning	**	9.1 Organisational Planning	*
	9.2 Staff Acquisition	***	9.2 Staff Acquisition	**	9.2 Staff Acquisition	*
	10.1 Communication Planning	**	10.1 Communication Planning	*	10.1 Communication Planning	*
	11.1 Risk Management Planning	***	11.1 Risk Management Planning	***	11.1 Risk Management Planning	***
	11.2 Risk Identification	***	11.2 Risk Identification	***	11.2 Risk Identification	***
	11.3 Qualitative Risk Analysis	**	11.3 Qualitative Risk Analysis	**	11.3 Qualitative Risk Analysis	**
	11.4 Quantitative Risk Analysis	**	11.4 Quantitative Risk Analysis	***	11.4 Quantitative Risk Analysis	**
	11.5 Risk Response Planning	**	11.5 Risk Response Planning	***	11.5 Risk Response Planning	**
	12.1 Procurement Planning	**	12.1 Procurement Planning	**	12.1 Procurement Planning	**
	13.1 Safety Plan Development	***	13.1 Safety Plan Development	**	13.1 Safety Plan Development	***
	14.1 Environmental Planning	**	14.1 Environmental Planning	**	14.1 Environmental Planning	***
	15.1 Financial Planning	*	15.1 Financial Planning	***	15.1 Financial Planning	*
	16.1 Claim Identification	None	16.1 Claim Identification	**	16.1 Claim Identification	None
	16.2 Claim Quantification	None	16.2 Claim Quantification	**	16.2 Claim Quantification	None
3- EXECUTING	4.2 Project Plan Execution	***	4.2 Project Plan Execution	***	4.2 Project Plan Execution	***
	6.6 Activity Weights Definition	**	6.6 Activity Weights Definition	**	6.6 Activity Weights Definition	**
	8.2 Quality Assurance	**	8.2 Quality Assurance	**	8.2 Quality Assurance	**
	9.3 Team Development	***	9.3 Team Development	None	9.3 Team Development	**
	10.2 Information Distribution	*	10.2 Information Distribution	**	10.2 Information Distribution	*
	12.4 Source Selection	**	12.4 Source Selection	***	12.4 Source Selection	**
	13.2 Safety Plan Execution	***	13.2 Safety Plan Execution	**	13.2 Safety Plan Execution	**
	14.2 Environmental Assurance	*	14.2 Environmental Assurance	*	14.2 Environmental Assurance	***
4- CONTROLLING	4.3 Integrated Change Control	*	4.3 Integrated Change Control	*	4.3 Integrated Change Control	*
	5.4 Scope Verification	***	5.4 Scope Verification	***	5.4 Scope Verification	***
	5.5 Scope Change Control	***	5.5 Scope Change Control	***	5.5 Scope Change Control	***
	6.5 Schedule Control	**	6.5 Schedule Control	**	6.5 Schedule Control	**
	7.7 Progress Curve Development	None	7.7 Progress Curve Development	None	7.7 Progress Curve Development	None
	7.8 Progress Monitoring	None	7.8 Progress Monitoring	None	7.8 Progress Monitoring	None
	7.4 Cost Control	*	7.4 Cost Control	***	7.4 Cost Control	*
	8.3 Quality Control	**	8.3 Quality Control	**	8.3 Quality Control	**
	10.3 Performance Reporting	*	10.3 Performance Reporting	**	10.3 Performance Reporting	*
	11.6 Risk Monitoring & Control	**	11.6 Risk Monitoring & Control	**	11.6 Risk Monitoring & Control	**
	14.3 Environmental Control	*	14.3 Environmental Control	*	14.3 Environmental Control	***
	15.2 Financial Control	*	15.2 Financial Control	***	15.2 Financial Control	*
	16.3 Claim Prevention	*	16.3 Claim Prevention	*	16.3 Claim Prevention	*
5- CLOSING	Relevance of Sustainability Approach to this Process Group is significantly minor not only because this stage consists mainly of the legal aspects of the project but also because it is too late to incorporate sustainability at this phase of administrative closure and contract closeout (ineffective leverage points). The only relevance for future projects is to document and record all lessons learned including gained sustainability benefits.					

Figure 5.14: Mapping Sustainable Development Opportunities to PM Processes & Knowledge Areas

COLOR KEY OF PM KNOWELDGE AREAS:
4- Project Integration Management
5- Project Scope Management
6- Project Time Management
7- Project Cost Management
8- Project Quality Management
9- Project Human Resource Management

10- Project Communications Management
11- Project Risk Management
12- Project Procurement Management
13- Project Safety Management
14- Project Environmental Management
15- Project Financial Management
16- Project Claim Management

The matrix lays out the knowledge areas and their processes in terms of any project's main five process groups (Initiating to Closing).

In line with the theories of systems thinking and leverage points, it is apparent that the highest relevance and potential for integrating sustainable development exists within the Initiating and Planning Process Groups. This is the most efficient leverage point where the project is still in its early phases of creating the scope, generating the project's plans, identifying the risks and producing the rules. As explained earlier, these process groups keep repeating the cycle from Initiating processes to Closing processes for every stage of the project, hence the appearance of high relevance and potential points during the Executing and the Controlling Processes (e.g. `14.2 Environmental Assurance` for the Environmental bottom line, `5.5 Scope Change Control` for the three bottom lines and `7.4 Cost Control` for the Economic bottom line). The high potential for integration at this stage is underpinned by the significance of the process itself and its contribution to and authority over the following process.

As an example, for the executing process group, although it comes after long procedures of planning (i.e. the Planning Process Group) it holds within it very significant processes which affect the overall definition of the project's general scope (e.g. 4.2 Project Plan Execution). In this case, the process of Project Plan Execution offers significant chances to identify social, economic and environmental risks which were not anticipated previously in the `Risk Management Planning` process (Planning Process Group), and this is where, during the Executing process group, the opportunity exists to amend the changes according to the sustainability guidelines.

236

As a further example, for the controlling process group, although it provides controlling and monitoring process to activities which have already taken place, it holds within its processes, powerful opportunities to reconsider general aspects of the project such as the scope, cost and quality if these are found not to be satisfying the original plans. In this case, introducing the desired change within this process is an efficient leverage point although its impact will not be as positive, as it would have been, had the change been introduced at an earlier phase of the project.

Following passage through the process groups, the closing process group is reached where, according to the PMBOK description, it is related mainly to closing procedures of the project, fulfilling the legal aspects of all contracts and finally ensuring the documentation and regular recording of all lessons learned which will becomes the source of `historical information` for future similar projects. The closing process group does not hold within its processes any significant leverage points for introducing sustainable development to the system because it represents the final stage of all projects where no change at that stage is possible and therefore it has minor relevance to the approach. But, the only sustainable relevance to this process would be in ensuring the documentation of all lessons learned including all gained benefits from the sustainability approach to serve as inputs of historical information in any subsequent similar project or activity.

Although the matrix presents the possibilities of integrating sustainable development into project management process provided in the PMBOK (2000 Edition), a chance was provided for PM practitioners, professionals, academics and researchers to introduce their own professional opinions on this integration's hypothesis in an online questionnaire[347] on the world wide web which will be discussed in further details in the next chapter.

The hypothesis of this research, explained in the introduction, is based on that project management is a fertile ground of practice which would enhance any industry's performance in terms of its commitment to sustainable development. The importance of project management practices to construction as well as the contribution of the construction industry to our quality of life has been established in the first part of this research. Compelling evidence have been displayed to fortify his point of view on living up to the project management challenge. The potential for sustainable project management is immense. The challenge is for the PM practitioners, researchers and professionals to address this potential and benefit from its outcomes. This vast potential benefit will not only profit the project management practice but in the bigger perspective, implies a lot of positive change to our quality of life.

Global commitment to a better quality of life for human kind is an open invitation to all to contribute in any way possible. Adopting a sustainable approach to the project management process is the responsibility and indeed, duty of the project management community to follow the global agenda and demonstrate that contributing to such a cause underpins the moral objective of general management; i.e. doing things better.

---

[347] www.caad.ed.ac.uk/projects/eid

5.9 The Way Forward

With this chapter, the second part of this research is initiated; demonstrating the research's arguments in bringing together the construction industry, sustainable development and project management in a tri-dimensional integration facilitated by a systems thinking and leverage points approach.

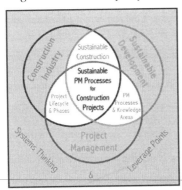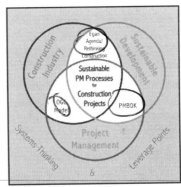

Figure 5.15: Replacing the outcomes of the Tri-Dimensional Integration with the practical examples discussed earlier in this chapter

One of the main objectives of this chapter was to demonstrate how the proposed hypothesis could be implemented and examined practically. Figure (5.15) summarises the research work on which this chapter is based. The hypothesis has been examined on existing initiatives (i.e. the Egan Agenda/ Rethinking Construction), construction projects' phases (i.e. the OGC Procurement Model) and PM standards (i.e. PMBOK).

The Venn diagram portrayed the proposed integration to point out the interconnections between the three dimensions of this research and to show that the integration is aided by a milieu of systems thinking and leverage points theories for introducing change to a system. The reasons behind choosing the systems thinking approach to the proposed integration were

explained and fortified the hypothesis by displaying the advantages which such an approach would provide to the framework, including the portrayal of the new characteristics it introduced to the general view of processes.

The integration diagram displayed the potential of the hypothesis by examining not only the main four pillars of the research but also the interconnections between and among them. Hence, the impact of such integration does not only affect the construction industry in general but also, as leads the hypothesis to demonstrate the impact on the initiatives of sustainable construction and enhancing the Egan drivers.

The principle objective was not only to propose a new integration and embedment of sustainable development but also to demonstrate practical means for this integration. Currently, major needs exist for demonstrating different ways of implementing the theories and testing them into practical life because it is no longer simply about proposing new strategies; rather it is about fulfilling the need for practical demonstration on real life examples.

Illustrative examples of integrating the three dimensions of the research have been carried out by examining the impacts of the framework on existing functioning systems. The demonstration started with the OGC procurement process model to identify the crucial need for a sustainable approach to its processes. In this case, the OGC procurement model is currently used by the UK government as a mandatory model for construction procurement but, it fails to follow the guidelines of government's initiative for sustainable construction. The new proposed model represents a practical solution for integrating sustainable development into the core processes of procurement.

The research progressed with the arguments to include the project management processes which are considered to be huge stepping stones to construction projects. Therefore, the arguments continued with the examination of a systems thinking approach to project management and demonstrated the benefits which it offers to the practice.

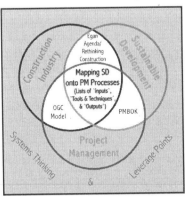

Figure 5.16: `Mapping SD onto PM Processes` demonstrated the significant opportunity for bringing together all the elements of the research.

The case for integrating sustainable development into project management processes on which the hypothesis is based has been made. The processes listed in the PMBOK do not address the issues of sustainability. This minimises the contribution project management can make to the global commitment to the sustainable development agenda. An extensive examination of all the processes listed in the PMBOK was led to identify the opportunities for sustainable change. The change is introduced to the framework of the processes through the core origins of inputs, tools and techniques and outputs out of which the processes arise and contribute to the general practice of project management.

Figure (5.14) illustrated the relevance of sustainable development criteria (the

Triple Bottom Line) to each of the processes which constitute the knowledge areas of PMBOK. There is a persisting need for the project management community to act upon the conviction that a sustainable approach is possible and as shown, it creates a whole new and significantly more powerful role for project management; to guide the industry to even better performance.

In order to examine further these possibilities and opportunities for sustainable project management processes, the research now moves forward to examine the results of an online survey made accessible to PM practitioners, professionals and academics which attempts to discover the potential and identification of a sustainable approach.

CHAPTER 6

THE QUESTIONNAIRE

"Concerns for sustainability need to become people's way of life."[348]

The Environmental and Natural Resources Policy and Training Project (EPAT)[349]

The broader case for sustainability is dependent on reforms which take place in a society's institutions.

In the case of the construction industry, it can be influenced through the contribution of project management to its cycles and practices. The previous chapters demonstrated the fundamental role which the construction industry plays in determining our quality of life and the fundamental relationship between successful construction projects and the early involvement of project management processes in these endeavours. This chapter examines the potentials within project management processes to positively influence our ways and quality of life.

As the Project Management Institute (PMI) is one of the main PM institutions worldwide, it is the main goal of this chapter to examine the most important PM standardisation publication of PMI; the Project Management Body of Knowledge (PMBOK) from a sustainable development point of view.

This final chapter is an analysis of an online questionnaire prepared to

---

[348] Hans M. Gregersen, Allen L. Lundgren and T. Anderson White, *Improving Project Management for Sustainable Development*, The Environmental and Natural Resources Policy and Training Project (EPAT), EPAT/MUCIA publication by University of Wisconsin, 1994

[349] It is A USAID-funded global program, the Environmental and Natural Resources Policy and Training Project (EPAT), is implemented, in part, by 15 Universities and development organizations through the Midwest Universities Consortium for International Activities, Inc. (MUCIA), the EPAT project ended in December 1995 www.wisc.edu/epat

identify the opportunities for a sustainable approach to the project
management processes contained in the PMBOK.

6.1 Introduction

The wide range of knowledge which the hypothesis covers, initiated the
essential need to incorporate the views of PM professionals, practitioners,
academics and researchers.

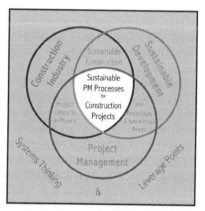

Figure 6.0: The Venn diagram that summarises the hypothesis of the research showing the
highlighted middle area which represents the main theme of the questionnaire.

An online questionnaire was created discussing the proposed set of
arguments as an invitation for all project management users to agree and/or
disagree with the hypothesis. The questionnaire is also an opportunity to
share the views of the international audience on the sustainable approach to
an international PM document publication such as the PMI's PMBOK.

Figure (6.0), illustrates the summary of the entire hypothesis of this research
with special highlights on the middle area of the integration which
represents the main theme of the questionnaire: Is a sustainable approach to

the project management processes, set out in the PMBOK and analysed earlier in chapter 3, possible for construction projects?

The chapter starts by describing the reasons behind the need for the questionnaire to demonstrate the views of invited PM professionals, practitioners, researchers and academics and to examine whether they share the same views of this research or disagree with the hypothesis.

The design criteria are then displayed for the questionnaire in addition to the guidelines in creating the layout and question sequence. The chapter then examines into the analysis of the methodology and the format of the questionnaire. This analysis portrays the different choices of the questionnaire and describes how it fortifies the theme and makes it an easier task for the respondents to complete the assignment following the two chosen answering techniques.

The final version of the questionnaire is then analysed, out of which the online survey was created. A full analysis is displayed to describe the reasons behind each question and the targeted outcome of results followed by a statistical analysis of the responses received.

The conclusion surveys the outcome from the received responses and determining the impact of the analysis on the proposed hypothesis of the research.

6.2 The Need for a Questionnaire

Since the Venn diagram of the integration acknowledges the wide area which the research covers, and because of the importance of such topics, introducing such fundamental changes on the PMBOK as the main publication of project management standards is a very crucial task which should be fortified by the endorsement of PM practitioners, professionals, academics and researchers as the targeted audience/respondents.

The views of the targeted respondents have been investigated via a questionnaire created to highlight the way forward for further research and development activities within the project management profession.

Chapter 5 described the proposed integration would be implemented within the fifty two project management processes combined from the PMBOK (2000 Edition) generic processes and the additional ones from the Construction Extension to PMBOK. At this point, it is important to point out that at the time of creating and launching the questionnaire (30th of June 2003), the Construction Extension to PMBOK was not yet published by PMI until it was officially released and distributed by early October 2003. Therefore, the questionnaire does not encompass any of the thirteen processes from the Construction Extension added to chapter 3 but only relies on the thirty nine processes displayed in the PMBOK (2000 Edition).

There are two versions of the questionnaire; a detailed version in Appendix 4 and a reduced shorter one which became the online version shown in Appendix 5.

The detailed version of the questionnaire is the original work of this research where it illustrates the detailed integration of sustainable development into each PM process in the PMBOK. The proposed integration targets the fundamentals of each process through adding sustainable development guidelines as an additional item on the lists of 'Tools and Techniques' which transform the lists of 'Inputs' to 'Outputs' for each process.

As there are fifty two numerous processes, the detailed version of the questionnaire -shown in Appendix 4- resulted in a very long document (forty three pages) which demanded the inputs and full dedication of certain type of respondents to complete it. This thorough and comprehensive document proved to be extremely difficult if not impossible to be effectively marketed among individuals who would be interested in taking part in any survey. This does not undermine the quality of the research in anyway but demonstrates the difficulty in requesting individuals to take part in such time consuming task. Therefore, the detailed questionnaire document was summarised into a less detailed version that on average takes 20 minutes to complete. The short, final version of the questionnaire is shown in Appendix 5; it follows the same design, methodology, format and answering techniques of the detailed version. The primary difference is that the final version does not contain the detailed illustration of the interactions of each process from 'Inputs' to 'Outputs' through the involvement of the lists of 'Tools and Techniques' but rather a general outlook on the process without its lists of interactions.

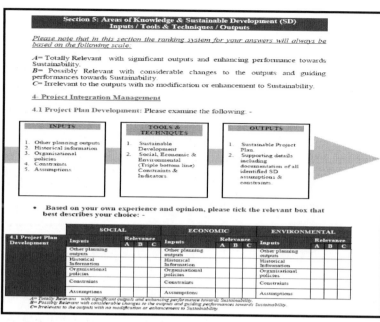

Figure 6.1: Snapshot of the detailed version questionnaire showing the proposed SD integration for `Project Plan Development` process within its correspondent knowledge area[350]

As an example, figure (6.1) shows a snapshot of the detailed proposed integration in the case of the process of `Project Plan Development` within the `Project Integration Management` knowledge area. It shows the in depth analysis of the PMBOK interactions of the process and how the proposed integration would influence its outcomes. For a dedicated respondent, the task would be in contemplating the proposed new approach to the transformation of `Inputs` to `Outputs` when sustainable development guidelines are added to the list of `Tools and Techniques` (the arrow figure) then provide his/her point of view on the integration within the matrix provided below the arrow figure.

---

[350] Appendix 4, pp.5

249

A shorter version of the same proposition would be a possible alternative to encourage respondents to actually take part. Figure (6.2) shows the modified approach of the questionnaire to the same process illustrated in figure (6.1). In the short version, the questionnaire requests the feedback of individuals on the process in general assuming that the respondent has read the introduction added to each section of the short version and also possesses a clear understanding of the manner in which the PMBOK displays the interactions within the processes.

Section 5: Areas of Knowledge & Sustainable Development (SD) Inputs / Tools & Techniques / Outputs

This section aims to evaluate the possibility of integrating each area of knowledge with sustainable development considering its inputs with sustainable development as an added tool &technique to attain outputs which are more sustainable.

Please note that in this section the ranking system for your answers will always be based on the following measure:
A = Significant sustainable outputs, enhancing performance towards Sustainability.
B = Considerable changes to outputs and guiding performance towards Sustainability.
C = Resulting outputs with no modification or enhancement of Sustainability.

1. Applying sustainable development as an added tool & technique to the inputs of each of the following elements, please specify the effect of this application on the outputs of the following major processes:-

Project Integration Management	**SUSTAINABILITY** A	B	C
1. Project Plan Development	○	○	○
2. Project Plan Execution	○	○	○
3. Integrated Change Control	○	○	○

Figure 6.2: A snapshot of the short version questionnaire illustrating the proposed SD integration for `Project Plan Development` process within its knowledge area[351]

The final version shown in Appendix 5 was launched on June 30th 2003 as on online questionnaire[352] on the World Wide Web (WWW).

Both versions attached in Appendices 5(A) and (B) follow the same guidelines of creating any questionnaire since the final short version is literally drawn from the long version; both following the published good

[351] Appendix 5, pp.4
[352] www.caad.ed.ac.uk/projects/eid

survey practice of Tull and Hawkins[353]. The following analysis refers to the final version published on the internet as an online web survey.

6.3 Design of the Questionnaire

Because of the broad nature of questions and subject areas, it was necessary to design a questionnaire which professionally helps the respondent to answer all the questions quickly but efficiently. The questions were designed so as to abide by the guidelines of good survey practice following the strategies shown in figure (6.3).

The question sequence was carefully considered to encourage the respondents to complete the questionnaire, while maintaining their interest in the contents.

Figure (6.3) below, highlights the guidelines of Tull and Hawkins followed in the design of the questionnaire. The guidelines portray the importance of seven main areas starting from the preliminary decisions stage until the Pre-test and revise stage. Each stage is broken down to essential questions which should be asked by the creating team to be fulfilled by the created questionnaire.

For this online survey, it was very important to be as clear as possible about all the guidelines but with special focus on the second stage of guidelines (Decisions about Question Content), the fifth guideline (Decisions Concerning the Question Sequence) and finally, the sixth guideline

---

[353] Donald Stanley Tull and Del I. Hawkins, Marketing Research-Measurement and Method, 5th edition, Maxwell Macmillan International Editions, London, 1990

251

discussing the layout of the questionnaire.

For the second guideline, the content of the questionnaire was clearly covering several areas and concluding to the integration of these areas. This presented a clear challenge when creating the survey; a challenge to maintain a clear perspective of the specific required information without loosing perspective of the supposedly unbiased nature of the questionnaire.

In choosing the sequence of the questions, the guidelines propose a logical manner that avoids the introduction of errors. This was maintained by the online survey as a major goal in order to encourage the respondents to sustain their interest in completing the questionnaire without confusing them about the logical progression of the questions.

This concern has directly affected the layout of the questionnaire to maintain the chosen logical sequence of questions while preserving the overall perspective of the goals of the questionnaire in order to minimise confusion and recording errors.

The guidelines were very helpful in the design process of the online survey as they tackle and focus on general ideas that ensure the fulfilment of the designed questionnaire to the basic requirement of the guidelines. In several cases, when following the guidelines, this would result in favouring certain questions that fulfil the desired objectives over others which could introduce confusion, misguidance or errors.

```
┌────────────────────────────────────────────────────────────────────┐
│ 1- Preliminary Decisions                                             │
│     Exactly what information is required?                            │
│     Exactly who are the target respondents?                          │
│     What method of communication will be used to reach these respondents? │
└────────────────────────────────────────────────────────────────────┘
                                  ↓
┌────────────────────────────────────────────────────────────────────┐
│ 2- Decisions about Question Content                                  │
│     Is this question really needed?                                  │
│     Is this question sufficient to generate the needed information?  │
│     Can the respondent answer the question correctly?                │
│     Will the respondent answer the question correctly?               │
│     Are there any external events that might bias the response to the question? │
└────────────────────────────────────────────────────────────────────┘
                                  ↓
┌────────────────────────────────────────────────────────────────────┐
│ 3- Decisions Concerning Question Phrasing                            │
│     Do the words used have but one meaning to all the respondents?   │
│     Are any of the words or phrases loaded in any way?               │
│     Are there any implied alternatives in the question?              │
│     Are there any unstated assumptions related to the question?      │
│     Will the respondents approach the question from the frame of reference desired by the │
│     researcher?                                                      │
└────────────────────────────────────────────────────────────────────┘
                                  ↓
┌────────────────────────────────────────────────────────────────────┐
│ 4- Decisions about the Response Format                               │
│     Can this question best be asked as an open-ended, multiple choice or rating scale │
│     questions?                                                       │
└────────────────────────────────────────────────────────────────────┘
                                  ↓
┌────────────────────────────────────────────────────────────────────┐
│ 5- Decisions Concerning the Question Sequence                        │
│     Is the questionnaire designed in a logical manner that avoids introducing errors? │
└────────────────────────────────────────────────────────────────────┘
                                  ↓
┌────────────────────────────────────────────────────────────────────┐
│ 6- Decisions on the Layout of the Questionnaire                      │
│     Is the questionnaire designed in a manner which avoids confusion and minimise │
│     recording errors?                                                │
└────────────────────────────────────────────────────────────────────┘
                                  ↓
┌────────────────────────────────────────────────────────────────────┐
│ 7- Pre-test and Revise                                               │
│     Has the final questionnaire been subjected to thorough pre-test, using respondents │
│     similar to those who will be included in the final survey?       │
└────────────────────────────────────────────────────────────────────┘
```

Figure 6.3: Guidelines for creating questionnaires extracted from Tull and Hawkins[354]

---

[354] ibid.

Researching for questionnaire guidelines has been extremely helped by studying the research of work of Scott William Baker in his PhD Thesis on "Risk Management in Major Projects" University of Edinburgh, 1998. Baker's thesis relies mainly on a major Risk Management Questionnaire (RMQ) which he created and that the author found extremely helpful and resourceful in terms of questionnaire guidelines and helping models.

6.4 Methodology of the Questionnaire

The overall objective of the questionnaire was to investigate the views of the respondents on the possibilities and the opportunities for integrating sustainable development into project management processes listed in the PMBOK (2000 Edition). The broad as well sophisticated nature of the area covered by the questionnaire meant that the targeted audience should represent a specific class of respondents; PM practitioners, professionals, academics and/or researchers. The questionnaire examines specific aspects of project management with specific interest in the PMBOK processes; this implied that the respondents should be familiar of the contents of the PMBOK and preferably well into practicing its guidelines.

This implied a selected and specifically targeted audience, hence, the Project Management Institute was contacted through their website research coordinator team to link the questionnaire website to the official PMI website and more specifically to the 'Project Management Survey Links'. The questionnaire fulfilled all their requirements and was linked to the PMI Survey Links[355].

The UK audience was also included more specifically because of the earlier emphasis of this research on the UK construction industry, therefore, the PMI Chapter in the UK was contacted and a collective invitation was extended to all the UK members via email lists to join the survey and include their views. The questionnaire also fulfilled the requirements of the UK lists of members.

In order to reach the PM researchers and academics, the Project Management

---

[355] http://www.pmi.org/info/PP_ResearchSurveyLinks.asp

Specific Interest Group (PM SIG) manager as well the Students of Project Management Specific Interest Group (Students of PM SIG) were contacted and they both provided linked access to the questionnaire through their official websites[356].

Finally, the questionnaire was sent via email invitation to selected audience in the field of project management, whom the author met through project management conferences, personal contacts and/or upon their requests.

The participants who requested the results would have been informed of the summary.

6.5 Format of the Questionnaire

The questionnaire starts with an invitation summary of the contents and short analysis of the hypothesis of the research. Although, the final version published on the web link was the less detailed version, an access was provided for individuals interested in further detailed analysis of the integration to the comprehensive version of the questionnaire via a click button on the front page of the web link. Whoever chooses to access the longer version, the link opens up the complete file to be examined, studied and/or filled out with the option of mailing it back to the author.

The questionnaire was designed in five distinctive yet interlinked section: -

• **Section 1:** Asks for information to establish the background and experience of the respondent.

• **Section 2:** Discusses the knowledge of the participants and their attitudes

---

[356] http://www.pmsigcentral.org/Surveys.htm and
http://www.studentsofpm.org/Surveys.htm

towards Sustainable Development (SD).

- **Section 3:** Seeks to find out about the level of familiarity of the respondents with PMBOK and their opinion of its current contents.

- **Section 4:** Is aimed at trying to identify different ways for integrating PM and SD.

- **Section 5:** Evaluates the possibility of integrating sustainable development within each knowledge area when considering its lists of inputs.

The overall format of the questionnaire is meant to be inviting for respondents to complete and easy to understand. The five sections are illustrated in figure (6.4) showing the nature of the information gathered from each section and the transition from each section to the other. Within the framework of the questionnaire shown in the figure, it was an essential goal to display the different sections in a way which maintains the line of thought of the respondent. It does not lead the participant to any answer in any biased way, but introduce him/her to each section from a logical progression point of view.

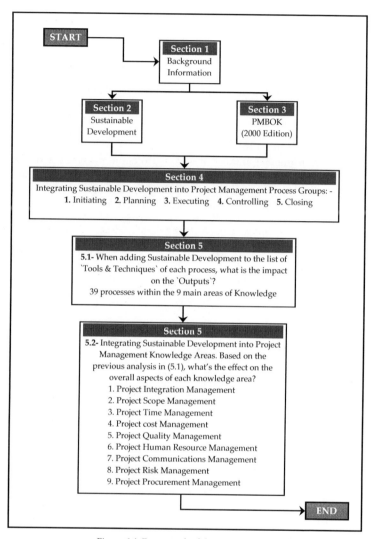

Figure 6.4: Framework of the questionnaire

The framework also follows the same logical progression used in laying out this book; hence, the questionnaire starts with some simple questions about the respondent background information. Then, it examines the correspondent's points of view and level of knowledge/familiarity on the two main issues of the survey; Sustainable Development and PMBOK. Each issue is examined separately in a corresponding section, and then the following section discusses bringing both issues together and examines the respondent's feedback on this integration.

First, the integration is looked at from the perspective of the five main process groups. Then the respondent is asked to move into the final section of the questionnaire where the integration is examined in terms of component processes to the knowledge areas. This transition inspects the impact of the proposed integration on the components parts of the system (i.e. the 39 processes) then examines the impact on the bigger perspective (i.e. the whole areas of knowledge).

6.6 Answering Techniques

In order to reinforce the objectives of the questionnaire and maintain the ideology behind its design, format and methodology, the questionnaire uses only two answering techniques;
- Multiple choice
- Rating Scales

The first questions (Section 1 and 4) follow the multiple choice technique because they are easy to answer and therefore encourage the respondent to move from one question to the other. They are designed to enquire about basic information about the participant's background experience and current career and responsibilities. Although, these questions seem easy to answer with minimal information, they do have a significant impact on the analysis of the responses as we will discuss later in this chapter.

The remainder of the questions (Section 2, 3 and 5) follow the rating scale technique; this allows the respondent to be more involved in the answer. This technique acts as an invitation to the participant to think, concentrate and then choose the required the answer in his/her opinion following a clear rating scale which is defined at the beginning of each section.

The answering techniques were intentionally mixed among the entities of the five sections in order to make the overall experience of the questionnaire more interesting. Not following one simple technique from start to finish was introduced in order to avoid monotony while serving the planned objectives.

Once the respondent had finished the questionnaire, an open ended answering box was created (feedback/comments box) to invite the respondents to share their views, expand and/or comment on any of the sections of the questionnaire. This option gave the participants the chance to endeavour on the opportunity of praising, criticising and/or enquiring about the hypothesis of the research and also the questions within the survey.

6.7 Analysing the Responses

The online questionnaire was launched on June 30th, 2003. The following statistics are based on the responses received from the online questionnaire until the closing date (November 14th, 2003).

The author recognises that the total number of respondents is relatively small compared to the scale of the construction industry as well as the project management profession in terms of working force worldwide and within the UK. As explained earlier, the online questionnaire was linked to three major PM international websites and to one of the main lists of PM professionals in the UK, therefore the small interest in taking part in the questionnaire, is not, by any means, because of lack of publicity.

In fact, the participants were selectively targeted by introducing the survey online link to these professional PM Websites. The following is the analytical summary of the replies.

6.7.1 Respondents' Background Information

Section 1, Questions 1, 2 and 3

Occupation and Responsibilities	General PM	Construction	Academia / Research & Development
No. of Respondents	20	10	6
Total no. of responses	36		

Table 6.1: Summary of the total number of responses

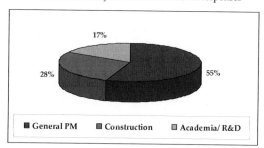

Figure 6.5: Summary of the total number of responses

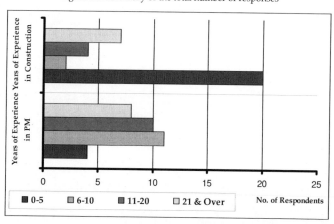

Figure 6.6: Breakdown of no. of respondents relative to their years of experience

Table (6.1), figures (6.5) and (6.6) are the statistical representations of the first section of the questionnaire entitled 'Section 1: Background Information'. They demonstrate that the questionnaire attracted a majority of respondents who are currently working within general PM practice.

In figure (6.6), the graph shows that this majority has past experience in the construction industry. Out of 33 replies to question 3 from this section, 20 respondents (60.6%) had only 0-5 years of experience in the construction industry which may indicate that the construction industry has been attracting more project managers into its practices in the last 5 years. This demonstrates the growing relationship between current construction practices and project management, where the industry is calling for more involvement from PM professionals into construction projects to ensure successful completion.

6.7.2 Respondents' Feedback on Sustainable Development

Section 2, Questions 1, 2, 3 and 4

This section discusses the responses received for 'Section 2: Sustainable Development' which aims to examine the respondents' general knowledge of SD and their perception of linking SD to the quality of life. Then, the questions look at establishing the respondents' point of view on the relationship between the construction industry and the integration of sustainable development into its practices. For this section, the answers were all following a rating scale technique defined for every question.

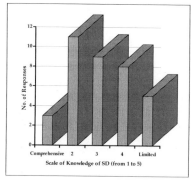
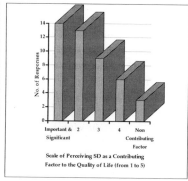
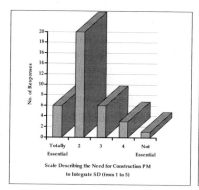
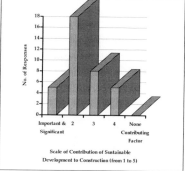

Figure 6.7: Respondents' feedback on Sustainable Development (SD)

In figure (6.7), the graphs show that the majority of the respondents have good knowledge of what sustainable development means and its implications of the quality of life. Only 5 respondents said they had limited and superficial knowledge of SD. None of the respondents denied the interconnection between sustainability and the quality of life. This feedback had good implications on the subsequent questions. The respondents agreed that the construction industry needed to integrate sustainable development into its practices with a majority of 32 responses (88.9%). Another majority described sustainable development as a very important and significant factor in terms of changing the outcomes of construction projects with a majority of 31 responses (86.1%).

These statistics support the arguments when establishing the relationships between the four pillars of the research and more specifically, between the construction industry and the sustainability agenda. This also endorses that the need for embracing `change` within the construction industry had to start from within the core of its culture and individuals' belief of the importance of the existing relationships between sustainable development, construction and project management.

6.7.3 Respondents' Feedback on the PMBOK (2000 Edition)

Section 3, Questions 1, 2 and 3

This section examines the responses from `Section3: PMBOK - 2000 Edition`. The questions aim at establishing the level of familiarity of the respondents with the PMBOK and query the respondent's knowledge of the contents of PMBOK and its linkage to sustainable impacts and construction projects.

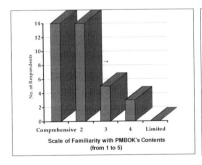
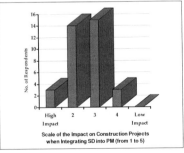

Figure 6.8: Respondents' feedback on the 2000 Edition of PMBOK in terms of its contents

264

In figure (6.8), the graphs demonstrate the majority of the respondents describe their familiarity with the contents of PMBOK as comprehensive and up-to-date. This acknowledgement endorses the integrity of the information gathered from the questionnaire because of the respondents' good knowledge of the PMBOK which is vital to the creditability of the conclusions derived from the responses. It demonstrates the targeted nature of the questionnaire's participants.

A significant majority of respondents agreed on the high impact on construction projects which would emerge from integrating sustainable development into project management practices. The graph on the right in figure (6.8) mirrors a majority of 32 responses (88.9%) leaning towards the high impact part of the rating scale (scale step 1, 2 and 3 combined).

Contrary to the results arising from the remainder of the questionnaire, a conflicting majority of (61.1%) agrees that the aspect of PM context of `Social-Economic-Environmental Influences` in the PMBOK (explained in chapter 3, section 3.6) does adequately covers the integration of sustainable development into project management (Section 3, Question 2) and is, indeed, a significant addition to ensure guiding PM practices towards sustainable performance. This result, obviously, conflicts with the research's arguments regarding the need for more involvement of SD into PM practices. This recent addition to the PM context aspects in the 2000 Edition of PMBOK is not enough to endorse a sustainable approach to PM processes and practices.

Although the majority of respondents disagree with this argument, the remainder statistics of the responses conflicts completely with this outcome.

265

This originated from one or more of the following reasons: -

- The author acknowledges that the phrasing of this specific question could be considered as ambiguous. It might have confused the respondents in ways which instigated their choice.

- Although a majority of respondents conceded to a good knowledge of the contents of PMBOK, the question was very specific to one of five aspects of the PM context. The section of the PMBOK in question is a one page sub-section within the first introductory part of the PMBOK; therefore, it is unlikely for respondents to relate to the same section that the question was meant to refer to.

- The question was intended as an aspirational indicator which would demonstrate the respondents' desire to accept the concept of `change`. But at this stage of the questionnaire, the author's approach has not been yet revealed and therefore, the respondents could have chosen (Yes) as a passive endorsement of the status quo. The (No) answer could have signalled a demanding `action` on their behalf which was not the case. Individuals reject what they do not know rather than embrace the unknown.

The inconsistency in the respondents' points of view may be due to a degree of ambiguity in the question, suggest that its implications should not imply a great deal of significance. This does not undermine the value of the remaining answers provided by the respondents but it seems logical and wise to disregard the result of this specific question as it has the potential to misinterpret the arguments from which the survey arises.

6.7.4 Respondents' Feedback on PM Processes and SD

Section 4, Questions 1, 2, 3, 4 and 5

This section examines the respondents' viewpoint on integrating sustainable development into project management processes. Based on the PMBOK categorisation of PM process groups (Initiating - Planning - Executing - Controlling - Closing), this section examines five possible `places to intervene` when introducing SD guidelines into each process group.

These five opportunities for integration are: -

A= Scope, **B**= Objectives, **C**= Core Processes, **D**= Facilitating Process or finally, the respondents were given the choice to disagree with this argument if they decide to choose the fifth option (œ).

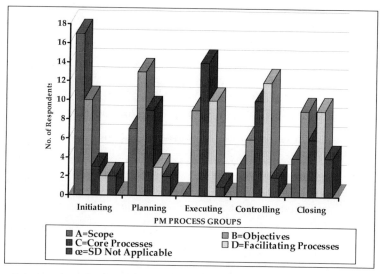

Figure 6.9: Respondents' Feedback on `places to intervene` when introducing SD to PM

- **For the Initiating Process Group:** 47.2% of the respondents chose the scope of the initiating process as the best place to introduce sustainable development into PM. This outcome endorses the earlier argument, which advocates the integration starting from within the origins out of which a process or a system arises. In this case, the scope of initiating process would identify sustainable development as integral part of the overall scope of the whole project.

- **For the Planning Process Group:** 36.1% of the respondents selected the objectives of the planning process as the best opportunity for integrating SD into project management. This majority choice indicates that when planning processes start, the objectives of the planning activities identifies itself as the best chance for including sustainable development guidelines which supports the findings detailed in chapter 5.

- **For the Executing Process Group:** 38.9% of the responses indicated that when reaching the executing phase, sustainable development is best integrated in its core processes such as `Project Plan Execution`. This choice also originates from the logic of introducing `change` from within the most effective part of the process which is, in this case, its core processes.

- **For the Controlling Process Group:** 33.3% of the respondents selected the facilitating processes as the best opportunity to embrace sustainability within the controlling process group. This choice follows some respondents' conviction that when controlling projects' activities, the facilitating processes arise as the possible likelihood for introducing the change in approach to a more sustainable one.

- **For the Closing Process Group:** 50% of the responses were split evenly between the choice of `objectives` and `facilitating processes` as the best places to intervene when introducing sustainable development. Since the closing process is the final phase of any projects, this undermines the level of impact that could be inflicted if SD was introduced. The differences between the five possibilities in terms of the number of respondents for each choice are relatively diminutive. In other words, the distribution of number of responses between the five options is narrowly small. Number of respondents who selected A= 4, B=9, C=6, D=9 and œ=4. This might jeopardise a conclusive assumption, but among all the process groups, the closing process had the highest number of entries for (œ) and its inconclusiveness suggests that the respondents perceived the closing process as the least appealing opportunity for integrating SD endorses the research's arguments from a systems thinking point of view.

6.7.5 Respondents' Feedback on PM Knowledge Areas and SD

Section 5, Questions 1 and 2

This section is divided into two questions as illustrated in figure (6.4) defining the framework of the questionnaire. The first question examines the opportunities for integrating sustainable development into the component processes within each knowledge area based on their lists of inputs, tools & techniques and outputs listed in the PMBOK. The second question discusses the same integration process but in terms of the general overview of each knowledge area as a whole.

Question 1

The first question is a detailed series of choices asking the respondents to choose one of three possible answers to determine, when sustainable development guidelines are added to the lists of 'tools & techniques', the impact the integration would have on the lists of 'outputs' for each process. This also meant that the respondents were selecting the best opportunities, in their own point of view, which would embrace sustainable development as a fundamental part of the corresponding process.

The answers followed a rating scale based on: -

- **A**= Significant sustainable outputs which enhance sustainable performance.
- **B**= Considerable changes to outputs and guiding performance towards sustainability.
- **C**= Resulting outputs have no modification or enhancement of sustainability.

Respondents Who Chose / PM Process Groups	SELECTION A		SELECTION B		SELECTION C	
	PM Processes	%	PM Processes	%	PM Processes	%
1- INITIATING	5.1 Initiation	82.4	5.1 Initiation	11.8	5.1 Initiation	5.9
2- PLANNING	4.1 Project Plan Development	76.5	4.1 Project Plan Development	20.6	4.1 Project Plan Development	2.9
	5.2 Scope Planning	82.4	5.2 Scope Planning	17.6	5.2 Scope Planning	0
	5.3 Scope Definition	67.6	5.3 Scope Definition	32.4	5.3 Scope Definition	0
	6.1 Activity Definition	41.2	6.1 Activity Definition	41.2	6.1 Activity Definition	17.6
	6.2 Activity Sequencing	20.6	6.2 Activity Sequencing	52.9	6.2 Activity Sequencing	26.5
	6.3 Activity Duration Estimating	11.8	6.3 Activity Duration Estimating	44.1	6.3 Activity Duration Estimating	44.1
	6.4 Schedule Development	20.6	6.4 Schedule Development	50	6.4 Schedule Development	29.4
	7.1 Resource Planning	55.9	7.1 Resource Planning	32.4	7.1 Resource Planning	11.7
	7.2 Cost Estimating	44.1	7.2 Cost Estimating	44.1	7.2 Cost Estimating	11.8
	7.3 Cost Budgeting	17.7	7.3 Cost Budgeting	64.7	7.3 Cost Budgeting	17.7
	8.1 Quality Planning	59.4	8.1 Quality Planning	37.5	8.1 Quality Planning	3.1
	9.1 Organisational Planning	23.5	9.1 Organisational Planning	47.1	9.1 Organisational Planning	29.4
	9.2 Staff Acquisition	20.6	9.2 Staff Acquisition	52.9	9.2 Staff Acquisition	26.5
	10.1 Communication Planning	35.3	10.1 Communication Planning	50	10.1 Communication Planning	14.7
	11.1 Risk Management Planning	61.8	11.1 Risk Management Planning	38.2	11.1 Risk Management Planning	0
	11.2 Risk Identification	67.6	11.2 Risk Identification	29.4	11.2 Risk Identification	3
	11.3 Qualitative Risk Analysis	26.5	11.3 Qualitative Risk Analysis	64.7	11.3 Qualitative Risk Analysis	8.8
	11.4 Quantitative Risk Analysis	20.6	11.4 Quantitative Risk Analysis	61.8	11.4 Quantitative Risk Analysis	17.6
	11.5 Risk Response Planning	35.3	11.5 Risk Response Planning	55.9	11.5 Risk Response Planning	8.8
	12.1 Procurement Planning	48.5	12.1 Procurement Planning	48.5	12.1 Procurement Planning	3
	12.2 Solicitation Planning	33.3	12.2 Solicitation Planning	60.6	12.2 Solicitation Planning	6.1
3- EXECUTING	4.2 Project Plan Execution	26.5	4.2 Project Plan Execution	67.6	4.2 Project Plan Execution	5.9
	8.2 Quality Assurance	30.3	8.2 Quality Assurance	63.6	8.2 Quality Assurance	6.1
	9.3 Team Development	20.6	9.3 Team Development	52.9	9.3 Team Development	26.5
	10.2 Information Distribution	32.6	10.2 Information Distribution	50	10.2 Information Distribution	17.6
	12.3 Solicitation	15.2	12.3 Solicitation	57.6	12.3 Solicitation	27.2
	12.4 Source Selection	33.3	12.4 Source Selection	51.5	12.4 Source Selection	15.2
	12.5 Contract Administration	21.2	12.5 Contract Administration	57.6	12.5 Contract Administration	21.2
4- CONTROLLING	4.3 Integrated Change Control	23.5	4.3 Integrated Change Control	70.6	4.3 Integrated Change Control	5.9
	5.4 Scope Verification	35.3	5.4 Scope Verification	55.9	5.4 Scope Verification	8.8
	5.5 Scope Change Control	29.4	5.5 Scope Change Control	70.6	5.5 Scope Change Control	0
	6.5 Schedule Control	11.8	6.5 Schedule Control	44.1	6.5 Schedule Control	44.1
	7.4 Cost Control	23.5	7.4 Cost Control	50	7.4 Cost Control	26.5
	8.3 Quality Control	30.3	8.3 Quality Control	45.5	8.3 Quality Control	24.2
	10.3 Performance Reporting	11.7	10.3 Performance Reporting	55.9	10.3 Performance Reporting	32.4
	11.6 Risk Monitoring & Control	15.2	11.6 Risk Monitoring & Control	66.7	11.6 Risk Monitoring & Control	18.1
5- CLOSING	10.4 Administrative Closure	5.8	10.4 Administrative Closure	47.1	10.4 Administrative Closure	47.1
	12.6 Contract Closeout	3	12.6 Contract Closeout	60.6	12.6 Contract Closeout	36.4

Figure 6.10: Illustration of the respondents' selections concerning 'Mapping the opportunities and the impact of integrating SD into PM processes

A= Significant sustainable outputs which enhance sustainable performance.
B= Considerable changes to outputs and guiding performance towards sustainability.
C= Resulting outputs have no modification or enhancement of sustainability.

COLOR KEY OF PM KNOWELDGE AREAS: -
4- Project Integration Management
5- Project Scope Management
6- Project Time Management
7- Project Cost Management
8- Project Quality Management

9- Project Human Resource Management
10- Project Communications Management
11- Project Risk Management
12- Project Procurement Management

Figure (6.10) summarises the answers retrieved from the first part of section 5 of the questionnaire. To illustrate all the answers, the same matrix used

271

before in chapter 5 (figure 5.14) has been re-introduced to map the opportunities and the relevancy of sustainable development to each of the PM processes. In this section, but with minor changes although following the same framework, the responses were compiled to calculate the percentage of respondents who chose any of the possible selections (A, B, C).

The outcome of the compilation demonstrates that `B` is the most popular choice. Hence, for 79.5% of the listed processes, the respondents thought that when sustainable development guidelines would be added to the list of `tools and techniques` of these processes, there will be considerable changes to their lists of outputs and therefore guide the overall performance towards sustainability. This significant majority supports the argument that endorses the integration of SD into PM processes. The analysis of the responses clearly shows that the respondents agree that the processes hold within them efficient leverage points for introducing SD to PM practices.

From figure (6.10), another conclusion is apparent; among the other two selections (A, C); the respondents seem more leaning towards choosing (A) rather than (C). In fact, only two processes out of the thirty nine had a majority choice of (C) denying them the opportunity for SD enhancement (i.e. Activity Duration Estimating and Schedule Control). In this case, the majority of choice was equally divided between (B) and (C) and never for (C) alone. This analysis underpins the research's findings of the great potential that exists within the processes to embrace sustainable development guidelines and therefore, enhance the overall performance of project management.

With a closer look at figure (5.14) in chapter 5 and figure (6.10) above, they both illustrate mapping the sustainable development opportunities within the PM processes and knowledge areas. Figure (5.14), demonstrates these opportunities on a detailed level, therefore the integration of sustainable development is examined in terms of its triple bottom line; social, economic and environmental levels. Figure (6.10) illustrates the mapping of opportunities for integrating the concept of sustainable development as a whole because it represents the respondents' feedback on the online version of the questionnaire which is less detailed in terms of addressing the integration as whole and not on each level of sustainability as achieved in figure (5.14).

PM Knowledge Areas	PM Component Processes	Majority of Respondents Chose: -	%
Project Integration Management	Project Plan Development	A	76.5
	Project Plan Execution	B	67.6
	Integrated Change Control	B	70.6
Project Scope Management	Initiation	A	82.4
	Scope Planning	A	82.4
	Scope Definition	A	67.6
	Scope Verification	B	55.9
	Scope Change Control	B	70.6
Project Time Management	Activity Definition	A/B	41.2
	Activity Sequencing	B	52.9
	Activity Duration Estimating	B/C	44.1
	Schedule Development	B	50
	Schedule Control	B/C	44.1
Project Cost Management	Resource Planning	A	55.9
	Cost Estimating	A/B	44.1
	Cost Budgeting	B	64.7
	Cost Control	B	50
Project Quality Management	Quality Planning	A	59.4
	Quality Assurance	B	63.6
	Quality Control	B	45.5
Project Human Resource Management	Organisational Planning	B	47.1
	Staff Acquisition	B	52.9
	Team Development	B	52.9
Project Communications Management	Communications Planning	B	50
	Information Distribution	B	50
	Performance Reporting	B	55.9
	Administrative Closure	B/C	47.1
Project Risk Management	Risk Management Planning	A	61.8
	Risk Identification	A	67.6
	Qualitative Risk Analysis	B	64.7
	Quantitative Risk Analysis	B	61.8
	Risk Response Planning	B	55.9
	Risk Monitoring & Control	B	66.7
Project Procurement Management	Procurement Planning	A/B	48.5
	Solicitation Planning	B	60.6
	Solicitation	B	57.6
	Source Selection	B	51.5
	Contract Administration	B	57.6
	Contract Closeout	B	60.6

Table 6.2: Highlighting the process with highest majority of respondents choosing it as the best opportunity to integrate SD within the corresponding knowledge area.

Among each knowledge area, the answers in table (6.2) were re-organised to highlight the respondents' popular choices of processes which they think hold within them the most efficient leverage points to introduce sustainable development to the corresponding knowledge area.

A significant observation from table (6.2) is that the highest percentage of respondents' choice (82.4%) among all processes is dedicated to the `Initiation Process` within the initiating process group and to the `Scope Planning Process` within the planning process group. These two processes are the first processes in all PM practices. The respondents chose selection (A) for these processes to indicate that they hold within their lists of interactions `significant sustainable outputs which would enhance an overall sustainable performance`.

This choice accredits the research's arguments, based on Donella Meadows' theory of systems thinking and leverage points, concerning the crucial theory of the sooner the implementation of sustainable development is introduced to the early stages of a system, the better and more efficient the outcome would be towards a more overall sustainable performance. Changing the initiation and scope planning processes to more sustainable processes would inflict sustainable implications on all of the subsequent processes; therefore the whole PM framework would change towards sustainable performance.

Question 2

The second question of section 5 of the questionnaire, asks the respondents for their point of view on the impact of sustainable development on the overall of each of the knowledge areas. Following the same scale as in

276

question 1, the respondents were asked to describe the ways in which the outputs of the knowledge areas would be affected when sustainable development guidelines are integrated within the component processes.

PM Knowledge Areas	Majority of Respondents Chose: -	%
Project Time Management	B	74.3
Project Scope Management	A	70.6
Project Procurement Management	B	70.6
Project Quality Management	B	60
Project Cost Management	B	58.8
Project Integration Management	B	54.5
Project Human Resource Management	B	54.3
Project Communications Management	B	50
Project Risk Management	A/B	44.3

Table 6.3: The PM Knowledge Areas in descending order based on the respondents feedback on question 5.2 in the questionnaire

Table (6.3) displays the analysis of the responses by listing the knowledge areas in descending order of percentage of respondents agreeing on the selected choice.

Again, the majority of respondents chose either (A) or (B), this affirms the significant potential that exists in enhancing sustainable PM performance and the respondents, obviously, identify with.

Although, this analysis endorses the argument, the descending order is not necessarily any favourable order which should guide the choice of which knowledge area to first integrate sustainable development with. But, this order only mirrors the respondents' awareness of the components of each knowledge area. Therefore, since `Project Risk Management` is a complicated

277

set of interactions between its processes, which demand specialization in practice, it came at the bottom end of the list because the majority of the respondents do not necessarily deal in risk management although they would be working in general aspects of PM.

In the same table, `Project Time Management, Project Scope Management and Project Procurement Management` took the lead in the majority choice. This demonstrates the respondents' viewpoint on the importance of these specific aspects of PM in controlling the whole practice and influencing the system of PM performance as a whole.

6.8 Critical Review of the Online Questionnaire

An important finding of this questionnaire is that the arguments of this research, discussed in the questions, were endorsed strongly by the respondents' responses. Although this does indeed fit with the hypothesis of the research, there is a necessity for a word of caution. Since most of the respondents are members of PMI (although not all), there is an obvious possibility that they would be biased to portray their view on the PMBOK processes. A more interesting result would be to examine the views of PM professionals who are not members of PMI to study their observations –as outsiders- on the PM processes included in the PMBOK.

Although the design of the questionnaire, in terms of outline structure and sequence of questions, was intended to be inviting and not confusing, there is a concern that the language of the questionnaire might have excluded certain respondents who are not familiar with the terminology used in the questions. At certain levels, this was controlled by the targeted respondents approach in marketing the questionnaire. Thus, it was made clear from the start that respondents are expected to be familiar with the subjects in questions. This turned out to be a subjective factor which would damage in certain cases the credibility of the answers.

A similar criticism can be levelled at the overall findings because of the limited number of respondents. This could query the importance of the findings based on the fact that the fields of PM, construction and SD attract a high number of professionals, researchers and academics which is not relatively presented by the limited number of respondents that the survey attracted. The significance of the findings is still of a high implication level but would benefit from an even wider scale of respondents to re-test the conclusions.

In terms of respondents' assessment of their knowledge of SD, this has suffered from a possible lack of objectivity which might have affected the respondents in testing their own knowledge of the subject. The language of the question itself may have favoured an answer over the other which was not on purpose but it has be accepted that creating the questionnaire in the first place was triggered by a possible subjective judgement.

One has to acknowledge that analysing the results of the questionnaire might have been subjected to a bias judgement as in all cases of any analysis following the nature and beliefs of the creating team, but an even more interesting exercise would be to test the answers in a wider context and possibly in a public or group session, thus, benefit from the collection of different perspectives.

6.9 The Way Forward

The fours pillars of this research (i.e. the construction industry, sustainable development, project management and systems thinking theories) are complex functioning systems. Bringing them all together in an efficient tri-dimensional integration, between construction practices, SD and PM, in a facilitating milieu of systems thinking and leverage points was the main objective for this research. Because of the complexity and the importance of each of the four pillars, involving the expert opinion, of professionals, practitioners, academics and researchers, plays a vital role in validating the arguments. The questionnaire was made available to respondents as an efficient mean for requesting the feedback of interested participants.

Creating the questionnaire followed the same logic used in creating this book. The first questions were to establish the respondents' knowledge and awareness of each element on its own then followed by the questions discussing the elements in interaction with each other in the form of the integration on which the research is based.

The respondents' feedback on each section of the questionnaire was very informative in many ways. This enhanced the outcome of the analysis of the responses. The responses were analysed with a clear approach in mind which allowed the statistical analysis to represent, in an honest and fair way, the participants' point of views and professional feedback.

From the statistical analysis of the responses, it is evident that the respondents acknowledge the possibilities for integrating sustainable development into project management processes and support the positive impact this integration would have on the overall performance of PM within construction in specific and in all fields in general.

Significant majority of the participants identified several valid opportunities within PM processes listed in the PMBOK which have been identified earlier within the approach of this research. The outcome of the questionnaire's analysis has strengthened this research's hypothesis and identified the ways in which project management, as significant profession in the current modern age, should contribute to the global commitment for sustainable development within all fields.

Therefore, since the PMBOK is considered as an international source of project management standards, a way forward for enhancing the PM pledge to embrace a sustainable approach to its practices, is to have sustainable criteria implications on the contents of the PMBOK. These implications have to be transferred and applied to the lists of PM processes and knowledge area. This would serve the whole PM profession with a document of standards that embraces sustainable development. In this case, changing PM practices to sustainable PM practices would have originated from the source out of which PM practices arise; the sustainable approach to PM standards.

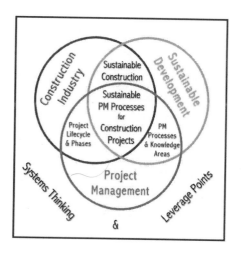

CONCLUSION

*"Rethinking Relationships in the Construction Industry:
Integrating Sustainable Development into Project Management Processes"*

Acknowledging that the construction sector is an indispensable industry for both developed and developing countries, it is imperative to recognise the considerable potential that the industry has for generating and influencing the quality of life to which individuals aspire globally. On the one hand, the construction industry has been the prime generator of wealth for several countries, governments, business owners and architects but on the other hand, it has also been the cause for social dissolution, environmental degradation and worldwide disapproval of its current standards of performance. The construction industry's strong performance, ironically, has become the problem and a challenge to which world societies have to find a sustainable answer.

Since the sector's impact is affecting the whole world, with significant evidence of contributing to the global climate change, the scale of action needed to confront the challenge has risen beyond national geographic boundaries to a global scale.

This study is a contribution to such a challenge. It has demonstrated that the involvement of sustainable development in all fields, to generate a better of quality of life for all now and for generations to come, can cross boundaries which have not been surmounted before. When approached from a systems

283

thinking point of view, sustainability becomes the impact creator that can engender change within existing functioning systems. Not only can it affect the construction industry's detailed activities and procurement of resources but, more significantly, it can influence the performance of the industry as a whole, notably when introduced to the origins of the decision making levels.

This research has discussed the decision making level of current construction projects including project management practice. The involvement of project management in construction projects is fundamental, although not exclusive, to the successful completion of projects. When embraced from the initial phases of a project, project management standards ensure a systematic breakdown of all activities to fit into a comprehensive, detailed plan for the project as a whole, from initiation to completion and closure.

This book has demonstrated that project management, when embedded in construction projects, has the capacity to be a significant leverage point of such great influence that it is the cornerstone for rethinking the relationships between the three main elements of the integration.

The research has defined and examined the proposal of a tri-dimensional integration between construction, project management and sustainable development when approached from a systems thinking point of view. The main focus of the research is not only to explain the potential and the benefits of such integration. It also tests the criteria on which the integration is based and offers guidance concerning the practical aspects of construction, and project management practices, in the form of illustrative examples taken from current initiatives and practice standards.

This final part of the research presents a series of conclusions which have been distilled from the work described above. The observations and recommendations are subdivided into two parts based on the general areas of research investigated (shown in figure 1* in 'Introduction') and are presented together to allow an overall appreciation of the findings.

Conclusions from Part I of the Book

"Establishing the Relationships"

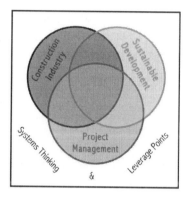

- The construction industry is a key element of influence bearing on our quality of life; economically, socially and environmentally. Although current performance standards are proving to be disappointing to all stakeholders, the potential for enhancing future performance is immense. The industry has shown considerable flexibility towards the implementation of governmental initiatives which have been introducing new approaches to the way projects are undertaken. Overall within the industry, there is much to be done not only in terms of construction practices but also in changing the culture of the industry. The focus should no longer be on the short-term economic profits but it should also embrace the social aspects and the environmental impact of projects' activities which influence long term profitability.

- On the international as well as national level, the challenges facing the industry are very similar; hence, new global construction initiatives call for the embodiment of a sustainable development approach in all practices. Although maintaining a sustainable construction agenda is the main focus, the research has demonstrated that these initiatives still fail to address the full potential of such an agenda. The problems facing the implementation are mainly based on the reluctance of businesses to embrace the sustainable approach, unless they are convinced of a successful business case for sustainability.

- One of the major concerns of the industry is to sustain its competitiveness; this research has explained that adopting sustainable construction endorses the competitiveness of the construction industry not only in terms of its economic future viability and successful business case but also in fortifying its social and environmental aspects. This adds to the competitive edge of businesses by satisfying the growing number of customers who demand environmentally sound products and services as well as clear indicators of respect to end users and employees.

- The Egan report `Rethinking Construction` does not directly mention sustainable development, although the drivers proposed define a sustainable approach. Integrating sustainability into rethinking construction has proven to be a valid and, indeed, an efficient agenda for future performance. The established relationship between both elements still hold within its core, greater potential for generating better practice by adopting an even deeper understanding of the notions of sustainable development from a systems thinking point of view.

- Sustainable development has been criticised despite the global endorsement of its guidelines. This research demonstrates that embracing a sustainable development agenda can only improve the conditions of the three pillars of society; civil, government and businesses. Sustainable development is now perceived within a global context fortified by international agendas which have significant impact on the local agendas of practice enhancing the quality of people's life.

- The business case for sustainable development has proved crucial to the implementation phase, underpinned by the adoption of sustainable construction agendas. Sustainability generated to businesses a new competitive advantage to the level of practice.

- The relationship between project management and the successful completion of construction projects is evident. The involvement, from start to completion, has proven vital to the exploration of the full extent of project management's potential in supporting all project's activities and, more specifically, from the decision making level.

- The PMBOK® 2000 Edition and the Construction Extension to PMBOK, represent the standardisation authority of project management practice on the international level. Although they provide a comprehensive framework and context for PM standards, they fail to seriously address the sustainability agenda. Both documents forsake the influence of sustainability on PM practice and therefore disregard the possible impact such an approach could have on the involvement of project management in construction projects and more specifically on the decision making level.

- Project management processes and knowledge areas fall short of committing to a sustainable approach. This research has argued that the potential within these processes is significant in terms of its impact on the overall performance. Since project management is involved in construction projects, with such significant impact on the overall performance, it has therefore to comply with current sustainable construction initiatives. This compliance is far from being demonstrated by the current description of PM processes and knowledge areas which ignores, to a very large extent, sustainable development guidelines.

- The research has demonstrated that within the PM processes, lie efficient leverage points to introduce sustainable development to project management standards. There is a crucial need for rethinking the involvement of PM processes within construction projects to satisfy and endorse the sustainable agendas from a systems thinking point of view.

- Systems thinking and leverage points theories have demonstrated that the bottom line in changing existing functioning systems lies within the identification of places, within these systems, to intervene and introduce the desired change. Donella Meadows' list of twelve leverage points, identified within systems, has proved to be the cornerstone concept for introducing change. It is understood, from Meadows' approach, that the order of efficiency, which the list displays, applies to all systems. However, the author believes that the environment, in which any system takes place, plays a fundamental role in interpreting the scenario that controls its activities and processes.

- The earlier a desired change is introduced to the phases of any system, the better and more efficient the impact is on the subsequent phases of the system in question. This is the basis on which the second part of the research allows the four pillars of the research to work collectively and in a more efficient manner to answer to sustainable development agendas.

- The criteria driving the research are based on an examination of the possibilities of creating a sustainable approach to the PM processes and knowledge areas currently playing a significant role in construction projects. Also considered is the impact this approach would have, on delivering a more sustainable construction performance, when systems thinking and leverage points theories are followed in introducing such approach.

Conclusions from Part II of the Book

"Rethinking the Relationships"

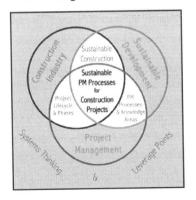 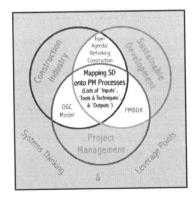

- Based on the arguments considered in the first part of the research, chapter 5 illustrates how the hypothesis brings together the four pillars of the research to endorse the proposed tri-dimensional integration between sustainable development, construction and project management in a facilitating milieu of a systems thinking approach.

- Project management is an efficient vehicle to introduce a more profound change not only to the construction industry's practice but more importantly to the industry's culture. Project management's involvement in construction projects tackles, and indeed dominates, the decision level making which the research describes as the best place to intervene in the way projects are undertaken. Project management processes are especially effective at the early stages of construction initiation and planning stages.

- Bringing together the three dimensions of the integration, generates a new set of common issues among the elements. The research examines these resulting issues from a systems thinking point of view. The above Venn diagram illustrating the hypothesis, integrating sustainable development and construction generates new sustainable construction agendas. Another interaction is between project management and construction through the projects' lifecycle and phases. Finally, the PM processes and knowledge areas were identified as being the most efficient leverage for embracing a sustainable approach.

- These three areas, when approached from a systems thinking point of view, create the resulting centre of the hypothesis; sustainable project management processes for construction projects. Systems thinking, and leverage points theories, act as the catalyst for such integration to take place and generate an efficient impact on the three dimensions of the integration by bringing them together to create a sustainable approach to the PM processes which are used to define the different phases of all construction projects. The impact therefore of such an approach has the potential to inflict a sustainable outcome from initiation to completion.

- The hypothesis has been tested on three separate examples fulfilling the three generated areas before concluding to the centre area of the integration. When examining the Egan agenda, from a systems thinking point of view, the drivers in questions embrace an even wider context to incorporate the triple bottom line guidelines. When investigating the impact of the integration on projects' phases, the procurement model used by the Office of Government Commerce (OGC) illustrates the importance of procurement processes and therefore it represents the best example for testing the hypothesis. Sustainability gaps were identified within the processes and therefore a new approach was introduced to promote a more serious commitment to sustainability which was facilitated by the identification of leverage points within each Gateway Review within the model. The analysis of the incorporation of sustainability guidelines proved to generate an enhanced model driven by the triple bottom line guidelines. For the PMBOK, sustainable development had to be implemented within its fundamental basics in order to ensure a more efficient impact on the overall performance.

- Mapping sustainable development onto project management processes, and knowledge areas, was the final step of examination which led to an extensive study of each process, its lists of Inputs, Tools & Techniques and Outputs. The results of the mapping process identified all the opportunities for introducing the sustainability guidelines into all PM processes in a comprehensive matrix shown in chapter 5 (figure 5.14). The matrix illustrates the processes with four degrees (high – medium – low - none) of relevancy scale in terms of their potential to embrace a sustainability approach with their lists of interactions.

- From the matrix's analysis, it demonstrates that the highest potential, and most efficient leverage points, exist within the early stages of project management such as for example, initiation processes. This does not deny the potential that exists within the other processes but endorses the systems thinking theory of more efficient impact from the early stages rather than the later stages.

- From the questionnaire analysed in chapter 6, PM professionals, practitioners, academics and researchers were given the chance to share their own views on the proposed hypothesis through the online questionnaire made available to a large selection of possible participants. A significant majority of respondents agreed with the hypothesis and indeed chose similar processes as analysed in the matrix shown in figure (5.14), to be the best and most efficient processes, such as initiation and scope planning, to integrate sustainable development guidelines.

- The questionnaire was successful in reinforcing the strength of the hypothesis in terms of its feasibility and efficient impact on the real life projects. The outcome of the arguments in chapter 5 and the results of the questionnaire in chapter 6 compliment each other in significant measures that endorse the proposed hypothesis.

The Way Forward "Recommendations for Further Work"

Expanding Research and Development to Embrace Sustainability

"The process of finding, implementing and improving sustainable development indicators will not be done right at first. Nevertheless, it is urgent to begin"[357]

The main objective of this research was to demonstrate that great potential exists for the project management profession to contribute to a global commitment to sustainable development agendas through its standards. This will underpin the delivery of sustainable processes and projects in all fields and more specifically in the construction industry. The research calls for introducing a sustainable development approach to all project management standards publications worldwide and especially the new version of PMBOK (expected to be published in 2004) should embrace a more serious sustainable agenda as demonstrated by this research.

The built environment could benefit from the involvement of several disciplines in its creation. The construction industry is the main executer of the elements which define the built environment, but the involvement of sustainable development guidelines should not be limited to construction practices or the contribution of project management processes into construction projects, but future work should tackle the other elements which contribute to the built environment such as architecture, commerce, and manufacturing. Further research should look into the progress of these disciplines along the years to reveal different ways of improving their performances. This would ultimately result in a better quality of life which

---

[357] Donella Meadows, *Indicators and Information Systems for Sustainable Development*, The Sustainability Institute (www.sustainabilityinstitute.org), Vermont, USA, 1998, pp.78

does not only rely on the impact of construction but an overall response from the built environment.

In the practice of construction projects, new case studies should be identified to demonstrate the potential benefits which exist in the implementation of sustainable PM guidelines. This research introduced and tested the desired change of SD guidelines into the standards of PM. This change was intended to be introduced to the policies and strategies of practice before heading to the real life projects. The research makes the initial step towards the implementation phase but it is no longer about enforcing new initiatives on the construction sector, and expecting stakeholders to justify their business cases within these regulations. Further research should be done to examine the practical implementation of this research's recommendation on real life case studies. Future work should concentrate on the identification of stakeholders/clients who would be interested in implementation such recommendations on different scales of projects (i.e. large, medium or small scale projects). This would add an additional dimension to the findings to reveal whether or not the scale of the impact of such change in policies would differ in the case of large scale projects from its impact in the case of small scale projects.

Case studies used in this research, such as the OGC procurement model and the PMBOK processes, demonstrated good use of leverage points and efficient means of application. New case studies should represent a platform for the demonstration of positive impacts of such changes in approach on the three levels of sustainability.

Economically, the business case of such case studies should embrace long term profitability rather than the short term success. Socially, all individuals involved, should exemplify the potential of a successful social agenda whether for the employees or end users. Environmentally, where these case studies are taking place is no longer limited by the construction site, an environmental agendas should be included within the financial, marketing and social management aspects.

The research examined the notions of the integration and its possible impact on the initiative of the EU with special focus on the UK's agendas. Further research should consider a global approach to the industry. Therefore, future work should examine the performance of the construction industry in several other countries in order to draw a global strategy for change which could embrace the globalisation agenda.

For developing countries, in the preliminary implementation of sustainable regulatory frameworks, there is a greater opportunity and a more efficient leverage point than in the case of developed economies. For the latter, it is a chance to reshape existing frameworks and disseminating such knowledge to the developing countries. The developing world, paradoxically, has greater prospects for effective change in the application of existing expertise through new frameworks, conceived with sustainability as a key integral component. This contrasts with the difficulties the western hemisphere has in grafting sustainable policy to entrenched methodologies.

Inspired by the most efficient leverage point on Meadows' list; `the power to transcend paradigms`, in the early phases of all new initiatives, there is no right or wrong in proposing solutions to current problems, but the key is to find the appropriate context in which these propositions can be tested. This fortifies the recommendations for future work to be executed on further case studies to examine the real life nature of the proposed change. This would identify the level of benefits gained on each level of the triple bottom line and also highlight the practical possibility of achieving the ultimate goals of change.

This research has proposed a tri-dimensional integration in an effort to enhance construction practices, and thereby improve the impact of projects economically, environmentally and socially while requesting the endorsement and involvement of all stakeholders to generate and sustain a better quality of life for current and future generations worldwide.

BIBLIOGRAPHY

Adams, G. and Schvaneveldt, J., *Understanding Research Methods*, Longman Publications, New York, 1985

Addis, B. and Talbot, Roger D., *Sustainable Construction Procurement*, CIRIA Publications, London, 2001

Akiyama, K. *Function Analysis: Systematic Improvement of Quality and Performance*, Cambridge, MA, Productivity Press, 1991

Allen, Warren E. *Establishing some basic project management body of knowledge concepts*, International Journal of Project Management Vol. 13, No. 2, ELSEVIER Science Ltd., Great Britain, 1995

Archer. G.T. *Sustainable Construction: Targets and Indicators*, CIRIA Publications, London, 2001

Argyris C. & Schön D., *Organizational Learning: A theory of action perspective*, Addison-Wesley Publication, Reading Massachusetts, 1978

Aronson, Daniel. *Introduction to Systems Thinking*, The Thinking Page, Online Publication, 1999

Baker, Scott William. *Risk Management in Major Projects*, PhD thesis, University of Edinburgh, Edinburgh, 1997

Bartelmus, Peter. *Environment, growth and development: the concepts and strategies of sustainability*, Routledge Publishing, London, 1994

Bernstein, Peter L. *Mastering Risk*, Financial Times, U.K, April 25, 2000

Blockley, David and Patrick Godfrey, *Doing It Differently; systems for rethinking construction*, London: Thomas Telford Publishing, 2000

Boersema, Jan J. and Joeri Bertels, *Sustainable Development in the Developed Countries: Will Theory and Practice Meet?*, published in *"Global Sustainable Development in the 21st Century"*, edited by Keekok Lee, Alan Holland and Desmond McNeill, Edinburgh University Press, Edinburgh, 2000

Bouma, G.D. *The Research Process*, Oxford University Press, Australia, 1993

British Prime Minister (Tony Blair), Forward by the Prime Minister for *"A Strategy for Sustainable Development for the United Kingdom"*, Sustainable Development – the UK's government approach – *Achieving a Better Quality of Life*, The Stationery Office, London, 1999

British Research Establishment (BRE), *Environmental Issues in the construction sector, Construction Materials in the Environment*, BRE, London, 1999

Brookfield, H. *Environmental Sustainability with Development: What Prospects for a Research Agenda?*, Frank Cass Publications, London, 1991

Brundtland, Gro Harlem. *Our Common Future and Ten Years after Rio: How Far Have We Come and Where Should We Be Going?* , Article part of the book: *Earth Summit 2002, A New Deal*, (Edited by Felix Dodds), United Nations Environment and Development-UK Committee (UNED-UK), Earthscan Publications Ltd., 2000

Building Research Establishment, MaSC, *Managing Sustainable Construction – Profiting from Sustainability*, Report produced by MaSC Team, first published in 2002 by CRC Ltd, BRE, 2002

Busby, J.S., *An assessment of post-project reviews*, Project Management Journal, PMI Publications, Volume 30, Number 3, 1999

Buttrick, Robert. *Fundamentally Speaking (Part One)*, Project Manager Today, published by Larchdrift Projects Ltd., Volume XIII Issue 9, September 2001

Cavaleri, S.A. & Fearon, D.S., *Systems integration through concurrent learning*, Industrial Management Journal, Volume 36, issue 4, 1994

Clayton, Anthony M H and Nicholas J Radcliffe, *Sustainability: A Systems Approach*, The Institute for Policy Analysis and Development and WWF-UK, Earthscan Publications Limited, UK, London, 1997

Clough, Richard H. *Construction Project Management*, Wiley-Interscience, New York, 1985

Commission of the European Communities, *A Sustainable Europe for a Better World: A European Union Strategy for Sustainable Development; Communication from the Commission to the Gothenburg European Council*, European Union, Brussels, 2001

Commission of the European Communities, *Communication's proposal to the Gothenburg European Council*, European Union, Brussels, 2001

Commission of the European Communities, *Ten Years After Rio: Preparing for the World Summit on Sustainable Development (WSSD)*, Communication from the Commission to the Council and European Parliament, European Union, Brussels, 06 February 2000

Communication from the Commission of the European Parliament, The Council, The Economic and Social Committee and the Committee of the Regions on: *"The Competitiveness of the Construction Industry"*, The European Union Online, Europa

Construction Confederation and CIRIA, *The Towards Sustainable Construction Conference -Building a Better Way of Life*, Conference proceedings, Queen Elizabeth Conference Centre, London, July 2000

Construction Industry Council (CIC), *Construction Project Management Skills*, CIC publications, London, 2000

Construction Research and Innovation Strategy Panel (CRISP), *Integrating Sustainability and "Rethinking Construction"*, Environmental Resources Management (ERM), CRISP, London, 1999

Construction Task Force, *Rethinking Construction*, DETR, London, 1998

Cook, D.L. *Certification of project managers-Fantasy or reality?*, Project Management Quarterly, Volume 8, No.2, PMI publishing, PA, USA, 1977

Cooper, G., Lyneis, J. & Bryant, B., *A clever approach to selecting a knowledge management strategy*, International Journal of Project Management, Volume 20, 2002

Cummings T.G., *Systems theory of organizational development*, Wiley Publications Ltd, New York, 1980

Davenport T.H., *Process Innovation: Reengineering work through information technology*, Harvard Publications, Boston, U.S.A, 1993

Day, Robert M. *Beyond Eco-Efficiency: Sustainability as a Driver for Innovation*, Sustainable Enterprise Perspectives, part of the publications of the World Resources Institute (WRI), March, 1998

De Valence, Gerard and Rick Best (Editors), *Building in Value* (Pre-design Issues), University of Technology, Sydney, Australia, 1999

Department of Environment, Trade and the Regions (DETR), *Opportunities for Change, Sustainable Construction*, (DETR), London, 1998

Department of the Environment, Transport and the Regions, *Building a better quality of life; A strategy for more sustainable construction*, DETR, London, 2000

Department of the Environment, Transport and the Regions, *Construction Research and Innovation Business Plan; Promoting innovation in the construction industry*, London, 1999

Department of the Environment, Transport and the Regions, *Rethinking Construction*, The Construction Task Force, DETR, London, 1998

Department of the Environment, Transport and the Regions, *Sustainable Development Fact sheets; The UK Government's Policy for SD for UK Businesses*, Her Majesty's Stationery Office, (DETR), London, 1999

Department of Trade and Industry (DTI), *A Quick Guide to Value Management*, DTI Publications Online, UK, 1999

Department of Trade and Industry (DTI), *What is Sustainable Development*, DTI Publications, UK, 1998

Department of Trade and Industry *Construction Statistics Annual* 2002 Edition, DTI Online Publication, UK, 2002

Dodds, Felix. *Earth Summit 2002; A New Deal*, Earthscan Publications, London, 2000

Dowd, Kevin. *Beyond Value at Risk: the new science of risk management*, Wiley publications, Chichester, 1998

Drucker, P.F., *Managing in a time of great change*, Truman Talley Ltd., New York, 1995

E, Adam. *Value Management Cost Reduction Strategies for the 1990's*, Melbourne: Longman Professional, 1993

Eid, Mohamed. *A review of "Project Management" & "Sustainable Development" for Construction Projects*, (EAR) Journal, Volume 27, September 2000

Eid, Mohamed. *A Sustainable Approach to the Project Management Odyssey*, PMI Research Conference, Seattle, Washington USA, Contributing paper, conference proceedings, July 2002

Eid, Mohamed and Roger D. Talbot, *Rethinking Project Management; The Business Case for Sustainable Construction*, Project Management Institute (PMI) Conference, contributing paper, Conference Proceedings, London, June 2001

Eid, Mohamed. *Sustainable Management Systems; Embedding Sustainable Development into Project Management Processes*, Sustainable Development Forum, Conference proceedings, Alexandria-Egypt, January 2003

Elkington, John. *Cannibals with Forks; The Triple Bottom Line of 21st Century Business*, Capstone Publishing, Oxford, 1999

Environmental Resources Management Ltd, *Analysis of the responses to the UK Government's consultation paper on Sustainable Development; Opportunities for Change*, the UK Government consultation document in preparation of the UK strategy for SD, London, 1999

European Economic and Social Committee (EESC), *Opinion of the EESC on the Lisbon Strategy and Sustainable Development*, The European Commission, Official Journal of the European Union, Brussels, April 2003

European Union Online, *Towards Sustainability*, European Community Programme of policy and action in relation to the environment and sustainable development, Online Publication Europa, 2000

Fawthrop, Nigel. *Sustainable Construction; Approaches, Drivers and Barriers*, Dissertation for the Degree of Master of Science, Department of Building, Engineering and Surveying, Heriot-Watt University, 1999

Flanagan, R. and G. Norman, *Risk Management and Construction*, Black Well Scientific Publications, 1993

Flood, Robert Louis. *Rethinking The Fifth Discipline; Learning within the unknowable*, London, Routledge – Taylor and Francis Group, 1999

Forrester, Jay W. *Urban Dynamics*, Portland, Productivity Press, 1969

Forrester, Jay W. *World Dynamics*, Portland, Productivity Press, 1971

Fussler Claude. *The Role of Environmental Management Tools, Session 1: The contribution of Business to Sustainable Development; the Views from Stakeholders*, World Business Council for Sustainable Development, Proceedings of International Workshop, the European Commission, Lisbon, 2000

Gardiner, Paul D. *Project Management*, Heriot Watt University Publications, Edinburgh, 1999

Gardner, B.H. & Demello, S., Systems thinking in action, Healthcare Forum Journal, Volume 36, issue 4, 1993

Government Centre for Information Systems (GCIS), *Management of Project Risk*, CCTA, Norwich, U.K, 1994

Grant, R.M., *Toward a knowledge based theory of the firm*, Strategic Management Journal, Volume 17, 1996

Gregersen, Hans M. and Allen L. Lundgren and T. Anderson White, *Improving Project Management for Sustainable Development*, The Environmental and Natural Resources Policy and Training Project (EPAT), EPAT/MUCIA publication by University of Wisconsin, 1994

Griffith, Alan. *Environmental Management in Construction*, Macmillan Publications, Basingstoke, 1994

Hammer M. & Champy J, *Reengineering the corporation: A manifesto for business revolution*, Harper Business School Press, New York, 1993

Hill, J. Towards Good Environmental Practice; a Book of Case Studies, Institute of Business Ethics, London, 1992

Holland, Alan. Sustainable Development: The Contested Vision, Introduction to Global Sustainable Development in the 21st Century, Edinburgh University Press Ltd., Edinburgh, 2000

Holliday, Charles O. and Stephen Schmidheiny and Philip Watts, Walking the Talk; the Business Case for Sustainable Development, Greenleaf Publishing Limited, part of the WBCSD publications, Sheffield, UK, 2002

Hood C.C., D.K.C. Jones, N.F. Pidgeon and B.A. Turner, Risk Management – Risk: Analysis, Perception and Management, Royal Study Group, London, 1992

Hood, Christopher and David K.C. Jones (Editors), Accident and Design Contemporary Debates in Risk Management, UCL Press, London 1996

Institution of Civil Engineers, The organisation of civil engineering work, post-war national development, Report VI, UK, 1944

Institution of Civil Engineers and the Faculty and Institute of Actuaries, Risk Analysis and Management for Projects, Thomas Telford Publications, London, 1998

Intergovernmental Panel on Climate Change (IPCC), Synthesis Report Climate Change 2001, IPCC website publications, 2001

Intergovernmental Panel on climate Change, Third Assessment Report, Climate Change Report 2001, Impacts, adaptation and Vulnerability, IPCC, Geneva 2001

International Council for Research and Innovation in Building and Construction (CIB), Sustainable Development and the Future of Construction, Report Working Group 82, CIB Publication 225, Netherlands, May 1998

International Organisation for standardization. ISO 8402, Quality Management and Quality Assurance, Geneva, Switzerland: ISO Press, 1994

James, Peter. Business, Eco-Efficiency and Sustainable Development, report done for the European Commission, Lisbon, 2000

Kamara J., Anumba C. & Carillo P., *Learning to learn, from past to future*, International Journal of Project Management, Volume 20, 2002

Kuhn, Thomas S. *The Structures of Scientific Revolutions*; International Encyclopaedia of Unified Science, Volume 2-Number 2, The University of Chicago Press, USA, 1970

Langford, D., M. R. Hancock, R. Fellows and A.W. Gale, *Human Resources Management in Construction*, Longman Scientific and Technical Publications, Harlow, 1995

Lee, Keekok and Alan Holland and Desmond McNeil (Editors), *Global Sustainable Development In The Twenty-First Century*, Edinburgh University Press Ltd., Edinburgh, 2000

Leff, Enrique. *Sustainable Development in Developing Countries: Cultural Diversity and Environmental Rationality*, Keekok Lee, Alan Holland and Desmond McNeil (Editors), *Global Sustainable Development in the Twenty-First Century*, Edinburgh University Press Ltd., Edinburgh, 2000

Lock, Dennis. Project Management, Gower Publishing Company Ltd., England, 1981

McNeill, Desmond. *The Concept of Sustainable Development*, Keekok Lee, Alan Holland and Desmond McNeil (Editors), *Global Sustainable Development In The Twenty-First Century*, Edinburgh, Edinburgh University Press Ltd., 2000

Meadows, Donella. *Indicators and Information Systems for Sustainable Development*, The Sustainability Institute, Vermont, USA, 1998

Meadows, Donella. *Leverage Points: Places to Intervene in a System*, The Sustainability Institute, 1999

Miles, L.D. *Techniques in Value Analysis and Engineering*, Value Foundations, USA, 1989

Moore, Meg Mitchell. *Green is Good*, Darwin Magazine, Massachusetts, USA, September 2001

Morris, Peter W.G. *Managing Project Interfaces: Key Points for Project Success*, Project Management Handbook, 2nd ed., Englewood Cliffs, N.J: Prentice-Hall, 1988

Morris, Peter W.G. *Updating the Project Management Bodies of Knowledge*, Project Management Journal Volume 32, Number 3, Pennsylvania-USA, The Professional Journal of the Project Management Institute (PMI), Publishing Division, Pennsylvania, USA, September 2001

Movement for Innovation (M4I), *Sustainability Indicators*, Department of the Environment, Transport and the Regions (DETR), UK, 1999

National Audit Office, *Modernising Construction*, published January 2001

Office of Government Commerce (OGC), *Gateway Review; Leadership Guide*, OGC Best Practise, Published by the OGC, UK, 2003

Office of Government Commerce (OGC), *The Gateway Reviews Procurement Model*, OGC Online Publication, UK, 2003

Official Journal of the European Union, *Opinion of the European Economic and Social Committee on "the Lisbon Strategy and Sustainable Development"*, The European Union Bulletin online, April 2003

Pepper, John and A.G. Lafley, CEO and Chairman's Statement in P&G, *Sustainability Report*, Procter & Gamble, Cincinatti, 2001

Process Quality Associates Inc., *History of Project Management and CCPM*, Online publications, August 2002

Project Management Institute (PMI), A *Guide to the Project Management Body of Knowledge* (PMBOK®Guide2000 Edition), PMI publications, Pennsylvania, USA, 2000

Project Management Institute (PMI), *Construction Extension to A Guide to the Project Management Body of Knowledge* (PMBOK® Guide – 2000 Edition), PMI Publications, Pennsylvania, USA, September 2003

Project Management Institute, *Introduction to the Project Management Institute*, Project Management Institute (PMI) official website, PA, USA

Project Management Institute, *Practice Standard for Earned Value Management*, PMI Online Publication, Pennsylvania, USA

Redclift Michael. *Global Equity: The Environment and Development*, published in *"Global Sustainable Development in the 21st Century"*, edited by Keekok Lee, Alan Holland and Desmond McNeill, Edinburgh University Press, Edinburgh, 2000

Richardson G.P., *Feedback thought in social science and systems theory*, University of Pennsylvania Press, Philadelphia, 1991

Royal Commission on Environmental Pollution (RCEP), *Energy – the Changing Climate*, RCEP, London, 2000

Royal Society Study Group, Risk: Analysis, Perception and Management, Royal Society Publications, London, 1992

Sanders, Norman. Article *"and finally..."*, Project Manager Today, Issue October 2000

Schen, L.Y. *Application of Risk Management to the Chinese Construction Industry*, PhD Thesis, University of Reading, U.K, 1990

Schen, L.Y. *Building in Value* (Pre-design Issues), New York, 1999

Senge, Peter. *The Fifth Discipline Field book; Strategies and Tools for building a Learning Organization*, London, Nicholas Brealey Publishing Limited, 1999

Senge, Peter. *The Fifth Discipline; the Art & Practice of the Learning Organization*, London, Random House Business Books, 1999

SIGMA Project Website, *The SIGMA Project Guidelines*, Online publication, Pilot Draft, May 2001

Smith, M. K. *Peter Senge and the learning organization, the encyclopaedia of informal education*, Online Publication, 2001

Sneider, Keith f. & Nissen, Mark E., *Beyond the Body of Knowledge: Knowledge-Flow approach to Project Management Theory and Practice*, Project Management Journal, PMI Publications, Volume 34, Number 2, Pennsylvania, 2003

Spender J.C., *Making Knowledge the basis of a dynamic theory of the firm*, Strategic Management Journal, Volume 17, 1996

Stretton A., *Australian competency standards*, International Journal of Project Management, Volume 13, Issue 2, 1995

Sustainable Development International, *Strategies and Technologies for Agenda 21 Implementation*, ICG Publishing, London, 2001

Taylor, Malcolm and H. Hosker, *Quality Assurance for Building Design*, Longman Scientific & Technical Publications, Harlow, 1992

Thompson, P. and J. Perry, *Engineering Construction Risks: A Guide to project Risk Analysis and Assessment Implications for projects Clients and Project Managers*, Telford Publications, 1992

Thomson, I. and Roger D. Talbot, *New Business, New Scotland; Foundations for a Sustainable Scottish Economy*, Scottish Borders Enterprise, Scotland, 1998

Thorpe, Brian and Peter Sumner and John Duncan, *Quality Assurance in Construction*, Gower, Aldershot, 1996

Tull, Donald Stanley and Del I. Hawkins, *Marketing Research-Measurement and Method*, 5th edition, Maxwell Macmillan International Editions, London, 1990

UK Government's Policy for SD, *A Better Quality of Life; Sustainable Development – the UK's Government Approach*, The Stationery Office, London, 1999

United Nations Conference on Environment and Development, *Rio Summit*, Conference proceedings, United Nations Publications online, Istanbul, 1992

United Nations Environmental Programme (UNEP), *Global Environmental Outlook 2000*, UNEP GEO, Nairobi, 2000

United Nations Second conference on Human Settlements, *Habitat II*, United Nations Publications online, Istanbul, 1996

Walker, Anthony. *Project Management in Construction*, Granada Publishing, London, 1984

Wideman, R Max. *Criteria for a project management body of knowledge*, International Journal of Project Management, Volume 13, Number 2, ELSEVIER Science publishing, Great Britain, 1995

Wilson, B., *Systems: Concepts, Methodologies and Applications*, Wiley Publications Ltd., New York, 1984

Wirth, I. & Tryloff, D., *Preliminary comparison of six efforts to document the project management body of knowledge*, International Journal of Project Management, Volume 13, 1995

Wolstenholme, E. & Stevenson, R., *Systems thinking & systems modelling; New perspectives on business strategy & process design*, Management Services Journal, Volume 39, issue 2, 1994

World Business Council for Sustainable Development (WBCSD), *Eco-efficiency; creating more value with less impact*, WBCSD publications, Switzerland, October 2000

World Business Council for Sustainable Development (WBCSD), *Eco-efficient Leadership; for Improved Economic and Environmental Performance*, WBCSD core publications, 1996

World Business Council for Sustainable Development (WBCSD), *The Business Case for Sustainable Development; Making a difference toward the Johannesburg Summit 2002 and beyond*, World Business Council for Sustainable Development, Switzerland, 2002

World Commission on Environment and Development (WCED), *Our Common Future*, also known as (The Brundtland Report), United Nations Environment Programme (UNEP) Press, U.S.A, 1987

World Summit on Sustainable Development (WSSD), *Plan of Implementation*, Johannesburg, United Nations Earth Summit 2002

ELECTRONIC BIBLIOGRAPHY

Association for Project Management www.apm.org.uk

Australian Institute of Project Management http://www.aipm.com.au

Building Research Establishment *"Profiting from Sustainability"* Report http://projects.bre.co.uk/masc/index.html

CALIBRE – Performance Measuring Toolkit http://www.calibre2000.com/

Centre for Building Services Technology and Information www.bsria.co.uk

Centre for Business Practices http://www.cbponline.com/

Centre for Global Reporting Initiative www.globalreporting.org

Centre for Sustainable and Environmental Management www.csem.org.uk

Commission for Architecture and the Built Environment www.cabe.org.uk

Construction Best Practice Programme www.cbpp.org.uk

Construction Industry Research and Information Association www.ciria.org.uk

Construction Mall www.constructionmall.co.uk

Construction Research and Innovation Strategy Panel www.crisp-uk.org.uk

Construction Research Organisations www.construction.co.uk

Construction Statistics Annual http://www.dti.gov.uk/construction/stats/csa.htm

Darwin Magazine Online *"Green is Good"* Article http://www.darwinmag.com/read/090101/green.html

311

Department for Environment, Food and Rural Affairs – Sustainable Development Unit *"Achieving a Better Quality of Life"* Report http://www.sustainable-development.gov.uk/index.htm

Department for Environment, Food and Rural Affairs – Sustainable Development Unit *"Opportunities for Change"* Report http://www.sustainable-development.gov.uk/consult/construction/index.htm

Department for Environment, Food and Rural Affairs – Sustainable Development Unit – Facts Sheets http://www.sustainable-development.gov.uk/uk_strategy/factsheets/ukbus/index.htm

Department for Environment, Food and Rural Affairs www.defra.gov.uk

Department of Trade and Industry – UK Sustainable Development Strategy http://www.dti.gov.uk/sustainability/strategy/2.htm

Department of Trade and Industry – UK www.dti.gov.uk

Department of Trade and Industry *"Rethinking Construction"* http://www.dti.gov.uk/construction/rethink/report/index.htm

Department of Trade and Industry *"Value Management"* http://www.dti.gov.uk/mbp/bpgt/m9bd13001/m9bd130011.html

Dow Jones Sustainability Indexes www.sustainability-index.com

Earth Council Online – Learning Centre for Sustainable Development www.learnsd.org

Earth Technologies Forum http://www.earthforum.com/

Engineering Project Management Forum http://www.iee.org.uk/EPMF

Environmental and Natural Resources Policy and Training Projects www.wisc.edu/epat

European Commission's Communication on the Competitiveness of the EU Construction Industry http://europa.eu.int/comm/enterprise/construction/compcom/compcom.htm

European Construction Industry
http://europa.eu.int/comm/enterprise/construction/

European Construction Network www.connet.org

European Education Training and Image of the Construction Industry
http://europa.eu.int/comm/enterprise/construction/educim/educan1.htm

European Union Online – European Sustainable Development Strategy
http://europa.eu.int/comm/sustainable/index_en.htm
http://europa.eu.int/comm/environment/eussd/

European Union Online – The Amsterdam Treaty
http://europa.eu.int/scadplus/leg/en/lvb/a15000.htm

European Union Online – The Fifth EU Community Environmental Action
Programme http://europa.eu.int/comm/environment/actionpr.htm

European Union Online   www.europa.eu.int

Fédération de L'industrie Européenne de la Construction www.fiec.org

Global Hub for Carbon Commerce http://www.co2e.com/

Global Resource Action Centre for the Environment www.gracelinks.org

Her Majesty's Treasury – UK www.hm-treasury.gov.uk

Institution of Civil Engineers www.ice.org.uk

Intergovernmental Panel on Climate Change – Climate change graphical
Representations http://www.ipcc.ch/present/graphics.htm

Intergovernmental Panel on Climate Change www.ipcc.ch

International Consultancy in Business Strategy and Sustainable Development
www.sustainability.com

International Cost Engineering Council http://www.icoste.org

International Council for Local Environmental Initiatives – Local Agenda 21
http://www.iclei.org/ICLEI/la21.htm

International Council for Local Environmental Initiatives
www.iclei.org/SB1.HTM

International Council for Research and Innovation in Building &
Construction www.cibworld.nl

International Institute for Sustainable Development www.iisd.org

International Journal of Project Management
http://www.elsevier.com/locate/issn/02637863

International Organisation for Standardisation www.iso.org

International Project Management Association http://www.ipma.ch

Movement for Innovation – Publications
http://www.m4i.org.uk/m4i/publications/reports.asp

Movement for Innovation www.m4i.org.uk

Office of Government Commerce *"Achieving Excellence in Construction"*
http://www.ogc.gov.uk/sdtoolkit/reference/achieving/achievin.html

Office of Government Commerce *"Gateway Process"* www.ogc.gov.uk

Process Quality Associates *"History of Project Management"*
http://www.pqa.net/ccpm/W05002001.html

Project Development Disciplines http://members.aol.com/AllenWeb/

Project Management Institute – Research Survey Links
http://www.pmi.org/info/PP_ResearchSurveyLinks.asp

Project Management Institute – Students of Project Management Survey
Links http://www.studentsofpm.org/Surveys.htm

Project Management Institute – UK Chapter http://www.pmi.org.uk/

314

Project Management Institute *"Practice Standard for Earned Value Management"* http://www.pmi.org/prod/groups/public/documents/info/pp_practicestandardforevm.asp

Project Management Institute www.pmi.org

Project Management Specific Interest Group – Survey Links http://www.pmsigcentral.org/Surveys.htm

Project Sigma www.projectsigma.com

Rethinking Construction in Scotland http://www.pullingtogether.co.uk/

Sustainability Institute http://sustainer.org/resources.html www.sustainabilityinstitute.org

Sustainable Architecture – Resources http://www1.arch.hku.hk/research/BEER/sustain.htm

Sustainable Development Indicators for Scotland http://www.scotland.gov.uk/library5/environment/sdin-00.asp

Sustainable Development International www.sustdev.org

Systems Thinking – Peter Senge www.infed.org/thinkers/senge.htm

Systems Thinking – Resources http://www.thinking.net/Systems_Thinking/systems_thinking.html

Thinking Page www.thinking.net

UK National Audit Office www.nao.gov.uk

UK Trade & Investment http://www.tradepartners.gov.uk/

United Nations Conference – World Summit of Sustainable Development www.johannesburgsummit.org

United Nations Conference on Environment and Development http://www.un.org/geninfo/bp/enviro.html

United Nations Conference on Human Settlements
http://www.un.org/Conferences/habitat/

United Nations Department of Economic and Social Affairs – Sustainability
Indicators http://www.un.org/esa/sustdev/natlinfo/indicators/isd.htm

United Nations Development Programme – Clean Development Mechanism
www.cdm-connect.org

United Nations Development Programme www.undp.org

United Nations Environment Programme – Construction Sector Report
http://www.uneptie.org/outreach/wssd/contributions/sector_reports/sectors/
construction/construction.htm

United Nations Environment Programme Finance Initiatives
http://www.unepfi.net/

United Nations Environment Programme www.unep.org

United Nations www.un.org/

World Business Council for Sustainable Development www.wbcsd.org

The World Conservation Union "Caring for the Earth"
http://www.ciesin.org/IC/iucn/CaringDS.html

World Resources institute http://www.wri.org/wri/meb/sei/beyond.html

World View of Global Warming
http://www.worldviewofglobalwarming.org/

World Wide Web Virtual Library – Sustainable Development Resources
http://www.ulb.ac.be/ceese/meta/sustvl.html

Appendix 1: RISK MANAGEMENT

APPENDIX 1

RISK MANAGEMENT

"Risk Management" within the Construction's Culture

"Risk is ubiquitous and no human activity can be considered risk free."[358]

Risks depend on the uncertainties of the future and their potential consequences. Individuals routinely accept 'risks' and take measures to minimise them in our daily activities. This can be defined as a simple form of `Risk Management`.

In the construction industry, whether on small scale or major projects, Risk Management has different dimensions and is dealt with in cautious, studied and organised steps. The importance of Risk Management in the construction industry has been growing and showing dramatic increase in affecting decision making in small scale and major projects. This growing interest is probably justified by the increases in technology, tighter financial constraints, the augmented number of larger and more complex projects, public demands to decrease risk and improve safety and finally, the increase in time and costs overruns.

Figure (1) defines Risk Management and its different steps and identifies the way the construction industry is currently dealing with this process.

---

[358] C.C. Hood, D.K.C. Jones, N.F. Pidgeon, B.A. Turner, Risk Management – Risk: Analysis, Perception and Management, Royal Study Group, London, 1992

318

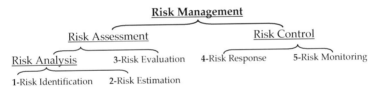

Risk Management

Risk Assessment   Risk Control

Risk Analysis   3-Risk Evaluation   4-Risk Response   5-Risk Monitoring

1-Risk Identification   2-Risk Estimation

Figure (1) the Risk Management Framework [359]

The outcome of the five steps identified in figure (1) should be a `Controlled Risk Environment` in which those steps should be working in a continuous loop to retain a sustainable system.

"Human beings will continue to interact, make choices and respond to those choices in unpredictable ways that are the ultimate sources of uncertainties. This is where the heart of risk management lies." [360]

For the construction industry, as for all other fields dealing with risk management, there are three basic elements which should apply to this system as with any other controlled system; goal setting (whether explicit or implicit), information gathering and interpretation and actions to influence human behaviour or modify physical structures or both. [361]

"Virtually anything that people do has some degree of risk attached, whether it is something that is inherently dangerous in a physical sense or something that carries a risk of financial loss. People carry out simple forms of risk analysis in their daily lives when deciding. What we are doing when making such decision is actually risk management, we identify the costs and benefits associated with alternative choices, assess the likelihood of those costs and benefits being realised, and make a balanced

---

[359] Scott William Baker, *Risk Management in Major Projects*, PhD thesis, University of Edinburgh, Edinburgh, 1997
[360] Peter L. Bernstein, Mastering Risk, Financial Times, U.K, April 25, 2000
[361] Christopher Hood 7 David K.C. Jones (Editors), *Accident and Design Contemporary Debates in Risk Management*, UCL Press, London 1996

decision on the basis of our analysis.

Risk Management does not eliminate risk, but it does offer decision-makers a range of tools for identifying and assessing risk. Clients can select those tools, which are most appropriate to their particular project, with respect to other factors such as their general attitude to risk and prevailing economic conditions."[362]

By its very nature the construction industry is considered to be subject to more risks than other industries. Getting a project from the initial investment appraisal stage, to completion and into use, involves a complex and time-consuming process. A variety of unexpected events may occur during the process of building procurement and many can cause losses to the client or other interested parties - these events are commonly called risks. The principle of risk management is widely used in the construction industry and applied at various stages during the procurement process as well as in general processes. Proper application of risk management techniques can significantly improve the investment performance of construction projects.

"In particular, it is widely accepted that risk management is most valuable during the initial appraisal phase as, at this stage, a great deal of flexibility in both design and planning remains and that allows consideration of ways in which various risks might be avoided or controlled."[363]

It is at this stage, however, that there is the greatest degree of uncertainty about the future, yet the client must make decisions about such fundamental concerns as the investment budget, the size and quality of the project, financing strategies and so forth. Risk management techniques can be an

---

[362] L.Y. Shen, Building in Value (Pre-design Issues), New York, 1999
[363] P. Thompson & J. Perry, *Engineering Construction Risks: A Guide to project Risk Analysis and Assessment Implications for projects Clients and Project Managers*, Telford Publications, 1992

effective tool which clients can use to assist them in making allowance for future uncertainties.[364] Consequently, the clients can be more confident in their decision-making as they have information which identifies possible uncertainties and their likely impact on a potential project.

The proper application of risk management methods can also improve the effectiveness of other project management techniques. Risk analysis can improve the accuracy of the project's cash flow analysis by assessing, properly and systematically, the future uncertainties and risks.

The clients can make their decision to invest in a project on the basis of achieving the greatest value for money. It is during the initial project appraisal stage that the client will try to establish project parameters which will ensure that he/she realises this basic aim. At the very least, they want to be certain that the potential returns from the project will balance the risks. If a project proposal includes a risk profile for various investment options this will be of great benefit to the clients in appraising the proposal, giving information such as the likely outcomes of all possible risks in case they occur.[365]

The analysis of risks during the initial project appraisal stage enables the client to make two important decisions; the first decision is whether to invest in a project, or reject it. This is clearly the most important decision as it determines whether the project proceeds at all. This decision will be based on

[364] The Government Centre for Information Systems (GCIS), Management of Project Risk, CCTA, Norwich, U.K, 1994
[365] Mohamed Eid, A review of "Project Management" & "Sustainable Development" for Construction Projects, (EAR) Journal, Volume 27, September 2000

the constructive analysis and evaluation of potential risks such as technical, economic, financial, political and legal. The second decision is the nature of the project objectives; the clients must decide their objectives in terms of budget, time scale, function, return on investment, and quality standards. These will be based on the client's investment expectations and their evaluation of various alternative investment options where such evaluation depends on projections of performance, cost and schedule with in-depth risk analysis carried out on those projections.[366]

The concept of risk is related to the activities that flow from decisions made by the clients where the outcomes of those activities may differ from expectations. These differences are the result of uncertainties that are inherent in the information on which the client bases his or her decision-making. This information includes historical data, predictions of the future and the decision maker's subjective judgement and, therefore, by its very nature displays degrees of uncertainty.

Broadly, risk, as it applies to building, can be defined as the possible occurrence of an uncertain event or outcome which, should it occur, will cause significant variation or consequences such as extra cost or delayed completion. Thus, the typical risks in a construction project include cost and time overruns as well as poor quality.[367]

These typical risks indicate the consequences commonly referred to as risk

---

[366] P. Thompson & J. Perry, *Engineering Construction Risks: A Guide to project Risk Analysis and Assessment Implications for projects Clients and Project Managers*, Telford Publications, 1992
[367] C.C. Hood, D.K.C. Jones, N.F. Pidgeon, B.A. Turner, Risk Management – Risk: Analysis, Perception and Management, Royal Study Group, London, 1992

effects, which are the result of possible occurrences called risk causes or risk factors.

Flanagan and Norman identify the risk factors which may affect construction projects as including[368]: -

- Failure to obtain approvals from relevant authorities within the time allowed in the project program.
- Unforeseen adverse ground conditions.
- Inclement weather resulting in delays.
- Industrial action.
- Unexpected price rises.
- Failure to let.
- Accidents on site resulting in injury or death, causing delays and/or extra costs.
- Latent defects due to poor workmanship or inadequate supervision.
- *Force majeure.*
- Late production of design information leading to claims by the contractor for loss or expense.
- Labour, material and/or equipment shortages.
- Disputes between project parties causing extra cost and/or project delays.

Generally, if these risks occur, it will result in financial loss to the client and often to other team members. Clients' advisers at the initial project appraisal stage are expected to be able to identify all possible risk causes, to analyse their implications for the project and to develop a risk management strategy to assist their clients in their evaluation of project proposals. The nature and

---

[368] R. Flanagan and G. Norman, *Risk Management and Construction*, Black Well Scientific Publications, 1993

identification of risk displays three attributes. Firstly, a range of possible outcomes are considered; the optimistic outcome, the pessimistic outcome and the most likely outcome. All the possible outcomes may be in discrete or continuous distribution, however, only one possible outcome in the range will actually happen. Secondly, the individual consequences of each possible outcome can be assessed and thirdly the probability of the occurrence of each outcome can be assessed and allocated.[369]

Obviously the decision maker's subjective judgement will have a significant effect on the assessment of the nature of risks. In general, those risks with lower probability of occurrence will have greater impact on a project while those with higher probability of occurrence will have smaller impact.

The earlier that the client recognises the nature of the risks involved with a project the more confident he or she will be about his or her chosen investment option.

Risk analysis not only assists clients in decision-making but also provides other parties involved in the project, such as the contractor, with an appropriate framework for managing and responding to risk. It allows construction managers to identify not only the risk allocated to him or her in the contract but also those risks inherent in the nature of the construction work. A better understanding of the forward risk situation can improve decision-making for all project participants.

Risk identification is a diagnostic process in which all the potential risks that

---

[369] L.Y. Schen, Application of Risk Management to the Chinese Construction Industry, PhD Thesis, University of Reading, U.K, 1990

could affect a construction project are identified and investigated, thus, enabling the client to understand the potential risk sources at an early stage in the project.

Risk can be broadly grouped into the following categories[370]: -

Business risk: indicates the probability that the expected level of investment return will not be achieved.

Pure risk: (static risk, non-market risk or unsystematic risk) is related to physical and technical causes. Subsequent losses occur at random and are beyond the control of the decision-maker.

Speculative risk: (dynamic risk, market risk or systematic risk) involves the possibility of either gain or loss should an uncertain event occur. These risks can cause variations in project development cost, operating cost or the value of built property, thus, changing the rate of investment return.

Financial risks: relates to the loss of financial capital and increase whenever the amount of debts or related charges increases.

A number of techniques have been developed for risk identification where the most common method involves compiling a list of risks for a particular project based on records of past projects as in project historical data.

Risk analysis is used to evaluate risk quantitatively and to ascertain the importance of each risk based on an assessment of the probability and

---

[370] ibid.

possible consequences of its occurrence. It assesses both the effects of individual risks and the combined consequences of all the risks on the project objectives. The major purpose of risk analysis is to provide a project risk profile that the client can use to look ahead at possible events and assess the probability of them occurring. The most common actions in risk management include avoiding risks, transferring risks to other parties and minimising the effects of those retained should they occur.[371]

During the early stages of a project the client may take preventative action to reduce, avoid or transfer risks. Rejecting a proposal is an obvious way of avoiding risk; however, if the client wishes to proceed with a project then risks should be reduced wherever possible.

[371] P. Thompson & J. Perry, *Engineering Construction Risks: A Guide to project Risk Analysis and Assessment Implications for projects Clients and Project Managers*, Telford Publications, 1992

Appendix 2: PMI & the PM Knowledge Areas

APPENDIX 2

INTRODUCTION TO THE PROJECT MANAGEMENT INSTITUTE & THE PM KNOWLEDGE AREAS

The appendix comprises two sections; Section I is an introduction to the history of the Project Management Institute (PMI) to demonstrate its leadership among project management institutions worldwide. The brief history provided below is an extract of the official website of PMI (www.pmi.org).

Section II represents fundamental extracts from the PMBOK (2000 Edition) as well as the Construction Extension to the PMBOK; the PM knowledge areas. This section is a combination of the knowledge areas provided in both documents. The background information of these knowledge areas are extracts from both publications including the introduction of each knowledge area and its corresponding processes preceding each figure.

Section I: The History of the Project Management Institute

Established in 1969 and headquartered outside Philadelphia, Pennsylvania USA, the Project Management Institute (PMI) is the world's leading not-for-profit project management professional association, with over 125,000 members worldwide. It was founded by five volunteers. The Commonwealth of Pennsylvania USA issued Articles of Incorporation for PMI which signified the official inception of the organization.

In the 1970s the first issue of Project Management Quarterly (PMQ) was published and later renamed Project Management Journal® (PMJ). The first Annual Seminars & Symposium was held outside of the USA, the first PMI Chapter was chartered and the PMI Professional Awards Program was established. By the end of the decade PMI membership totalled over 2,000 individuals worldwide.

During the 1980s, PMI's membership, programs and services continued to grow. A Code of Ethics was adopted for the profession and the first Project Management Professional (PMP®) Certification examination was administered. The first PMI project management standard was published as the PMQ Special Report on Ethics Standards and Accreditation. PMI's publishing products and services also grew rapidly during this decade. The first PMI book was co-published and PM Network®, PMI's monthly magazine was born. Due to this growth, the PMI Publishing Division was established in North Carolina USA.

By 1990, PMI's membership totalled over 8,500 and by 1993 the annual membership growth rate rose to over 20 percent per year. During the 1990s,

Specific Interest Groups and Colleges were formed and Seminars USA, a series of educational programs on project management was initiated (later renamed World Seminars). PMI also established a presence on the World Wide Web and published the project management standard, A Guide to the Project Management Body of Knowledge (PMBOK® Guide). PMI Today®, PMI's monthly newsletter was printed for the first time and the Professional Development Program (PDP) was established for PMP certificate holders to maintain their credential.

By the beginning of the 21st century, PMI had over 50,000 members, over 10,000 certified Project Management Professionals and over 270,000 copies of the PMBOK® Guide in circulation.

Currently, PMI supports over 125,000 members in 140 countries worldwide. PMI members are individuals practicing and studying project management in many different industry areas, including aerospace, automotive, business management, construction, engineering, financial services, information technology, pharmaceuticals and telecommunications.

Over time, PMI has become, and continues to be, the leading professional association in project management. Members and project management stakeholders can take advantage of the extensive products and services offered through PMI.

Professional Standards

PMI provides global leadership in the development of standards for the practice of the project management profession throughout the world. PMI's premiere standards document, A Guide to the Project Management Body of Knowledge (PMBOK® Guide), is a globally recognized standard for managing projects in today's marketplace.

The PMBOK® Guide is approved as an American National Standard (ANS) by the American National Standards Institute (ANSI).

Certification

Since 1984 PMI has been dedicated to developing and maintaining a rigorous, examination-based, professional certification program to advance the project management profession and to recognize the achievements of individuals in project management. PMI's Project Management Professional (PMP®) certification is the world's most recognized professional credential for individuals associated with project management.

In 1999, PMI became the first organization in the world to have its Certification Program attain International Organization for Standardization (ISO) 9001 recognition.

Research

PMI is focused on the expansion of the body of knowledge of the project management profession. Project management research is encouraged through a biennial project management research conference, external research grants, research books, a research database and identification of research topics. Additionally, current needs, information, knowledge and wisdom about the profession are collected and disseminated, the future of the profession is assessed and the evolution of the profession is encouraged.

Publications

PMI produces three periodical publications for the benefit of individuals in project management. PM Network® is a monthly professional magazine, Project Management Journal® is a quarterly professional journal and PMI Today® is the monthly newsletter of PMI.

PMI is the world's leading publisher of project management books, training tools, and learning products.

With the help of eight language teams, consisting of 10-35 project management professionals, translators, editors and proofreaders, PMI has released eight official translations in Mandarin Chinese, Spanish, Brazilian Portuguese, Japanese, Italian, German, French and Korean.

These new PMI translations have standardized the glossary and terminology for speakers of these eight target languages and will help global participants excel in future testing. Each easy-to-use translation is of the highest quality and is consistent with the content of the English language PMBOK® Guide– 2000 Edition.

Section II: The Project Management Knowledge Areas

The knowledge areas describe project management knowledge and practice in terms of their component processes. The component processes function on the basis of their list of inputs, tools & techniques and outputs.

The following demonstration of the PMBOK analysis of the knowledge areas and their component processes is essential to the reader of this research as it represents a crucial reading to comprehend the impact of the arguments provided by this research.

First, the nine knowledge areas from the PMBOK (2000 Edition) are presented, and then followed by the examination of the four additional knowledge areas provided by the construction extension to PMBOK. The new publication `Construction Extension to PMBOK` has particularly enhanced the original list of nine knowledge areas in terms of their component lists and provided the new four areas to illustrate the unique aspects applicable to the construction industry.

In the following illustrating figures extracted from the PMBOK, the additional processes to the original lists of PMBOK 2000 Edition are highlighted in bold font.

Project Integration Management

"It involves making tradeoffs among competing objectives and alternatives to meet or exceed stakeholder needs and expectations."[372]

This knowledge area is based on the function of three component processes:-[373]

- **Project Plan Development:** - integrating and coordinating all project plans to create a consistent, coherent document.

- **Project Plan Execution:** - carrying out the project plan by performing the activities included therein.

- **Integrated Change Control:** - coordinating changes across the entire project.

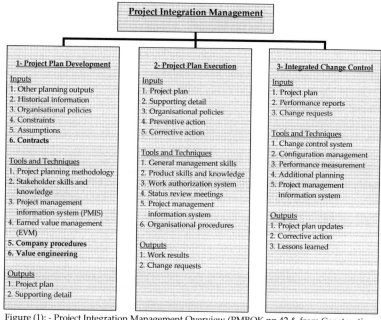

Figure (1): - Project Integration Management Overview (PMBOK pp.42 & from Construction Extension pp. 20 Bold Font)

---

[372] Project Management Institute (PMI), *A Guide to the Project Management Body of Knowledge (PMBOK® Guide)*, Newtown Square, Pennsylvania USA, 2000 Edition, pp.41
[373] ibid.

334

Project Scope Management

"It is primarily concerned with defining and controlling what is or is not included in the project."[374]

Project Scope Management includes: -[375]

- **Initiation:** - authorizing the project or phase.
- **Scope Planning:** - developing a written scope statement as the basis for future project decisions.
- **Scope Definition:** - subdividing the major project deliverables into smaller, more manageable components
- **Scope Verification:** - formalising acceptance of the project scope.
- **Scope Change Control:** - controlling changes to project scope.

---

[374] ibid. pp.51
[375] ibid.

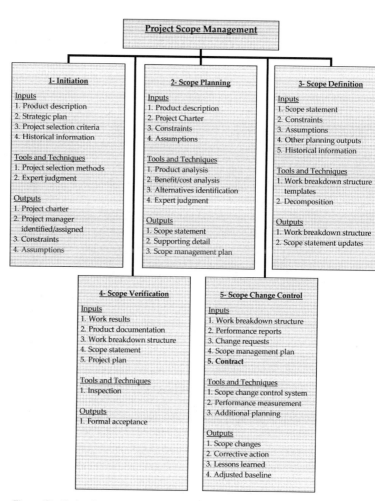

Figure (2): - Project Scope Management Overview (PMBOK pp.52 in & from Construction Extension pp. 31 in **Bold** Font)

336

Project Time Management

In developing the project time schedule, the component processes are: [376]

- **Activity Definition:** - identifying the specific activities that must be performed to produce the various project deliverables.

- **Activity Sequencing:** - indemnifying and documenting interactivity dependencies.

- **Activity Duration Estimating:** - estimating the number of work periods that will be needed to complete individual activities.

- **Schedule Development:** - analysing activity sequences, durations and resource requirements to create the project schedule.

- **Schedule Control:** - controlling changes to the project schedule.

And from the Construction Extension to PMBOK, the following processes have been added to the original list: [377]

- **Activity Weights definition:** - determining the relative and absolute weights for each project activity.

- **Progress curves development:** - Analysing activity weights and project schedule to create progress curves.

- **Progress monitoring:** - Monitoring project progress.

---

[376] ibid. pp.65
[377] Project Management Institute (PMI), Construction Extension to *A Guide to the Project Management Body of Knowledge (PMBOK® Guide- 2000 Edition)*, Newtown Square, Pennsylvania USA, 2003, pp.33

Project Time Management		

1- Activity Definition

Inputs
1. Work breakdown structure
2. Scope statement
3. Historical information
4. Constraints
5. Assumptions
6. Expert judgment

Tools and Techniques
1. Decomposition
2. Templates
3. **Concurrent engineering**

Outputs
1. Activity list
2. Supporting detail
3. Work breakdown structure updates

2- Activity Sequencing

Inputs
1. Activity list
2. Product description
3. Mandatory dependencies
4. Discretionary dependencies
5. **External dependencies**
6. **Constraints**
7. **Assumptions**

Tools and Techniques
1. Precedence diagramming method (PDM)
2. Arrow diagramming method (ADM)
3. Conditional diagramming methods
4. Network templates

Outputs
1. Project network diagrams
2. Activity list updates

3- Activity Duration Estimating

Inputs
1. Activity list
2. Constraints
3. Assumptions
4. Resource requirements
5. Resource capabilities
6. Historical information
7. Identified risks

Tools and Techniques
1. Expert judgment
2. Analogous estimating
3. Quantitatively based duration
4. Reserve time (contingency)

Outputs
1. Activity duration estimates
2. Basis of estimates
3. Activity list updates

4- Schedule Development

Inputs
1. Project network diagrams
2. Activity durations estimates
3. Resource requirements
4. Resource pool description
5. Calendars
6. Constraints
7. Assumptions
8. Leads and lags
9. Risk management plan
10. Activity attributes

Tools and Techniques
1. Mathematical analysis
2. Duration compression
3. Simulation
4. Resource levelling heuristics
5. Project management software
6. Coding structure

Outputs
1. Project schedule
2. Supporting detail
3. Schedule management plan
4. Resource requirement updates

5- Schedule Control

Inputs
1. Project schedule
2. Performance reports
3. Change requests
4. Schedule management plan
5. **Progress monitoring curves**

Tools and Techniques
1. Schedule change control system
2. Performance measurement
3. Additional planning
4. Project management software
5. Variance analysis

Outputs
1. Schedule updates
2. Corrective action
3. Lessons learned
4. **Progress curves updates**

6- Activity Weights Definition

Inputs
1. **Work breakdown structure**
2. **Activity attributes**

Tools and Techniques
1. **Expert judgement**
2. **Percentage calculation**

Outputs
1. **Relative weights**
2. **Absolute weights**

7- Progress Curves Development

Inputs
1. **Relative weights**
2. **Absolute weights**
3. **Project schedule**
4. **Weights distribution standard curves**

Tools & Techniques
1. **Mathematical analysis**
2. **Project management software**

Outputs
1. **Progress curves**
2. **Progress curves management plan**

8- Progress Monitoring

Inputs
1. **Progress curves**
2. **Work results**
3. **Schedule monitoring**

Tools & Techniques
1. **Progress curves development**
2. **Progress measurement criteria**
3. **Progress curve analysis**

Outputs
1. **Actual progress**
2. **Progress monitoring curves**
3. **Schedule updates**
4. **Corrective action**
5. **Lessons learned**

Figure (3): - Project Time Management (PMBOK & in **bold** from Construction Extension)

338

Project Cost Management

It comprises the following component processes: -[378]

- **Resource Planning:** - determining the resources and the quantities which should be used to perform project activities.

- **Cost Estimating:** - developing an estimate of the costs of the resources needed to complete project activities.

- **Cost Budgeting:** - allocating the overall cost estimate to individual work activities.

- **Cost Control:** - controlling changes to the project budget.

---

[378] Project Management Institute (PMI), *A Guide to the Project Management Body of Knowledge (PMBOK® Guide)*, Newtown Square, Pennsylvania USA, 2000 Edition, pp.83

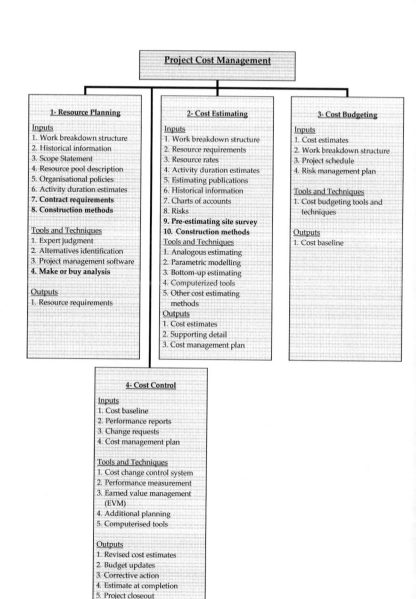

Project Cost Management

1- Resource Planning

Inputs
1. Work breakdown structure
2. Historical information
3. Scope Statement
4. Resource pool description
5. Organisational policies
6. Activity duration estimates
7. Contract requirements
8. Construction methods

Tools and Techniques
1. Expert judgment
2. Alternatives identification
3. Project management software
4. Make or buy analysis

Outputs
1. Resource requirements

2- Cost Estimating

Inputs
1. Work breakdown structure
2. Resource requirements
3. Resource rates
4. Activity duration estimates
5. Estimating publications
6. Historical information
7. Charts of accounts
8. Risks
9. Pre-estimating site survey
10. Construction methods
Tools and Techniques
1. Analogous estimating
2. Parametric modelling
3. Bottom-up estimating
4. Computerized tools
5. Other cost estimating
   methods
Outputs
1. Cost estimates
2. Supporting detail
3. Cost management plan

3- Cost Budgeting

Inputs
1. Cost estimates
2. Work breakdown structure
3. Project schedule
4. Risk management plan

Tools and Techniques
1. Cost budgeting tools and
   techniques

Outputs
1. Cost baseline

4- Cost Control

Inputs
1. Cost baseline
2. Performance reports
3. Change requests
4. Cost management plan

Tools and Techniques
1. Cost change control system
2. Performance measurement
3. Earned value management
   (EVM)
4. Additional planning
5. Computerised tools

Outputs
1. Revised cost estimates
2. Budget updates
3. Corrective action
4. Estimate at completion
5. Project closeout
6. Lessons Learned

Figure (4): - Project Cost Management Overview (PMBOK pp.84 & from the Construction
Extension pp. 45 in **Bold** Font)

340

Project Quality Management

"It includes all activities of the overall management function that determine the quality policy, objectives, and responsibilities and implements them by means such as quality planning, quality assurance, quality control, and quality improvement, within the quality system."[379]

The major project quality management component processes are: -[380]

- **Quality Planning:** - identifying which quality standards are relevant to the project and determining how to satisfy them.

- **Quality Assurance:** - evaluating overall project performance on a regular basis to provide confidence that the project will satisfy the relevant quality standards.

- **Quality Control:** - monitoring specific project results to determine if they comply with relevant quality standards and identifying ways to eliminate causes of unsatisfactory performance.

---

[379] International Organisation for standardization. ISO 8402, *Quality Management and Quality Assurance*, Geneva, Switzerland: ISO Press, 1994.
[380] Project Management Institute (PMI), *A Guide to the Project Management Body of Knowledge (PMBOK® Guide)*, Newtown Square, Pennsylvania USA, 2000 Edition, pp.95

Figure (5): - Project Quality Management Overview (PMBOK pp.96 & Construction Extension pp. 52 in **Bold** Font)

342

Project Human Resource Management

The major processes are: -[381]

- **Organisational Planning:** - identifying, documenting and assigning project roles, responsibilities, and reporting relationships.

- **Staff Acquisition:** - getting the needed human resources assigned to and working on the project.

- **Team Development:** - developing individual and group competencies to enhance project performance.

From the Construction Extension to PMBOK, the following process has been added specific to construction practices: -[382]

- **Project Completion/Team Closeout:** - managing the dissolution of project team; returning them to point of hire or to other assignments.

---

[381] ibid. pp.107
[382] Project Management Institute (PMI), Construction Extension to *A Guide to the Project Management Body of Knowledge (PMBOK® Guide- 2000 Edition)*, Newtown Square, Pennsylvania USA, 2003, pp.55

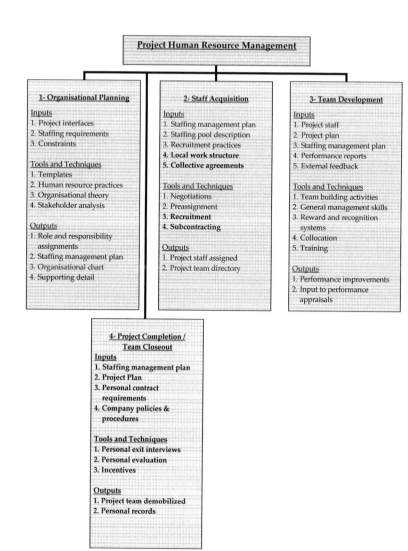

Figure (6): - Project Human Resource Management Overview (PMBOK pp.108 & Construction Extension pp. 63 in **Bold** Font)

Project Communications Management

"Everyone involved in the project must be prepared to send and receive communications, and must understand how the communications in which they are involved as individuals affect the project as a whole."[383]

The following are the major component processes: -[384]

- **Communication Planning:** - determining the information and communications needs of the stakeholders.

- **Information Distribution:** - making required information available to project stakeholders in a timely manner.

- **Performance Reporting:** - collecting and disseminating performance information, including status reporting, progress measurement and forecasting.

- **Administrative Closure:** - generating, gathering, and dissemination information to formalise a phase or project completion.

---

[383] Project Management Institute (PMI), *A Guide to the Project Management Body of Knowledge (PMBOK® Guide)*, Newtown Square, Pennsylvania USA, 2000 Edition, pp.117
[384] ibid.

345

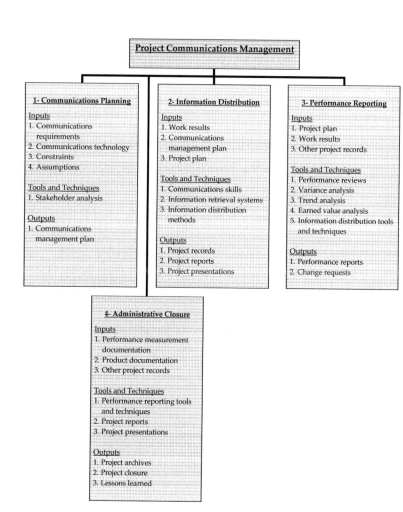

Project Communications Management

1- Communications Planning

Inputs
1. Communications
   requirements
2. Communications technology
3. Constraints
4. Assumptions

Tools and Techniques
1. Stakeholder analysis

Outputs
1. Communications
   management plan

2- Information Distribution

Inputs
1. Work results
2. Communications
   management plan
3. Project plan

Tools and Techniques
1. Communications skills
2. Information retrieval systems
3. Information distribution
   methods

Outputs
1. Project records
2. Project reports
3. Project presentations

3- Performance Reporting

Inputs
1. Project plan
2. Work results
3. Other project records

Tools and Techniques
1. Performance reviews
2. Variance analysis
3. Trend analysis
4. Earned value analysis
5. Information distribution tools
   and techniques

Outputs
1. Performance reports
2. Change requests

4- Administrative Closure

Inputs
1. Performance measurement
   documentation
2. Product documentation
3. Other project records

Tools and Techniques
1. Performance reporting tools
   and techniques
2. Project reports
3. Project presentations

Outputs
1. Project archives
2. Project closure
3. Lessons learned

Figure (7): - Project Human Resource Management Overview (PMBOK, pp.118)

346

Project Risk Management

"It includes maximizing the probability and consequences of positive events and minimizing the probability and consequences of adverse events to projects objectives."[385]

The major component processes are: -[386]

- **Risk Management Planning: -** deciding how to approach and plan the risk management activities for a project.

- **Risk Identification: -** determining which risks might affect the project and documenting their characteristics.

- **Qualitative Risk Analysis: -** performing a qualitative analysis of risks and conditions to prioritise their effects on project objectives.

- **Quantitative Risk Analysis: -** measuring the probability and consequences of risks and estimating their implications for project objectives.

- **Risk Response Planning: -** developing procedures and techniques to enhance opportunities and reduce threats to the project's objectives.

- **Risk Monitoring and Control: -** Monitoring residual risks, identifying new risks, executing risk reduction plans, and evaluating their effectiveness throughout the project life cycle.

---

[385] ibid. pp.127
[386] ibid.

Project Risk Management		

1- Risk Management Planning	**2- Risk Identification**	**3- Qualitative Risk Analysis**
Inputs	Inputs	Inputs
1. Project charter#	1. Risk management plan	1. Risk management plan
2. Organisation's risk management policies	2. Project planning outputs	2. Identified risks
3. Defined roles and responsibilities	3. Risk categories	3. Project status
4. Stakeholder risk tolerances	4. Historical information	4. Project type
5. Template for the organisation's risk management plan	Tools and Techniques	5. Data precision
6. Work breakdown structure (WBS)	1. Documentation reviews	6. Scales of probability and impact
7. Contract provisions	2. Information-gathering techniques	7. Assumptions
Tools and Techniques	3. Checklists	Tools and Techniques
1. Planning meetings	4. Assumptions analysis	1. Risk probability and impact
Outputs	5. Diagramming techniques	2. Probability/impact risk rating matrix
1. Risk management plan	Outputs	3. Project assumptions testing
	1. Risks	4. Data precision ranking
	2. Triggers	Outputs
	3. Inputs to other processes	1. Overall risk ranking for the project
		2. List of prioritised risks
		3. List of risks for additional analysis and management
		4. Trends in qualitative risk analysis results

4- Quantitative Risk Analysis	**5- Risk Response Planning**	**6- Risk Monitoring & Control**
Inputs	Inputs	Inputs
1. Risk management plan	1. Risk management plan	1. Risk management plan
2. Identified risks	2. List of prioritised risks	2. Risk response plan
3. List of prioritised risks	3. Risk ranking of the project	3. Project communication
4. List of risks for additional analysis and management	4. Prioritised list of quantified risks	4. Additional risk identification and analysis
5. Historical information	5. Probabilistic analysis of the project	5. Scope changes
6. Expert judgment	6. Probability of achieving the cost and time objectives	Tools and Techniques
7. Other planning outputs	7. List of potential responses	1. Project risk response audits
Tools and Techniques	8. Risk thresholds	2. Periodic project risk reviews
1. Interviewing	9. Risk owners	3. Earned value analysis
2. Sensitivity analysis	10. Common risk causes	4. Technical performance measurement
3. Decision tree analysis	11. Trends in qualitative and quantitative risk analysis results	5. Additional risk response planning
4. Simulation	Tools and Techniques	Outputs
Outputs	1. Avoidance 2. Transference	1. Workaround plans
1. Prioritised list of quantified risks	3. Mitigation 4. Acceptance	2. Corrective action
2. Probabilistic analysis of the project	Outputs	3. Project change requests
3. Probability of achieving the cost and time objectives	1. Risk response plan	4. Updates to the risk response plan
4. Trends in quantitative risk analysis results	2. Residual risks	5. Risk database
	3. Secondary risks	6. Updates to risk identification checklists
	4. contractual agreements	
	5. Contingency reserve needed	
	6. Inputs to other processes	
	7. Inputs to a revised project plan	

Figure (8): - Project Risk Management Overview (PMBOK pp.128 & Construction Extension pp. 77 in **Bold** Font)

Project Procurement Management

It includes the following component processes: -[387]

- **Procurement Planning:** - determining what to procure and when.

- **Solicitation Planning:** - documenting product requirements and identifying potential sources.

- **Solicitation:** - obtaining quotations, bids, offers, or proposals as appropriate.

- **Source Selection:** - choosing from among potential sellers.

- **Contract Administration:** - managing the relationship with the seller.

- **Contract Closeout:** - completion and settlement of the contract, including resolution of any open items.

---

[387] ibid. pp.147

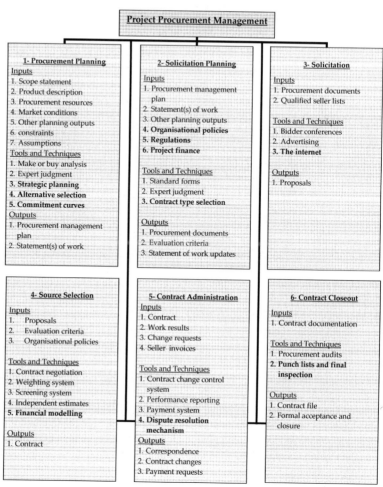

Project Procurement Management

1- Procurement Planning
Inputs
1. Scope statement
2. Product description
3. Procurement resources
4. Market conditions
5. Other planning outputs
6. constraints
7. Assumptions
Tools and Techniques
1. Make or buy analysis
2. Expert judgment
3. Strategic planning
4. Alternative selection
5. Commitment curves
Outputs
1. Procurement management
   plan
2. Statement(s) of work

2- Solicitation Planning

Inputs
1. Procurement management
   plan
2. Statement(s) of work
3. Other planning outputs
4. Organisational policies
5. Regulations
6. Project finance

Tools and Techniques
1. Standard forms
2. Expert judgment
3. Contract type selection

Outputs
1. Procurement documents
2. Evaluation criteria
3. Statement of work updates

3- Solicitation

Inputs
1. Procurement documents
2. Qualified seller lists

Tools and Techniques
1. Bidder conferences
2. Advertising
3. The internet

Outputs
1. Proposals

4- Source Selection

Inputs
1.   Proposals
2.   Evaluation criteria
3.   Organisational policies

Tools and Techniques
1. Contract negotiation
2. Weighting system
3. Screening system
4. Independent estimates
5. Financial modelling

Outputs
1. Contract

5- Contract Administration
Inputs
1. Contract
2. Work results
3. Change requests
4. Seller invoices

Tools and Techniques
1. Contract change control
   system
2. Performance reporting
3. Payment system
4. Dispute resolution
mechanism
Outputs
1. Correspondence
2. Contract changes
3. Payment requests

6- Contract Closeout
Inputs
1. Contract documentation

Tools and Techniques
1. Procurement audits
2. Punch lists and final
inspection

Outputs
1. Contract file
2. Formal acceptance and
   closure

Figure (9): - Project Procurement Management Overview (PMBOK pp.148 & Construction Extension pp. 94 in **Bold** Font)

350

Project Safety Management

Includes the following major processes: -[388]

- **Safety Planning:** - Development of the approach to manage the various hazards to safety inherent in the project.

- **Safety Plan Execution:** - Carrying out the safety plan by performing the activities included therein.

- **Administration and Reporting:** - Maintenance of safety records and reporting safety activities.

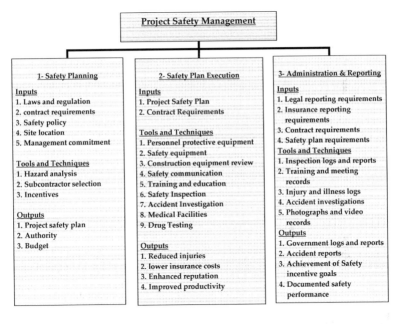

Figure (10): - Project Safety Management (Construction Extension to PMBOK pp. 101-106)

---

[388] Project Management Institute (PMI), Construction Extension to *A Guide to the Project Management Body of Knowledge* (PMBOK® *Guide- 2000 Edition),* Newtown Square, Pennsylvania USA, 2003, pp.101

351

Project Environmental Management

"It is related with identifying the environmental characteristics surrounding the construction site and the potential impacts the construction may bring to the environment"[389]

It includes the following processes: -[390]

- **Environmental Planning:** - identifying what are the characteristics of the environment surrounding the construction site and which environmental standards are relevant to the project and determining what impact will the project bring to the environment and how to satisfy the identified environmental standards.

- **Environmental Assurance:** - Evaluating the results of environmental management on a regular basis to provided confidence that the project will satisfy the relevant environmental standards.

- **Environmental Control:** - Monitoring specific project results to determine if they comply with relevant environmental standards and identifying ways to eliminate caused of unsatisfactory performance.

---

[389] ibid. pp.107
[390] ibid. pp.108

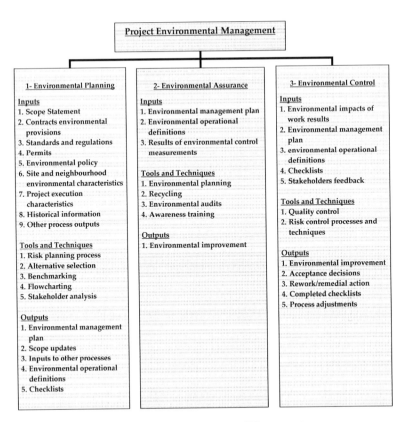

Project Environmental Management

1- Environmental Planning

Inputs
1. Scope Statement
2. Contracts environmental provisions
3. Standards and regulations
4. Permits
5. Environmental policy
6. Site and neighbourhood environmental characteristics
7. Project execution characteristics
8. Historical information
9. Other process outputs

Tools and Techniques
1. Risk planning process
2. Alternative selection
3. Benchmarking
4. Flowcharting
5. Stakeholder analysis

Outputs
1. Environmental management plan
2. Scope updates
3. Inputs to other processes
4. Environmental operational definitions
5. Checklists

2- Environmental Assurance

Inputs
1. Environmental management plan
2. Environmental operational definitions
3. Results of environmental control measurements

Tools and Techniques
1. Environmental planning
2. Recycling
3. Environmental audits
4. Awareness training

Outputs
1. Environmental improvement

3- Environmental Control

Inputs
1. Environmental impacts of work results
2. Environmental management plan
3. environmental operational definitions
4. Checklists
5. Stakeholders feedback

Tools and Techniques
1. Quality control
2. Risk control processes and techniques

Outputs
1. Environmental improvement
2. Acceptance decisions
3. Rework/remedial action
4. Completed checklists
5. Process adjustments

Figure (11): - Project Environmental Management
(Construction Extension to PMBOK pp. 107-116)

353

Project Financial Management

"Financial Management is distinctly different from Cost Management which relates more to managing the day to day costs of the project labour and materials...Financial management is more about the requirements to finance the entire project as a result of the use of several different types of project delivery methods such as Design-Build-Own-Operate (DBOO), Design-Build-Operate- Maintain (DBOM)"[391]

The major processes involved are: [392]

- **Financial Planning:** - Identifying key financial issues to be addressed and assigning project roles, responsibilities and reporting relationships.

- **Financial Control:** - Monitoring key influences identified from the financial planning and taking corrective measures if negative trends are recognized.

- **Administration and Records:** - Designing and maintaining a financial information storage/retrieval database to enable financial control to proceed in a smooth way.

---

[391] ibid. pp.117
[392] ibid.

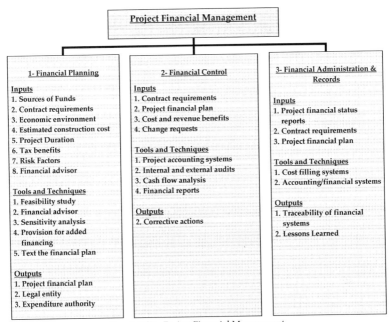

Project Financial Management

1- Financial Planning	2- Financial Control	3- Financial Administration & Records
Inputs 1. Sources of Funds 2. Contract requirements 3. Economic environment 4. Estimated construction cost 5. Project Duration 6. Tax benefits 7. Risk Factors 8. Financial advisor **Tools and Techniques** 1. Feasibility study 2. Financial advisor 3. Sensitivity analysis 4. Provision for added financing 5. Text the financial plan **Outputs** 1. Project financial plan 2. Legal entity 3. Expenditure authority	**Inputs** 1. Contract requirements 2. Project financial plan 3. Cost and revenue benefits 4. Change requests **Tools and Techniques** 1. Project accounting systems 2. Internal and external audits 3. Cash flow analysis 4. Financial reports **Outputs** 2. Corrective actions	**Inputs** 1. Project financial status reports 2. Contract requirements 3. Project financial plan **Tools and Techniques** 1. Cost filling systems 2. Accounting/financial systems **Outputs** 1. Traceability of financial systems 2. Lessons Learned

Figure (12): - Project Financial Management
(Construction Extension to PMBOK pp. 117-123)

355

Project Claim Management

This final knowledge area represents an outline of approach to claim management to stimulate a careful approach to contract preparation and expeditious handling of claims should they arise. It consists of: -[393]

- **Claim Identification:** - starts with sufficient knowledge of the scope and contract terms to be aware when some activity appears to be a change in scope or terms requiring a contract adjustment.

- **Claim Quantification:** - quantifying a claim is usually in terms of additional compensation or a time extension to the contract completion or other milestone date.

- **Claim Prevention:** -The emphasis is on how to avoid or prevent claims from arising

- **Claim Resolution:** - It is a step by step to resolve questions as to whether the claim is a change to the contract or not, or whether the claimed amount of compensation or time requested is correct.

---

[393] ibid. pp.125

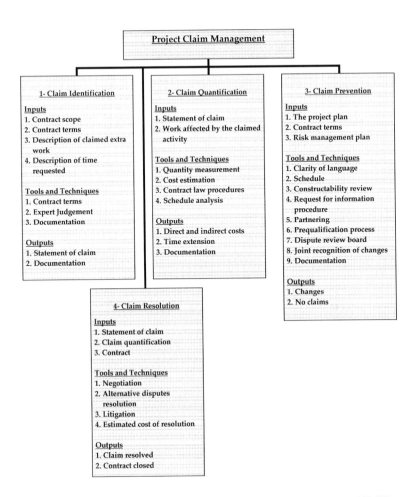

Figure (13): - Project Claim Management (Construction Extension to PMBOK pp. 125-131)

Appendix 3: The OGC Procurement Model

APPENDIX 3

THE OGC PROCUREMENT PROJECT PROCESS MODEL (EXISITING GATEWAY REVIEW 0 TO 5)

Procurement activities and processes represent a major part of all construction projects and project management processes, but the OGC model does not address any sustainable agenda and falls short of any mention of sustainable development as an objective or guideline for the Gateway reviews process.

The OGC Gateway Reviews

This appendix puts forward the description of the six Gateways as explained in the OGC reports of best practice (Chapter 5 - figure 5.7). The OGC description highlights the obvious lack of sustainable development guidelines which are, in fact, non existent in the description of any of the Gateways.

Although, the OGC Gateway Reviews Process represents a positive initiative for procurement and a significant step forward towards better future performance, it clearly falls short of showing any clear commitment to the incorporation of a sustainable development agenda in the processes.

1. Gateway Review 0 / Start Up: Strategic Assessment

Gateway 0 is to be expected at the start up of a project and is recommended practice for major projects which are of high risk. It produces a preliminary justification for the project based on a strategic assessment of business needs and a high level assessment of the project's costs and potential for success. This is done through an extensive phase of information gathering and data collection.

The Gateway Review comes after the business need has been identified and before any further development proposal goes before a project board or executive authority to proceed. It also provides assurance to the project board or the similar authority that the business requirement has been adequately researched and fits within the department's overall business strategy and examines how the planned projects' processes would deliver the overall objectives and that the management structure, monitoring and resourcing is appropriate.[394]

2. Gateway Review 1: Business Justification

In this Review, the project board determines that the project is feasible with a robust high level business case. The main purposes of this review are to:-[395]

- Confirm that the business case is strong through meeting the business needs, being affordable, achievable, with appropriate options explored

---

[394] The Office of Government Commerce (OGC), *Gateway Review 0: Strategic assessment*, OGC Best Practice, OGC Publication, UK, 2001. Latest version accessed at www.ogc.gov.uk , last visited October 2003
[395] The Office of Government Commerce (OGC), *Gateway Review 1: Business Justification*, OGC Best Practice, OGC Publication, UK, 2001

and likely to achieve value for money.

- Complete satisfactorily the feasibility study and establish the preferred way forward.

- Ensure that the different levels of authorities within the project support the project brief.

- Identify the major risks and outline risk management plans as well as quality management plans.

- Confirm that the scope and requirements specifications are realistic, clear of any ambiguities and serve the main objectives of the project.

- Identify project teams and team players while ensuring that the full scale, scope and intended outcomes are fully understood and considered when making decisions for the current and the following stages.

- Ensure the readiness of the plans for the next stage and that the project team can deliver them.

- Confirm that overarching and internal business and technical strategies have been taken into account

3. Gateway Review 2: Procurement Strategy

This phase defines the procurement strategy, focusing on establishing a clear definition of the project and a plan for its implementation. It assesses the project's viability, its potential for success and whether the project is ready to invite proposals or tenders from the market.[396]

This assures the project board that the selected procurement approach is appropriate for the proposed acquisition with special focus on procurement

---

[396] The Office of Government Commerce (OGC), *Gateway Review 2: Procurement Strategy*, OGC Best Practice, OGC Publication, UK, 2001

arrangements to offer value for money guidelines. The review also allows:-

- Confirmation of the full definition of the business case.

- Choice of appropriate procurement strategy in relation to the project's objectives.

- Confirmation of available funding, development and delivery approach and appropriate resources.

- Confirmation that the procurement will facilitate client/supplier relationships in accordance with government initiatives such as Achieving Excellence in Construction Procurement.

4. Gateway Review 3: Investment Decision

This third review should come before placing work orders with suppliers and before award of contract. After the potential suppliers and partners have submitted their proposals or tenders, an evaluation panel analyses them, and recommends the proposal which meets all the needs of clients and end-users and that offers the best value for money.[397]

A major part of this review is to ensure that management controls are in place to manage the project through to completion and confirm the proper implementation of the chosen procurement strategy. Finally, the review also confirms that the technical implications such as the `build-ability` for construction projects have been addressed.

---

[397] The Office of Government Commerce (OGC), *Gateway Review 3: Investment Decision*, OGC Best Practice, OGC Publication, UK, 2001

5. Gateway Review 4: Readiness for Service

"This review focuses on whether the solution is robust for delivery; how ready the organisation is to implement the business changes that occur before and after delivery; and whether there is a basis for evaluating ongoing performance."[398]

For construction projects, this review takes place after commissioning has been completed. The main purposes of the review are to:-

- Ensure that the current phase of the contract as well as the documentation is properly completed.
- Check that the business case is still valid and unaffected by internal or external events or changes.
- Ensure the original projected business benefits are likely to be achieved.
- Ensure that there are processes and procedures to ensure long-term success of the project.
- Ensure that the process is to the client's satisfaction and the client is ready to approve implementation.
- Check that lessons for future projects are identified and recorded.

6. Gateway Review 5: Benefits Evaluation

"This review focuses on ensuring that the project delivers the benefits and value for money identified in the business case and benefits plans."[399]

The main purposes of this review are to:-

- Assess whether the business case as well as the anticipated benefits are

---

[398] The Office of Government Commerce (OGC), *Gateway Review 4: Readiness for Service*, OGC Best Practice, OGC Publication, UK, 2001, pp.1
[399] The Office of Government Commerce (OGC), *Gateway Review 5: Benefits Evaluation*, OGC Best Practice, OGC Publication, UK, 2001, pp.1

being delivered.

- Where changes have been agreed, check that they do not compromise the original procurement.
- Check that there is ongoing contract development to improve value for money.
- Confirm that there are plans to manage the contract to its conclusion.

The above description of the OGC procurement process model, put forward as a generic procurement process, is applicable to all projects including construction projects.

Appendix 4: The Online Version of the Questionnaire

Integrating Project Management (PM) & Sustainable Development (SD) for Construction Projects

The Questionnaire is in Five Sections:

Section 1: Asks for information to establish your background and experience.
Section 2: Is about your knowledge of and attitudes towards Sustainable Development (SD).
Section 3: Seeks to find out about your level of familiarity with and opinion of Project Management Body of Knowledge (PMBOK).
Section 4: Is aimed at trying to identify different ways of integrating PM & SD.
Section 5: Evaluates the possibility of integrating each area of knowledge with sustainable development considering the inputs of each area.

Section 1: Background Information

Asks for information to establish your background and experience.

1- Name:

Organisation:

Contact details:

2- Please tick the box that best describes your responsibilities: -

☐ Architectural Design ☐ Construction ☐ R and D

☐ Initiating ☐ Planning ☐ Executing

☐ Controlling ☐ General PM ☐ Other

If Other Please Specify:

3- Kindly tick the relevant box describing: -

Experience (Years) in Project Management	Experience (Years) in Construction Industry
○ 0-5	○ 0-5
○ 6-10	○ 6-10
○ 11-20	○ 11-20
○ 21 & over	○ 21 & over

Section 2: Sustainable Development (SD)

This section aims to find your general point of views on sustainability issues where your answers are described by a scale of 1 to 5 representing different extremes shown on each answer line

1- How would you describe your knowledge of sustainable development?

Comprehensive & Up-to-date ○ 1 ○ 2 ○ 3 ○ 4 ○ 5 Limited and Superficial

2- How important, significant or contributing factor do you think sustainable development generally is to quality of life and to standards of living?

High Importance and Significance   ◯ 1 ◯ 2 ◯ 3 ◯ 4 ◯ 5   None Contributing Factor

3- How important, significant or contributing factor do you think sustainable development is to the outcomes of construction?

High Importance and Significance   ◯ 1 ◯ 2 ◯ 3 ◯ 4 ◯ 5   None Contributing Factor

4- How essential is it that the processes of construction project management fully integrate the principles and practices of sustainable development?

Totally Essential   ◯ 1 ◯ 2 ◯ 3 ◯ 4 ◯ 5   Not Essential at All

Section 3: Project Management Body of Knowledge (PMBOK) 2000 Edition

PMBOK is an internationally established guide also an inclusive term that describes the sum of knowledge within the profession of project management.
This section aims to know your level of familiarity with and opinion of PMBOK.

1- How would you describe your knowledge of PMBOK?

Comprehensive and Up-to-date   ◯ 1 ◯ 2 ◯ 3 ◯ 4 ◯ 5   Limited & Superficial

2- Social, Economic and Environmental impacts of construction have recently been added in section 2.5.4 in the new edition of PMBOK. Do you believe this adequately covers the integration of sustainable development and project management for the improvement of a sustainable performance?

◯   YES   ◯   NO

3- How would you value the impacts of this integration mentioned in section 2.5.4 on live construction projects?

High Value Impacts   ◯ 1 ◯ 2 ◯ 3 ◯ 4 ◯ 5   Low Value Impacts

Section 4: Project Management (PM) Processes & Sustainable Development (SD)

This section is aimed at identifying the different ways of integrating PM & SD by listing the Project management processes organised into Five groups and the four different interaction relationships among each process group.

Please specify, by ticking the appropriate box, the degree of integration of project management and sustainable development that you think is possible or achievable in order to improve overall performance

	A	B	C	D	œ
1-Initiating	◯	◯	◯	◯	◯
2-Planning	◯	◯	◯	◯	◯
3-Executing	◯	◯	◯	◯	◯
4-Controlling	◯	◯	◯	◯	◯
5-Closing	◯	◯	◯	◯	◯

4 Interaction relationships among each process group are:

A = Scope   B = Objectives   C = Core Processes   D = Facilitating Processes
œ = Integrating SD with this process is NOT applicable

Section 5: Areas of Knowledge & Sustainable Development (SD) Inputs / Tools & Techniques / Outputs

This section aims to evaluate the possibility of integrating each area of knowledge with sustainable development considering its inputs with sustainable development as an added tool &technique to attain outputs which are more sustainable.

Please note that in this section the ranking system for your answers will always be based on the following measure:

A = Significant sustainable outputs, enhancing performance towards Sustainability.
B = Considerable changes to outputs and guiding performance towards Sustainability.
C = Resulting outputs with no modification or enhancement of Sustainability.

1. Applying sustainable development as an added tool & technique to the inputs of each of the following elements, please specify the effect of this application on the outputs of the following major processes:-

Project Integration Management	SUSTAINABILITY		
	A	B	C
1. Project Plan Development	O	O	O
2. Project Plan Execution	O	O	O
3. Integrated Change Control	O	O	O

Project Scope Management	SUSTAINABILITY		
	A	B	C
1. Initiation	O	O	O
2. Scope Planning	O	O	O
3. Scope Definition	O	O	O
4. Scope Verification	O	O	O
5. Scope Change Control	O	O	O

Project Time Management	SUSTAINABILITY		
	A	B	C
1. Activity Definition	O	O	O
2. Activity sequencing	O	O	O
3. Activity Duration Estimating	O	O	O
4. Schedule Development	O	O	O
5. Schedule Control	O	O	O

368

Project Cost Management

	SUSTAINABILITY		
	A	B	C
1. Resource Planning	O	O	O
2. Cost Estimating	O	O	O
3. Cost Budgeting	O	O	O
4. Cost Control	O	O	O

Project Quality Management

	SUSTAINABILITY		
	A	B	C
1. Quality Planning	O	O	O
2. Quality Assurance	O	O	O
3. Quality Control	O	O	O

Project Human Resource Management

	SUSTAINABILITY		
	A	B	C
1. Organisational Planning	O	O	O
2. Staff Acquisition	O	O	O
3. Team Development	O	O	O

Project Communications Management

	SUSTAINABILITY		
	A	B	C
1. Communications Planning	O	O	O
2. Information Distribution	O	O	O
3. Performance Reporting	O	O	O
4. Administrative Closure	O	O	O

Project Risk Management

	SUSTAINABILITY		
	A	B	C
1. Risk Management Planning	O	O	O
2. Risk Identification	O	O	O
3. Qualitative Risk Analysis	O	O	O
4. Quantitative Risk Analysis	O	O	O
5. Risk Response Planning	O	O	O
6. Risk Monitoring & Control	O	O	O

Project Procurement Management

	SUSTAINABILITY		
	A	B	C
1. Procurement Planning	O	O	O
2. Solicitation Planning	O	O	O
3. Solicitation	O	O	O
4. Source Selection	O	O	O
5. Contract Administration	O	O	O
6. Contract Closeout	O	O	O

2. On the overview of each area of knowledge, please describe how applying the principles of sustainable thinking as tools & techniques would affect the outputs for the following areas: -

The PM Knowledge Areas

	SUSTAINABILITY		
	A	B	C
PROJECT INTEGRATION MANAGEMENT	O	O	O
PROJECT SCOPE MANAGEMENT	O	O	O
PROJECT TIME MANAGEMENT	O	O	O
PROJECT COST MANAGEMENT	O	O	O
PROJECT QUALITY MANAGEMENT	O	O	O
PROJECT HUMAN RESOURCE MANAGEMENT	O	O	O
PROJECT COMMUNICATIONS MANAGEMENT	O	O	O
PROJECT RISK MANAGEMENT	O	O	O
PROJECT PROCUREMENT MANAGEMENT	O	O	O

Where ...
A = Significant sustainable outputs, enhancing performance towards Sustainability.
B = Considerable changes to outputs and guiding performance towards Sustainability.
C = Resulting outputs with no modification or enhancement of Sustainability.

* Would you be willing to complete a subsidiary questionnaire should additional questions arise from the analysis of the results held in this questionnaire?

○ YES   ○ NO

* If there is anything you would like to expand on from any section of the questionnaire, please do so here:

You have now finished the questionnaire. I would like to thank you again for taking time in filling out this vital element of the research created and compiled by myself.

[Send]   [Clear]

Appendix 5: Excerpts from the Detailed Version of the Questionnaire

In this appendix, the author presents excerpts from the detailed version of the questionnaire to highlight the sample of questions used in section 5 of the questionnaire.

For a complete file of the detailed questionnaire, please contact the author.

Please note that in this section the ranking system for your answers will always be based on the following scale:

A= Totally Relevant with significant outputs and enhancing performance towards Sustainability.

B= Possibly Relevant with considerable changes to the outputs and guiding performances towards Sustainability.

C= Irrelevant to the outputs with no modification or enhancement to Sustainability.

4- Project Integration Management

4.1 Project Plan Development: Please examine the following: -

INPUTS	TOOLS & TECHNIQUES	OUTPUTS
1. Other planning outputs 2. Historical information 3. Organisational policies 4. Constraints 5. Assumptions	1. Sustainable Development 2. Social, Economic & Environmental (Triple bottom line) Constraints & Indicators.	1. Sustainable Project Plan. 2. Supporting details including documentation of all identified SD assumptions & constraints.

- **Based on your own experience and opinion, please tick the relevant box that best describes your choice: -**

4.1 Project Plan Development	SOCIAL				ECONOMIC				ENVIRONMENTAL			
	Inputs	Relevance			Inputs	Relevance			Inputs	Relevance		
		A	B	C		A	B	C		A	B	C
	Other planning outputs				Other planning outputs				Other planning outputs			
	Historical Information				Historical Information				Historical Information			
	Organisational policies				Organisational policies				Organisational policies			
	Constraints				Constraints				Constraints			
	Assumptions				Assumptions				Assumptions			

A= Totally Relevant with significant outputs and enhancing performance towards Sustainability.
B= Possibly Relevant with considerable changes to the outputs and guiding performances towards Sustainability.
C= Irrelevant to the outputs with no modification or enhancement to Sustainability.

373

4.2 Project Plan Execution: Please examine the following: -

INPUTS	TOOLS & TECHNIQUES	OUTPUTS
1. Project Plan 2. Supporting detail 3. Organisational policies 4. Preventive action 5. Corrective action	1. Sustainable Development 2. Social, Economic & Environmental (Triple bottom line) Constraints & Indicators.	1. Work results towards sustainable benefits (Economic, Social & Environmental). 2. Change requests.

- Based on your own experience and opinion, please tick the relevant box that best describes your choice: -

4.2 Project Plan Execution	SOCIAL				ECONOMIC				ENVIRONMENTAL			
	Inputs	Relevance			Inputs	Relevance			Inputs	Relevance		
		A	B	C		A	B	C		A	B	C
	Project Plan				Project Plan				Project Plan			
	Supporting detail				Supporting detail				Supporting detail			
	Organisational policies				Organisational policies				Organisational policies			
	Preventive actions				Preventive actions				Preventive actions			
	Corrective actions				Corrective actions				Corrective actions			

A= Totally Relevant with significant outputs and enhancing performance towards Sustainability.
B= Possibly Relevant with considerable changes to the outputs and guiding performances towards Sustainability.
C= Irrelevant to the outputs with no modification or enhancement to Sustainability.

4.3 Integrated Change Control: Please examine the following: -

INPUTS	TOOLS & TECHNIQUES	OUTPUTS
1. Project Plan 2. Performance Report 3. Change requests	1. Sustainable Development 2. Social, Economic & Environmental (Triple bottom line) Constraints & Indicators.	1. Project plan Updates 2. Corrective action towards sustainable performance 3. Lessons learned

- Based on your own experience and opinion, please tick the relevant box that best describes your choice: -

4.3 Integrated Change Control	SOCIAL				ECONOMIC				ENVIRONMENTAL			
	Inputs	Relevance			Inputs	Relevance			Inputs	Relevance		
		A	B	C		A	B	C		A	B	C
	Project Plan				Project Plan				Project Plan			
	Performance reports				Performance reports				Performance reports			
	Change requests				Change requests				Change requests			

A= Totally Relevant with significant outputs and enhancing performance towards Sustainability
B= Possibly Relevant with considerable changes to the outputs and guiding performances towards Sustainability.
C= Irrelevant to the outputs with no modification or enhancement to Sustainability.

- On the overall of this area of knowledge, How do you perceive Sustainable Development improving the performance of the project through this section?

SUSTAINABILITY

	A	B	C
4.1 Project Plan Development	☐	☐	☐
4.2 Project Plan Execution	☐	☐	☐
4.3 Integrated Change Control	☐	☐	☐

4.PROJECT INTEGRATION MANAGEMENT

12- Project Procurement Management

12.1 Procurement Planning: Please examine the following: -

INPUTS	TOOLS & TECHNIQUES	OUTPUTS
1. Scope statement 2. Product description 3. Procurement resources 4. Market conditions 5. Other planning outputs 6. Constraints 7. Assumptions	1. Sustainable Development 2. Social, Economic & Environmental (Triple bottom line) Constraints & Indicators.	1. Procurement management plan based on the needs of the project including SD 2. Statement of work

- **Based on your own experience and opinion, please tick the relevant box that best describes your choice: -**

12.1 Procurement Planning	SOCIAL				ECONOMIC				ENVIRONMENTAL			
	Inputs	Relevance			Inputs	Relevance			Inputs	Relevance		
		A	B	C		A	B	C		A	B	C
	Scope Statement				Scope Statement				Scope Statement			
	Product description				Product description				Product description			
	Procurement resources				Procurement resources				Procurement resources			
	Market conditions				Market conditions				Market conditions			
	Other planning outputs				Other planning outputs				Other planning outputs			
	Constraints				Constraints				Constraints			
	Assumptions				Assumptions				Assumptions			

A= Totally Relevant with significant outputs and enhancing performance towards Sustainability.
B= Possibly Relevant with considerable changes to the outputs and guiding performance towards Sustainability.
C= Irrelevant to the outputs with no modification or enhancement to Sustainability

12.2 Solicitation Planning: Please examine the following: -

INPUTS	TOOLS & TECHNIQUES	OUTPUTS
1. Procurement management plan 2. Statement of work 3. Other planning Outputs	1. Sustainable Development 2. Social, Economic & Environmental (Triple bottom line) Constraints & Indicators.	1. Procurement documents 2. Evaluation criteria 3. Statement of work updates

- Based on your own experience and opinion, please tick the relevant box that best describes your choice: -

12.2 Solicitation Planning	SOCIAL				ECONOMIC				ENVIRONMENTAL			
	Inputs	Relevance			Inputs	Relevance			Inputs	Relevance		
		A	B	C		A	B	C		A	B	C
	Procurement management plan				Procurement management plan				Procurement management plan			
	Statement of work				Statement of work				Statement of work			
	Other planning outputs				Other planning outputs				Other planning outputs			

A= Totally Relevant with significant outputs and enhancing performance towards Sustainability.
B= Possibly Relevant with considerable changes to the outputs and guiding performances towards Sustainability.
C= Irrelevant to the output with no modification or enhancement to Sustainability.

12.3 Solicitation: Please examine the following: -

INPUTS	TOOLS & TECHNIQUES	OUTPUTS
1. Procurement documents 2. Qualified seller lists	1. Sustainable Development 2. Social, Economic & Environmental (Triple bottom line) Constraints & Indicators.	1. Proposals

- Based on your own experience and opinion, please tick the relevant box that best describes your choice: -

12.3 Solicitation	SOCIAL				ECONOMIC				ENVIRONMENTAL			
	Inputs	Relevance			Inputs	Relevance			Inputs	Relevance		
		A	B	C		A	B	C		A	B	C
	Procurement documents				Procurement management plan				Procurement management plan			
	Qualified seller lists				Statement of work				Statement of work			

A= Totally Relevant with significant outputs and enhancing performance towards Sustainability.
B= Possibly Relevant with considerable changes to the outputs and guiding performances towards Sustainability.
C= Irrelevant to the output with no modification or enhancement to Sustainability.

12.4 Source Selection: Please examine the following: -

INPUTS	TOOLS & TECHNIQUES	OUTPUTS
1. Proposals 2. Evaluation criteria 3. Organisational policies	1. Sustainable Development 2. Social, Economic & Environmental (Triple bottom line) Constraints & Indicators.	1. Contract

- Based on your own experience and opinion, please tick the relevant box that best describes your choice: -

12.4 Source Selection	SOCIAL				ECONOMIC				ENVIRONMENTAL			
	Inputs	Relevance			Inputs	Relevance			Inputs	Relevance		
		A	B	C		A	B	C		A	B	C
	Proposals				Proposals				Proposals			
	Evaluation criteria				Evaluation criteria				Evaluation criteria			
	Organisational policies				Organisational policies				Organisational policies			

A= Totally Relevant with significant outputs and enhancing performance towards Sustainability.
B= Possibly Relevant with considerable changes to the outputs and guiding performance towards Sustainability.
C= Irrelevant to the outputs with no modification or enhancement to Sustainability.

12.5 Contract Administration: Please examine the following: -

INPUTS	TOOLS & TECHNIQUES	OUTPUTS
1. Contract 2. Work Results 3. Change requests 4. Seller invoices	1. Sustainable Development 2. Social, Economic & Environmental (Triple bottom line) Constraints & Indicators.	1. Correspondence 2. Contract Changes 3. Payment requests

- Based on your own experience and opinion, please tick the relevant box that best describes your choice: -

12.5 Contract Administration	SOCIAL				ECONOMIC				ENVIRONMENTAL			
	Inputs	Relevance			Inputs	Relevance			Inputs	Relevance		
		A	B	C		A	B	C		A	B	C
	Contract				Contract				Contract			
	Work Results				Work Results				Work Results			
	Change requests				Change requests				Change requests			
	Seller invoices				Seller invoices				Seller invoices			

A= Totally Relevant with significant outputs and enhancing performance towards Sustainability.
B= Possibly Relevant with considerable changes to the outputs and guiding performances towards Sustainability.
C= Irrelevant to the outputs with no modification or enhancement to Sustainability.

12.6 Contract Closeout: Please examine the following: -

INPUTS	TOOLS & TECHNIQUES	OUTPUTS
1. Contract documentation	1. Sustainable Development 2. Social, Economic & Environmental (Triple bottom line) Constraints & Indicators.	1. Contract file 2. Formal acceptance and closure

- Based on your own experience and opinion, please tick the relevant box that best describes your choice: -

12.6 Contract Closeout	SOCIAL				ECONOMIC				ENVIRONMENTAL			
	Inputs	Relevance			Inputs	Relevance			Inputs	Relevance		
		A	B	C		A	B	C		A	B	C
	Contract documentation				Contract documentation				Contract documentation			

A= Totally Relevant with significant outputs and enhancing performance towards Sustainability.
B= Possibly Relevant with considerable changes to the output and guiding performances towards Sustainability.
C= Irrelevant to the output with no modification or enhancement to Sustainability.

- On the overall of this area of knowledge, How do you perceive Sustainable Development improving the performance of the project through this section?

	SUSTAINABILITY		
	A	B	C
12.1 Procurement Planning	☐	☐	☐
12.2 Solicitation Planning	☐	☐	☐
12.3 Solicitation	☐	☐	☐
12.4 Source Selection	☐	☐	☐
12.5 Contract Administration	☐	☐	☐
12.6 Contract Closeout	☐	☐	☐
12. PROJECT PROCUREMENT MANAGEMENT	☐	☐	☐

Appendix 6: List of Published Papers (Until 2003)

LIST OF PUBLISHED PAPERS

- Edinburgh Architectural Research (EAR) Journal, Volume 27, 2000, University of Edinburgh, Department of Architecture: -

  Paper Title: *"A Review of `Project Management` & `Sustainable Development` for Construction Projects"*

- Project Management Institute (PMI) Europe 2001 Conference: *A Project Management Odyssey*, London, UK, 2001, Conference Proceedings: -

  Paper Title: *"Rethinking Project Management; the Business Case for Sustainable Construction"* in corporation with Roger D. Talbot

- Project Management Institute (PMI) Research Conference 2002: *Frontiers of PM Research & Applications*, Seattle, USA, 2002, Conference Proceedings: -

  Paper Title: *"A Sustainable Approach to the Project Management Odyssey"*

- Sustainable Development Forum in Cooperation with Alexandria University, 3rd Sustainable Development Forum (SDF-3) 2003: *Managing Sustainable Development in Emerging Markets*, Alexandria, Egypt, 2003, Conference Proceedings: -

  Paper Title: *"Sustainable Management Systems; Embedding Sustainable Development into Project Management Processes"*

  Award Received: Best Student Paper

894509

Printed in Great Britain by
Amazon.co.uk, Ltd.,
Marston Gate.